Reimagining Healthcare

How the Smartsourcing
Revolution Will
Drive the Future of
Healthcare and Refocus
It on What Matters
Most, the Patient

Thomas Koulopoulos

Post Hill
PRESS

A POST HILL PRESS BOOK
ISBN: 978-1-64293-557-8
ISBN (eBook): 978-1-64293-558-5

Reimagining Healthcare:
How the Smartsourcing Revolution Will Drive the Future of
Healthcare and Refocus It on What Matters Most, the Patient
© 2020 by Thomas Koulopoulos
All Rights Reserved

Post Hill Press
New York • Nashville
posthillpress.com

Published in the United States of America

TABLE OF CONTENTS

PART TWO: THE SOLUTION

PART THREE: THE FUTURE

ACKNOWLEDGMENTS

The origins of this book are the stuff of serendipity.

It began with a LinkedIn request I received nearly two years ago. Little did I know that accepting it would start a process of learning and exploration that would nearly devour me for the better part of the last two years as I delved into an industry so convoluted and disjointed that there were times I wondered if anyone really understood the magnitude of its dysfunction. I felt like a first-year medical resident, overwhelmed by the amount of information I needed to take in.

The only way I was able to make sense of it was through the incredible generosity, patience, and sharing of ideas with a long list of people to whom I am deeply indebted.

Any attempt to thank those people in these few pages is feeble when contrasted to the immense value they provided. Nonetheless I will offer my gratitude here to at least acknowledge those who helped the most.

Susan Worthy was the person who sent me that original LinkedIn request. She had come across a copy of another book I'd written in 2005, *Smartsourcing*, which, unbeknownst to me at the time, was making the rounds in the healthcare industry. When Susan and I first met she asked if I'd thought about writing a book on how my ideas about focusing on core competency could help to shape the healthcare conversation. I hadn't. Although I had experience in healthcare, I hadn't delved into its complexity. So, at first, I discounted her suggestion, but the spark she ignited with that initial conversation refused to be extinguished.

I spent the next few months trying to wrap my head around the challenge of understanding the intricacies of the healthcare industry. During those early months I had many moments of doubt when I wondered if I'd ever "get it." One of the principle reasons I stuck it out was that Susan's patience, deep insight about healthcare, and introduction to dozens of industry experts gave me the encouragement and the information I needed to put in place the foundation of the book.

Were it not for Susan's help and guidance, the many doors she opened, and the patience with which she helped me to shape the narrative of the book, it would never have been written.

If Susan was the kindling that kept the fire going, then Jon Russell, who was kind enough to write the forward for the book, was the spark that ignited it. Jon had been at John Muir Health for many years as their Chief Information Officer. He is one of those soft-spoken people whose work behind the scenes is the foundation without which little happens. Jon had come across a copy of *Smartsourcing* from an executive coach who recommended it. I came to find out later that in his capacity as CIO at John Muir Health he had a meeting with representatives of a prospective hospital service provider in which he told them that if they didn't smartsource he simply wasn't going to do business with them. The partner's reps left the meeting and promptly bought copies of the book.

Others at John Muir Health were also instrumental in helping me understand and navigate the healthcare maze, most notably: Chris Pass, Jane Willemsen, Michelle Lopes, Ray Nassief, Lisa Foust, Lee Huskins, Joshua Welch, Ben Drew, Dr. Steven Schlossberg, and Sanjib Dutt and Doug Robison who were instrumental in introducing my ideas to Jon.

Acknowledgments

John Muir Health's CEO Cal Knight provided me with virtually unlimited access to the doctors, clinicians, and administrators at John Muir Health. Cal's dedication to healthcare, his commitment to the important role of the community hospital, and his vision for the future of healthcare made a deep impression on me and helped set the trajectory of the book.

My longtime literary agent and dear friend John Willig has made the journey with me from idea to book an amazing ten times. When I think of those people who have been most instrumental in my professional life, John is one of a handful of people that I am most grateful for having had the good fortune to find and the greater fortune to continue to have in my circle. His professionalism, direct manner, and knowledge of publishing is simply without compare. While John's professional counsel has been invaluable, it is his kind friendship that I treasure most.

I'm especially grateful for the support of the amazing team at Post Hill Press: Anthony Ziccardi, Michael Wilson, Maddie Sturgeon, and my copyeditor Katie Post. Post Hill Press has a wonderfully refreshing entrepreneurial spirit that allows them to move quickly when they see an opportunity; and they do it all with extraordinary attention to detail and commitment to excellence. I've worked with many publishers, and while they all promise to focus on building a relationship with their authors, few do that as well as Post Hill Press.

Many people provided early comments and feedback on the book when it was still taking shape. Foremost among those was my friend Jill who took the time to read through the entire rough manuscript and provide invaluable commentary and advice from her time advocating tirelessly for healthcare reform as a legislator. While Jill and I often found ourselves on opposite sides of many political debates, we agreed on the fact that there is no excuse for the egregious inefficiencies of the healthcare system as it stands today.

Bill Shickolovich the CIO and EVP at Tufts Medical Center and Wellforce was one of the first people who showed me how smartsourcing related to healthcare, nearly fifteen years ago. Bill has also been kind enough to make himself available over the years to help me better understand the complexity of healthcare. Tufts also holds a special place in my past, having played a significant role in my own healthcare as a child at their Floating Hospital for Children.

My good friend Sunil Malhotra who took the time to do a full read through was one of the first people to support my work in smartsourcing over fifteen years ago. He saw its potential in ways I hadn't yet. Sunil is one of those people who has a consistently positive outlook and always greets you with a smile. His camaraderie, collaboration, ever-present wit and humor, and deep insight into business and life have enriched me in many ways and have become essential in shaping many of my perspectives.

Jim Champy has been a generous and staunch ally for decades. Without him the sale of my business to Perot and my subsequent foray into smartsourcing would never have happened. Jim was one of the people that I shared my very first published book with twenty-five years ago. Little did I know at the time that Jim would go on to be one of those people who would shape the trajectory of my own career in so many ways I could never have imagined. His unwavering support and friendship are a gift I continue to treasure.

Many other friends contributed as well. Nicole who was instrumental in recasting my own healthcare narrative by refocusing me on one of the core principles of this book, that I, and everyone else reading this book all share one common experience, we all have been and will be patients. Jack Rochester who helped breath life into the initial draft of the very early narrative, which turned into the baseline for the book. Jack has a wonderfully curious mind and is one of the best writers I know. My longtime friend Barry Chaiken gave me the benefit of his insider's knowledge and connections in healthcare, including his intro to Joe Restuccia at BU whose forty years of healthcare helped to validate many of my observations.

Thanks to my assistants Sharon and Aleise who keep me sane and grounded in the midst of the mayhem that is my life by making sure that the many things I should be doing while I'm sequestered in the author's cave still get done.

My international tribe of supporters, which includes Ralf from Germany, Adolfo from Italy, and Hirososhi from Japan provided encouragement and an international perspective on healthcare. And, of course, the many people who read through the final draft of the manuscript to provide insights and corrections. Thank you Denis, Darrell, Dmitry, Deborah, and most of all thank you to my father who has been among the first to read my many manuscripts over the years. Despite the obvious bias, his encouraging words are always welcome.

Special thanks to my daughter Mia who helped with the first full edit of the book. She immersed herself in the subject matter, was relentlessly detailed and precise in her comments, double-checked research and the many footnotes, and challenged many of my less-than-fully-formed ideas. Few things are as gratifying as coming to the realization that your child, who once learned from you, is now schooling you.

I recalled a time when Mia was a toddler and came into my library, which is lined with hundreds of books. With the curiosity and wonder of a child she looked at several of the books I had written and asked with awe, "Daddy, *how* do you make a book?" With a touch of pride I went on to offer a long-winded description of how one authors and publishes a book. "No, daddy," She said, clearly disappointed in my answer. "I mean how do you actually make the book?" Apparently, Mia was much more interested in how the pages of a book were held together than in how its ideas were held together, and more than a bit dismayed that I wasn't making each book by hand. Little did I know that a few decades later she would be the one I was in awe of.

Lastly, I owe an enormous debt of gratitude to both Mia and my son Adam for helping me to see the world through their far less biased eyes, which see more possibilities than obstacles. I have a small embroidered piece of cloth that hangs from my keychain which reads "Youth = Possibilities / Wisdom." It reminds me that for all the value we place on wisdom and experience, what drives us forward, disrupts our field of view, and ultimately causes change is a youthful outlook that is based less on wisdom than it is on an over-whelming abundance of possibilities; for that we should all be grateful.

FOREWORD

Several years ago I was in a strategy meeting with the senior leadership team from the hospital that I was then working at. We were struggling to find a way to build a future for ourselves and for the healthcare industry. The conversation was a common one among healthcare providers—how to maintain effective margins, while improving quality amid a pretty significant softening financial position, an increasingly sick population, and encroaching competition from very large and well-funded competitors; it was a pretty dismal scenario to say the least. Unfortunately, our situation was what doctors call "unremarkable," meaning that there was nothing significantly abnormal about it. Therein lies the problem with US healthcare: we accept what would in any other industry be unacceptable as the status-quo in healthcare.

Someone at the meeting suggested that we read a book he'd come across called *Smartsourcing*. He said it detailed a vision of how companies across all industries were using a new form of partnering to find additional efficiencies in their overall operations while increasing their ability to innovate their core. In our case that translated into increased focus on our mission of delivering affordable, quality care while also innovating the many administrative systems that supported that mission.

The challenge was that we had become bogged down in the "keep the lights on," day-in-and-day-out operational management that ultimately did nothing to drive value and quality, and certainly did not allow us to focus on maintaining or improving our financial performance so that we could invest in innovation or transformation.

I purchased the book that evening and started reading it by the next day. It didn't take long for me to realize that it was describing exactly the kind of transformation that we were searching for.

To get out of the zero-sum model that pitted investment in administration against investment in care we needed to focus on what the author called our core competency in order to drive transformation and innovation in our healthcare organization, while allowing partners to take responsibility for innovating non-core operations. *Smartsourcing* finally gave us a roadmap with which to do that; it was a transformative concept.

It suddenly dawned on me that we could have our cake and eat it too! Not only could we focus on the things that were most important to our mission, taking care of the health of our community, but we could also focus on innovation and transformation across every aspect of the patient experience. We could create the sort of digital health platform that our clinicians and patients expected, improve the doctor-patient relationship, leverage the deep data repositories we had to create predictive analytics, use artificial intelligence to assist our care teams in improving patient outcomes, streamline the patient's experience, and ease the burden of insurance and billing.

Most importantly, smartsourcing wasn't outsourcing. One thing that we were sure of was that we did not want to go down the path of outsourcing. The streets are littered with healthcare outsourcing failures. The leadership team had decided that we were not going to end up in that situation. Smartsourcing was an alternative that allowed us to leverage the strengths and core competencies of partners in a unique and novel way.

It was as though someone had just turned the lights on. We immediately began to look at the hospital through a very different lens, identifying opportunities and partners with deep core competencies that we would want to smartsource with.

While most partners we spoke with were still stuck in the world of outsourcing, we noticed that a few had already started to think about smartsourcing. The conversations that resulted with those progressive companies were a world removed from the concept of outsourcing, which basically distances the sourcing partner from the organization it's serving. These were relationships that were guided by common purpose. We quickly realized that there was significant additional value in partnering in a much more ambitious way than we had initially expected. This was not about the math of zero-sum, it was a classic case of 1 + 1 = 3.

This is the fundamental value that smartsourcing drives with the right partners; they are not just focused on their small part of the value chain, they are looking at the whole organization, raising their hand and saying, "Have you thought of this idea or that concept?" It significantly changes the way the organization functions in a very positive way that opens the door to innovation that would simply not have been possible otherwise.

Reimagining Healthcare builds on many of the ideas in *Smartsourcing*, but it goes well beyond them to provide not only a vision but a roadmap of how we can reengineer healthcare to refocus it on what matters most, the patient, while at the same time reducing the crippling administrative friction that drives up costs and undermines quality care. In the process we may well be able to transform American healthcare into a much more sustainable model than what we have today.

The current US healthcare model cannot continue to function in its current state. What's lacking is a practical strategy that guides healthcare into the future. I've lived in the healthcare industry long enough to know that won't be easy. The transition to a more sustainable model will not be a simple or painless process. So much of today's healthcare industry lives off of the friction that's been baked into the system. But the solution is there, hidden in plain sight, as Tom says. If we have the courage to follow some of the suggestions in this book we may finally be able to put healthcare on a trajectory towards affordable value and quality care for our communities, our patients, and ourselves.

Creating a sustainable healthcare system is the most important journey that the US, and the world, will be faced with for a generation and now we have a logical way to approach the transformation that must occur to make that journey.

Most importantly, *Reimagining Healthcare* offers a reason to be hopeful about the future of healthcare and the significant positive change that it can bring. But it will take healthcare leaders willing to step out of the traditional industrial age model of healthcare to embrace new ways of thinking about the role of the hospital, and a new generation of organizations, what Tom calls HSPs, that can take on the critical role of innovating all of the non-clinical activities that today make up over 30 percent of healthcare spending.

Reimagining Healthcare is a clear and straightforward guide to assist in that process.

As I look back to that original meeting, when I first learned about smartsourcing, I realize how fortunate we were to have someone at the table make the suggestion that we evaluate a new way of looking at healthcare. Every healthcare provider now has that same opportunity. And, if they take it— if we take it as an industry—I have no doubt that the result will be a remarkable future for healthcare.

> Jon Russell
> Senior Vice President &
> Chief Information Officer
> MultiCare Health System

INTRODUCTION

THE BLUE PILL
OR THE RED PILL

There's an iconic scene at the start of the Hollywood blockbuster movie *The Matrix* in which Morpheus asks the central character, Neo, in reference to the Matrix, "Do you want to know what it is?...It is the world that has been pulled over your eyes to blind you from the truth." Neo sits motionless as Morpheus reveals a blue pill in his left hand and a red pill in his right. "You take the blue pill and...you wake up in your bed and believe whatever you want to believe. You take the red pill...and I show you how deep the rabbit hole goes."

You don't need to have seen *The Matrix* to know which pill Neo chooses; that scene has become a social meme played out countless times. By picking up this book, you too have chosen the red pill and a backstage pass to the myriad disjointed and dysfunctional parts of the US healthcare system.

I'll warn you now that as you read this book, there will be times when you will wish you'd taken the blue pill. But as my own doctor of twenty years once said to me about a diagnostic procedure I was debating, "What's better, Tom—knowing, or not knowing?" The fact that you're reading this book tells me that your answer is the same as mine; knowledge, painful and disturbing though it may be, is always better—but only if you intend to do something with that knowledge.

The history of how I came to write on the topic of healthcare is important in understanding my own red-pill journey and the perspective of this book.

Fifteen years ago, I sold a very successful advisory services firm to Perot Systems—the company that the late Ross Perot had formed after selling Electronic Data Systems to GM. Ross was perhaps much better known for his run at the US presidency in 1992, in which he garnered 19 percent of the popular vote—more than any independent candidate since Theodore Roosevelt in 1912. But Perot was also a pioneer in building the outsourcing movement in technology. His idea was simple: since information technology required highly specific skills, it was better for large organizations to let someone whose core competency was computers and IT handle that part of their business.

Perot purchased my company to build a thought leadership practice within its global outsourcing services business. They were a just over billion-dollar player, and much of that revenue came from Perot's target industry, healthcare.

At the time, outsourcing and offshoring were experiencing rapid growth, having doubled in size over the previous ten years—1994 to 2004—to $77 billion.[1] Outsourcing is the practice of shifting work to a partner whose economies of scale, location, and expertise allow them to do this work for a lower cost. Offshoring is similar, but it's also meant to take advantage of wage arbitrage, the inherently lower wages in certain geographies and less developed economies.

The problem that Perot faced was threefold. First, outsourcing had developed a reputation as a euphemism for job destruction. Second, the much-touted benefits of wage arbitrage rarely proved sufficient to offset the added overhead of managing an offshore operation. Even when they were, the gap would decrease over time until the difference was negligible. Third, even though companies were outsourcing noncore activities, they still needed partners who were willing, able, and committed to driving innovation. In other words, innovating the core was critical, but these innovations could easily suffer if noncore activities were not keeping up with rapid technology and process innovation.

What's especially important to understand about outsourcing is that it is a relatively recent phenomenon. The move to computers and networks makes it possible to move a business process seamlessly across companies and geographies. So it's no coincidence that, as technology and connectivity have evolved, so has outsourcing.

When I coined the term *smartsourcing* in 2005 and then published a book by the same name, my premise was simple; rather than viewing outsourcing as a crude means by which to cut costs and eliminate jobs, we needed to look at a new model that maximized growth and innovation.

In the smartsourcing model, partners form a digital ecosystem with shared risks, shared rewards, and shared innovation across the entire ecosystem of activities. Everyone involved in a smartsourcing relationship focuses on their core competency while improving the overall quality and innovation of the ecosystem that they are also part of. In short, every player in a smartsourced ecosystem has a unique role in the creation of value, as is the case with every part of a natural ecosystem. And, as with any biological ecosystem, there are also the predators and parasites who take advantage of the frailties in the ecosystem. But we'll come back to that.

In the thirteen years since *Smartsourcing* was published, the concept has been used across industries from manufacturing to retail, transportation to hospitality. Having been a small part of that revolution was incredibly gratifying.

Yet, when I looked at the healthcare industry, it seemed to be lagging behind. Instead of shedding their noncore activities, many large healthcare providers were consolidating and acquiring smaller hospitals, private practices, and clinics. Community hospitals and community healthcare systems, which serve one of the most vital roles in healthcare by forging local bonds and developing a better understanding of their population's health risks, were barely getting by. Many were simply closing their doors due to an inability to achieve the economies of scale needed to operate a hospital with adequate services. This was especially true in cases where the physician group, hospital, or health system (a collection of hospitals and physician groups) were already stretched thin in terms of their resources and economic viability.

All the while, administrative processes were becoming increasingly more complex and frustrating for consumers, and the broader conversation about healthcare, often finding its way to the headlines of major media, centered mostly on policy and political agendas.

At around the same time that I sold my company to Perot Systems, my mother was starting a decade-long struggle with an illness that gave me painful first-hand insight into the sorry state of US healthcare. I witnessed the inordinate amount of effort that patients and their caregivers put into the coordination of the many disjointed pieces of the healthcare system, and the toll this took on the quality of healthcare, along with the economic horrors of the patient experience.

...healthcare is just different. I had spent thirty years hearing that same phrase uttered by every industry I'd ever worked with when a newer, more efficient, and more effective way of doing things was proposed to replace the way things had always been done.

It became abundantly clear to me, having seen smart-sourcing play such a vital role in reengineering so many other industries, that there were readily available options for improving the healthcare system. Smartsourcing would not only make fixing healthcare possible, *but possible within the coming decade.*

Most importantly, these were not solutions that required substantive changes to policy or the more draconian suggestion of rebuilding the healthcare system. Although that may make for colorful political diatribes, it is simply not practical. We need to work on improving the current healthcare system by eliminating the enormity of administrative friction that inhibits innovation in the business of healthcare: the same friction that distracts providers by siphoning valuable resources from the innovation and delivery of their clinical core competencies.

The question I repeatedly asked myself was, "If so many other industries could benefit from smartsourcing, why couldn't healthcare?" The answer I consistently received from healthcare insiders was this: healthcare is just different. Although I understood the essence of this belief, I had spent thirty years hearing that same phrase uttered in every industry I'd ever worked with when a newer, more efficient, and more effective way of doing things was proposed to replace the way things had always been done.

I embarked on a mission to understand healthcare, resolving to more credibly make the case that while healthcare may be "different," it is not different enough that we can excuse and ignore the benefits of reimagining healthcare that's affordable, accessible, and that drives the outcomes we all deserve from the single most expensive healthcare system in the world.

The point I make in this book—and repeat regularly—is that there's a clear path toward a sustainable healthcare

> What we will explore are readily available options that will not only make fixing healthcare possible, *but possible within the coming decade.*

system by applying methods and approaches that have been used and proven elsewhere, in other industries, with enormous success. However, these will only work if we choose to take action now.

I also want to be clear from the outset that when we look closely at healthcare, the fundamental force undermining its ability to scale has little to do with the quality of care, the availability of diagnostics and therapies, advances in pharmacology and genomics, or progress in research. All these areas have been evolving rapidly along a mostly positive trajectory.

Instead, the central challenge is continuing to scale the two-hundred-year-old industrial-era model of healthcare into the twenty-first century. The primary and pervasive culprit of the industrial model of healthcare is the invisible administrative friction that has been baked into the industry's highly fragmented processes. These are processes that lack sufficient innovation to keep pace with the increasing clinical complexity of healthcare.

The best way to describe what that friction feels like is an exercise I did many years ago while working as a nurse's aide. I was a college student in my late teens and had just landed a job assisting disabled patients whose movement was severely limited due to spinal cord injuries. To this day, I'm still not sure how my qualifications, which had little to do with a clinical setting, got me the job. But I've been forever grateful for the insights that experience provided.

As part of the orientation, I had to wear a disability-simulation suit that severely restricted my ability to move. The suit used a heavily weighted jacket, restrictive metal braces for arms and legs, stiff gloves, and a neck brace that prevented me from turning my head without turning my whole body. After a few minutes in the suit, trying to navigate even the simplest day-to-day activities became extraordinarily difficult and tiring. Here I was, in the best shape of my life, feeling otherwise invincible, and I couldn't even walk up a flight of stairs.

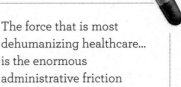

> The force that is most dehumanizing healthcare... is the enormous administrative friction created for patients, healthcare providers, and insurers—something that any sound business would relentlessly seek to drive out of its processes.

Healthcare today is similarly immobilized by having to wear a suit woven of administrative burdens that make the delivery of affordable and quality care nearly impossible.

The objective of this book is to first identify the culprits responsible for compromising and shackling the healthcare industry. We will then identify ways to shed the albatross that weighs down, and threatens to permanently disable, US healthcare.

Although the focus will admittedly be on the business of healthcare, improving the business of healthcare will also improve the patient experience, increase quality outcomes, and reduce costs.

We will look at the business of healthcare from the perspective of other industries: how new ways of partnering are driving significant efficiencies in these industries, and how these models can be used to also create a scalable healthcare system designed to meet the needs of the future. In that regard, I'll review how many of the concepts in the book that have been applied to other industries can also be applied to healthcare. That means we'll periodically embark on tangents that may at first seem to share little in common with healthcare. But that's only because we have developed a myopic view of healthcare. It is an insular industry that resists the opinions of outsiders and frequently puts up barriers of "not invented here." Those same barriers are among its biggest impediments to change.

I'm also well aware of the primary argument against much of what I've already said and what we'll discuss in this book: namely, that healthcare shouldn't be thought of as a business. The premise of the argument is that looking at healthcare as a business doesn't consider it a basic human right, and that it does not apply the most fundamental aspects of healthcare—compassion, caring, and healing—to how we approach any solution. What we will see is that these two points of view are not in conflict.

The force that is most dehumanizing healthcare, impeding the ability of a physician or clinician to focus on caring and healing, making healthcare unaffordable for so many, and ultimately disincentivizing patients from seeking healthcare, is the enormous administrative friction created for patients, healthcare providers, and insurers—something that any sound business would relentlessly seek to drive out of its processes.

Most importantly, keep in mind throughout the book that what we're describing isn't just an option, but rather a mandate for change that is unavoidable and which we put off at the peril of our social and personal well-being.

One last thing; a book of this sort cannot be written without asking the colloquial question, "Is this a prescription for healthcare?" The answer is that we are writing a new script for healthcare that will require off-label use of viable alternatives already in place in numerous other industries that are either unfamiliar to or rarely used in healthcare.

The good news is that there is a clear path forward to put healthcare on a track to serve the needs of the next hundred years if we have the courage and the resolve to take action now.

Everything we are about to discuss is already available as an option to create a future for healthcare that can set the standard for quality and value for the next century of change.

It won't be easy. Big change never is. It will require leadership with courage and vision on the part of those who are insiders, as well as the many more who live outside of the healthcare system. It will be messy, overwhelming at times, and painful for those who continue to fall through cracks that at times feel more like chasms. But the fact that you are reading this brings hope that we will fix US healthcare because of the efforts that you and so many others are taking. This book is at best a compass pointing in the direction of the change that needs to happen.

As Morpheus said to Neo just before Neo swallowed the red pill, "All I'm offering is the truth. Nothing more."

Welcome to the future of your healthcare.

Navigating the Book

To help you navigate the book, here's a rundown of what we'll cover in each of the book's three sections.

- **Part One, The Problem: Chapters 1–3** provide a summary of the trajectory of healthcare from the establishment of the first hospitals to its current state. We introduce the Ten Culprits of healthcare. We'll look at how the relationship between the patient and the healthcare provider has changed and the advent of health insurance and its evolution. We'll also begin to explore how healthcare complexity has increased to unsustainable levels and introduce the concepts of risk and smart-sourcing and the role both play in reimagining healthcare. We'll look at the specific costs of complexity, the demographic pressures that will force changes in the current system—including the government-funded, single-payer healthcare systems in other countries—and draw on examples from other industries that can be used as role models for the use of smartsourcing.

- **Part Two, The Solution: Chapters 4–5** introduce the importance of having healthcare providers focus on their core competency. We begin to deconstruct the current model of healthcare by presenting an alternative model of a "core competency" provider. We'll also look at how the trend toward core competency is evolving and changing every industry and use role models from other industries to better understand how we can apply these models to healthcare. We'll explore the challenges that smartsourcing will address as healthcare evolves into what we'll call Healthcare 2.0. We'll look at the changing role of the hospital, the myth behind the popular narrative that mergers and acquisitions are the best way to create economies of scale that reduce healthcare costs, and we'll begin to explore the move toward value-based healthcare. We start laying the groundwork for the concept of smartsourcing, which enables the formation of vast healthcare digital ecosystems that work together seamlessly by leveraging economies of scope, rather than economies of scale.

- **Part Three, The Future: Chapter 6** looks at the case study of John Muir Health and how it is using smartsourcing to build a sustainable community hospital for the future. Using John Muir Health as an example, we'll take a closer look at specific areas that can be smartsourced, such as the revenue cycle and information technology. We'll introduce and elaborate on the role of the healthcare services provider and how it directly addresses the Ten Culprits of healthcare.

Chapter 7 will offer a glimpse over the horizon at what the future of healthcare will look like. We'll delve into how the core competency model will be used to create the foundation for automated patient advocates, explore the possibility of hyperpersonalized medicine, take a look at some of the other disruptors to healthcare that will shape its future, and follow the evolution to what we'll call the hospital in the cloud.

At the end of each chapter, I've included a series of takeaways and lessons learned in the chapter, which we'll leverage as we move deeper into the book and the challenges of reimagining healthcare.

PART ONE: THE PROBLEM

*"It's time to build the future we want,
or one we don't want will be thrust upon us."*

—MICHAEL BENNET *(US Senator, Colorado)*

CHAPTER 1
ON THE PRECIPICE

Healthcare is on the precipice of enormous transformation brought on by three immutable forces: an aging demographic; the increasing sophistication and volume of diagnostic tools, therapies, and pharmaceuticals; and the exponential rate at which digital technology is advancing.

These changes are creating an unprecedented opportunity to build a future for healthcare that will put the patient at the center of a rich ecosystem with the power to positively impact the quality of life for each of us in dramatic ways.

As the demographics of the US and the world transition to a predominantly aging population and the diagnostic tools to uncover illnesses become prolific, we will experience a paradigm shift in how we view healthcare: from an acute service

> ...we need to make the transition from "sick care" to "health care."

meant to deal with injuries and sicknesses to an ongoing service that constantly monitors and maintains our well-being. Simply put, we need to make the transition from "sick care" to "health care."

> If we don't do something dramatic, courageous, and deliberate within the next decade, US healthcare will simply become economically unsustainable...

With the ability to capture and store data from every healthcare interaction, our digital genomes, and health patterns across vast populations, we will be able to predict disease and illness more accurately than we can currently predict tomorrow's weather forecast. It could be an amazing future in which healthcare becomes not only a fundamental human right, but one that is accessible and affordable for everyone.

Note that I said "could be" because healthcare is also at another precipice—one that threatens to send it, and all of this promise, plummeting out of control into an economic abyss.

Runaway administrative costs, dramatically shrinking margins for hospitals, the increasing burden on patients to pay for healthcare out of their own pockets, an equally onerous burden on doctors and clinicians to handle paperwork over patients, and systems that silo data in myriad proprietary repositories are crippling healthcare and the promise it could otherwise deliver.

If we don't do something dramatic, courageous, and deliberate within the next decade, the US healthcare system will simply become economically unsustainable and unable to provide quality care to an aging population with ever-increasing and ever more complex healthcare needs. What we think of as a crisis in healthcare today will pale in comparison to what lies ahead.

This may sound like fearmongering, but that is decidedly not the purpose or tone of this book. Instead, I've written this with the objective of providing insights into how healthcare organizations can apply proven methods, such as smartsourcing, to improve their underlying business, which in turn determines so much of the efficacy and the experience of healthcare for the patient and ultimately averts the crisis ahead.

Who's Who

It's important at the outset to clarify some core terminology that we will use throughout the book.

First off, the term *healthcare organization* or *system* refers to a variety of different players that make up the healthcare ecosystem. To keep things as simple and as straightforward as possible, we'll use the term *provider* to refer to those who are involved with the delivery of healthcare, such as hospitals, healthcare or hospital systems, doctors, doctor networks, clinicians, and clinics. We'll use the term *payer* to refer primarily to insurance companies or the government, which pays for healthcare through programs such as Medicare and Medicaid, also known as Centers for Medicare and Medicaid Services (CMS). However, a patient and an employer can also be a payer if the patient is paying out of pocket or if the employer is self-funding an insurance plan for a provider's services. Where needed, we'll make the distinction of which payers we're referring to.

Second, much of our focus will be on what's called smartsourcing. The easiest way to understand smartsourcing is by contrasting it to outsourcing. Outsourcing is driven purely by cost cutting. When an organization outsources a process, it sheds not only the process, but also all of its employees who were once responsible for that process. Unlike outsourcing, smartsourcing is driven by the need to innovate while keeping the employees of the original organization in place.

Smartsourcing is also a strategic decision by an organization to invest more of its resources into developing its core competency while partnering on those areas that are outside of the core.

Another term we will introduce is healthcare services provider (HSP). HSPs are third-party organizations that partner with a healthcare provider or payer to deliver smartsourcing services. These are private for-profit enterprises that have deep core competency in healthcare administration. As we'll see, HSPs are essential to slowing the high costs of administrative overhead, improving the patient experience, and allowing providers to focus on their core competencies. Ultimately HSPs will become a necessary part of the healthcare ecosystem.

Lastly, the use of two terms should be clarified. The first is the "business of healthcare," which refers specifically to the operational and administrative aspects of healthcare rather than to the clinical care itself. So, while a surgical procedure is not, in our use, the business of healthcare, the billing, claims processes, information technology, analytics, documentation of procedures, and payments are. The second is the term "consumer" or "patient-consumer." Although I realize that the word "consumer" carries connotations of commercialism, which may be off-putting to some, it also speaks to the focus on the individual as someone who needs to be understood and respected for their specific needs and wants. It is that ethos of empathy that we'll focus on in the use of the term within the book.

Before we go any further, it's helpful to make what we're discussing a bit more tangible by considering what healthcare could look like if we take the steps outlined in this book.

So let's take a quick jump into the future and imagine a healthcare system where each of the following is the norm.

What if...

- ...the patient experience and journey were stream-lined so that administrative friction, paperwork, documentation, and the burden on the patient of denied claims and erroneous and surprise billing were removed?

- ...providers actually treated patients like consum-ers with a simplified experience, alternative ways to access care, and online conveniences?

- ...providers were able to spend their time focusing exclusively on delivering care and healing rather than spending over half of their time documenting and justifying procedures?[1]

- ...providers and payers were able to eliminate the friction (effort, cost, and frustration) caused by the endless back-and-forth to determine the validity of coverage and claims?

- ...healthcare costs were reduced through the use of analytics and predictive models that leveraged large pools of data to better understand the short- and long-term costs of different outcomes on patient populations and individual patients?

No doubt, it's a stretch to imagine that sort of healthcare system in the next five to ten years. However, the unabash-edly bold claim presented here is that all of this is possible. The changes I'm suggesting will not only increase capacity and quality while decreasing the costs of healthcare, but also improve access to healthcare. Granted, that's a tall order, but it is not only achievable; it's achievable in the near term without a wholesale restructuring of healthcare, all the while preserving the option of choice for the patient and the benefit of significantly improved outcomes.

One last thing before we move on. The question I encountered regularly while researching and writing this book was, "Why now—what makes this point in time so critical to make a change?" As this book was being written, the US was still in the longest economic boom since the 1920s. GDP had been steadily rising for over a decade. Unemployment hadn't been this low since Diana Ross and the Supremes topped the Billboard charts. The fifteen largest companies in the US had nearly one trillion dollars of cash in the bank.[2] Although healthcare is no less broken because of this, its brokenness is much more tolerable in a healthy economy since more people have greater means to pay out of pocket. But that would imply that now is not a good time, right?

In 2010, when the ACA (the Affordable Care Act or Obamacare) was passed, the country was just coming out of a recession, with unemployment having reached 9.9 percent in the prior year. The nation was in pain, and political will and social support for change is almost always commensurate with the current degree of socioeconomic pain, which fuels the desire for change. However, if we wait for an economic crisis, the political will and public appetite to make drastic changes to healthcare may be adequate to push through nearly any policy change, but we will end up with crisis-mode decision-making, which is reactionary and rarely bodes well for the best long-term outcomes. Instead, as we'll see, it results in precisely the sort of patchwork healthcare policy that has led us to where we are today.

> Why not take advantage of this unique moment in time to put in place a foundation for healthcare that we can live with?

Today we have the luxury of making conscious and deliberate decisions about healthcare from a position of some economic strength on the part of providers, payers, and patients. None of this dismisses the importance of policy change. This will be necessary, and it will occur—but if history is any indication, it'll happen only when all other options have been taken off the table. Why not take advantage of this unique moment in time to start creating a healthcare system that we can live with?

The Ten Hidden Culprits of Quality Healthcare

Fixing the US healthcare system is one of the greatest challenges we face as a society. But trying to deconstruct the subject in a way that makes it meaningful and easy to understand can be daunting. To help us in our discussion, I'll use what I call the Ten Culprits of healthcare.

Although we all face these ten challenges on a regular basis, most of us feel helpless to do anything about them. As with so many of the costs involved in running any business, we accept them as simply the price to pay for the system we have, however dysfunctional it may be. Besides, we have no choice but to accept them since it's the only healthcare system the overwhelming majority of us have access to. Like the citizens of an impoverished economy, we wait in breadlines because that's the only place to get bread.

The irony is that we all know what the basic problems are. None of these Ten Culprits should come as a surprise. In

> We know what the elephant in the room is. We all agree it's there. We can all see it clearly. We just can't get it to move, no matter how many peanuts we throw at it!

fact, I expect you will nod your head in familiarity (or frustration) when you read through each one. As my friend Bill Shickolovich, CIO and executive VP at Tufts Medical Center, said to me, "We know what the elephant in the room is. We all agree it's there. We can all see it clearly. We just can't get it to move, no matter how many peanuts we throw at it!"

Well, in this case, there are ten elephants in the room. Notice, however, that I specifically call them the Ten Culprits and not the Ten Costs. That's because although they all have some negative impact on cost, the more critical effect they have is on the quality of care.

As we encounter each of these Culprits throughout the book, we will often call them out in order to point out how they individually and collectively undermine the US healthcare system. Later in the book, we will take them on one by one as we suggest ways to solve the US healthcare crisis.

1. **The Anonymous Patient.** Despite all the efforts to create medical records that are portable and shareable, there is still no single continuous repository of patient data that can be used to provide a reliable context for the treatment of patients and the projection of their outcomes. The problem lies in the fact that sharing of this data still happens within silos of provider organizations and insurers. As patients move from provider to provider and insurer to insurer, their continuity of care suffers as their health history is hidden in myriad healthcare systems.

2. **The Asymmetry Between Costs and Outcomes.** A lack of visibility into the relationship between costs and outcomes of a healthcare procedure, treatment, or therapy prevents patients and doctors from treating patients in a way that adequately balances cost and risk. Furthermore, large-scale studies have

shown that there is no correlation between the cost of healthcare and outcomes.[3] The result is an inherent asymmetry and lack of consistent alignment between the cost of a procedure and its impact on healthcare outcomes. Any relationship between the two is hidden and often incalculable. Try to come up with any other case when you are involved in a commercial transaction without being able to weigh costs against outcomes. It just doesn't exist because we would never tolerate it anywhere else.

3. **The Episodic Care Conundrum.** A disconnected healthcare life cycle creates vast opportunity for errors, redundancy, suboptimal treatments, and diagnostic failures. This goes beyond just having a single data source for a patient's history, as in Culprit #1. The disconnected nature of healthcare comes from the inability not only to share data, but also to coordinate a patient's life cycle of integrated care. This makes predictive methods to determine diagnostics and interventions nearly impossible. As a result, we are constantly stuck treating individual symptoms and not the underlying issues. This has an impact on both individual outcomes and public health issues such as diabetes, kidney disease, and Alzheimer's, which are among the most prevalent and costly diseases on the rise involving large populations of patients.

4. **The Complexity Crisis.** Our healthcare system has simply become too complex and sophisticated for humans to handle on their own without the use of much more sophisticated technologies such as data analytics, artificial intelligence (AI), and machine learning, which can quickly interpret the uniqueness of each patient's situation and handle

the enormity of administrative work required for each patient. Consider that a typical primary care doctor has a panel of 1,200–1,900 patients[4] to deal with on an ongoing basis. Attempting to diagnose, treat, coordinate care for, and document that many patients—especially as the number of diagnostic codes and the number of treatments increase radically—is next to impossible. And that's for patients lucky enough to have a primary care physician. According to a Kaiser Family Foundation report, 28 percent of US men (45 percent for Hispanic Americans) do not have a primary care doctor.[5] As we'll see, patients without a PCP increase the complexity and cost of healthcare by relying on specialists and emergency room visits. The complexity of medicine is not going to subside, especially as the population ages. As we'll see, it will not be solved by adding more PCPs—there just aren't enough of them. What we can do is radically decrease administrative complexity and costs.

5. **The Missing Link.** There is no single interorganizational entity to coordinate all the pieces of the healthcare system that need to be synchronized among patients, payers, and providers in order to coordinate care that both minimizes costs and optimizes outcomes. This sounds a lot like Culprits #1, #2, and #4. The difference is that it's not about the data as much as the hidden processes. Tracking the data and tasks needed to coordinate healthcare can never happen without an independent third party to streamline the care and management of administrative transactions and processes, as opposed to expecting it to happen organically through standards or a government-imposed entity.

6. **Drifting from the Core.** Healthcare providers have been forced to take on the responsibility of managing many administrative aspects of care, such as documentation, coding, and billing procedures, which detract them from their core competency of caring for the patient. For example, a physician spends two hours on the electronic health record[i] (EHR) and desk work for each hour of direct patient care.[6] Hospitals are also increasingly turning to mergers to alleviate eroding profit margins by at least leveraging shared services and buying power through the economies of scale of larger providers. Hidden in all of this is a dirty little secret about healthcare: economies of scale drive up costs. And, as we'll see, these mergers can actually have a negative impact on the overall quality of care and outcomes.

7. **The Tragedy of the Commons.** Healthcare is an inherently complex process that has evolved organically without a clear or well-designed overarching architecture. This has resulted in myriad participants (providers, physicians, clinicians, payers, and administrators) involved in the delivery of healthcare, each one attempting to optimize their own metrics for success. While this may appear to

---

i   An electronic health record (EHR) contains a patient's medical history in digital form. There is often confusion between the acronyms EHR and EMR (electronic medical record). An EHR is a more comprehensive view of the patient, while an EMR is a narrower view typically used for diagnosis and treatment of a specific illness by a doctor or specialist. EMRs are not typically meant to be shared outside of a practice, while the purpose of an EHR is that it can be shared across providers. In keeping with the book's focus on the overall healthcare system, and to keep things simple, we will use the acronym EHR unless we're using an outside reference specific to EMRs.

be advantageous for each individual participant, its overall effect is to erode the patient experience and dramatically increase costs and the potential for fraud through extensive gaming of the system.

8. **Defensive Medicine.** The practice of physicians ordering unnecessary tests and procedures in order to protect themselves from the potential of malpractice, although the tests have no benefit to the patient, results in up to 25 percent of all healthcare costs according to Gallup.[7] That comes to about $2,000 per person per year of unneeded procedures such as x-rays, blood tests, MRIs, and CT scans. A 2012 survey conducted by the American Academy of Orthopaedic Surgeons found that 96 percent of its doctors self-reported the practice of defensive medicine.[8] Researchers at Vanderbilt University found that the nation's orthopedic surgeons alone accounted for $173 million a month, nearly $2 billion annually, of defensive medicine. A 2015 survey conducted by the Congress of Neurological Surgeons found that 75 percent of neurosurgeons reported practicing defensive medicine to protect themselves from litigation. A 2017 survey of 2,106 physicians reported that 20.6 percent of overall medical care was unnecessary. The most common cited reason for overtreatment was fear of malpractice at 84.7 percent.

9. **The Primary Care Crisis.** There is a growing shortage of primary care physicians in the United States. According to the Association of American Medical Colleges, the US will see a shortage of up to 120,000 physicians by 2030.[9] Primary care physicians are potentially the single most important factor in determining quality healthcare and

patient longevity. Because they also balance the costs and benefits of treatment plans, primary care doctors also ultimately determine much of the cost effectiveness of the healthcare system. The lack of enough PCPs may well be one of the greatest hidden threats to the long-term effectiveness of any healthcare model, since the relationship between patients and their physicians is a foundational cornerstone of a patient-centered approach.

10. **The Aging of America.** An aging demographic will multiply the consequences of the above Culprits dramatically over the next two decades, ultimately making today's healthcare models economically unsustainable.

These Ten Culprits are at the heart of why the US healthcare system has become the most expensive in the world. However, they are also present to some degree in virtually every industrial-era healthcare system across the globe, regardless of the payer. As we look at the current state of healthcare and plot a trajectory for its future, we will come back to these regularly.

Friction(less)

Before we go much further it's important to clarify what I mean by the term friction because it's a central theme we will explore throughout the book.

In engineering, friction is a force that acts on a moving object and creates resistance, which slows the object down. Here, friction refers to the many administrative resources and systems that do not add value to the healthcare system. Administrative overhead creates resistance to change, slows the delivery of care, overcomplicates and frustrates the patient experience, creates impediments to delivering quality afford-able healthcare, and pits providers against payers and forces gaming of the system by both. Ultimately, friction restricts the innovation of new business models through which to deliver better healthcare outcomes.

Friction is always present in some fashion in every busi-ness process, as it is in every mechanical operation. The natural laws of physics, as well as those of commerce, dictate that you can never operate at 100 percent efficiency. The objective of an engineer or business manager is to mini-mize friction so that it's less than that of the competition and allows an organization to meet the demands of the market in a timely and affordable manner.

However, the irony of friction is that it's often hidden in plain sight. In other words, we know something is impeding a process, we can see it and describe it, but, we will accept it as necessary if we have become accustomed to it. In that sense, it becomes what we simply term "a cost of doing business." As a result, friction is always a relative measure.

So, by way of example, if I run a bank and the friction in my administrative paperwork means that a residential mortgage takes three weeks to process, that's only a problem if a com-petitor takes two weeks, or if I simply can't process enough mortgages within a three-week process to meet the demand. Other-wise, the friction is simply accepted as a necessary cost of doing business.

The existence of fric-tion also doesn't mean that all of the individ-ual tasks that make up a

In the case of healthcare, the sand causing friction is so finely ground and so pervasive that extri-cating it is considered impossible, so we've been pouring lubricant into the system by the bucketful.

process aren't otherwise exceptional, but rather that something is preventing the overall process from operating at a higher level of efficiency.

For example, think of a machine that uses gears to operate; perhaps it's a large clock. Imagine that these gears have been machined to impeccable Swiss watch-like precision. Somehow, sand has found its way into the clock's mechanism. As the clock operates and the gears turn, what happens? The sand will cause grinding and prevent the clock's mechanism from operating efficiently. It may also grind down the precision of the gears so that they begin to slip and fail. As the machine tries to go faster, the friction increases, as does the potential for damage to the gears.

We have two options at this point; we can stop the clock, disassemble it and remove the sand, or add lots of lubricant and accept that it just won't tell time as accurately as it otherwise could without the friction. Of course, if every other clock manufacturer had the same problem, it wouldn't worry us much since that would be what customers expected.

There is however, one other complication in the case of healthcare which does not fit neatly into our clock analogy. Time is precise and unchanging (with all due respect to Einstein). Therefore, clocks need to be totally predictable machines, and any change to a single gear or component has a predictable impact on every other part of the mechanism. That's not true of healthcare and medicine, which are constantly changing and evolving along with the sources of friction. A change to one part of the healthcare system has numerous unforeseen and unforeseeable implications to other parts of the healthcare ecosystem.

In the case of healthcare, we can't afford to stop the machine and disassemble the parts to find the source of the friction. The sand causing the friction is also so finely ground and so pervasive that extricating it, while not impossible, would be extremely expensive. So instead, we've been pouring lubricant into the system by the bucketful and dealing with an imprecise mechanism. That expensive lubricant is the administrative cost of labor and resources. And what about the imprecision of our hypothetical clock? Well, we can equate that to less-than-optimal healthcare outcomes.

That last point about outcomes often casts a long shadow over the perceived quality of US healthcare. As you'll see throughout the book, I'm going to take a hard stand on the fact that the US healthcare system is already more than capable of delivering high quality outcomes. In fact, what I'm about to suggest will, at first blush, strike you as anathema if you follow the conventional narrative about US healthcare, which positions US healthcare as being inferior in quality to many other health systems throughout the world.

The Healthcare Trade Balance

The "root cause" of the US healthcare problem is not a lack of quality for either the treatments provided or patient outcomes, but rather the administrative friction that drives up cost, hinders access to care, blocks innovation, and ultimately impacts patient outcomes. When you remove the friction, and overcome affordability, the system stands to deliver exceptional outcomes.

If you doubt this, consider the fact that over eight hundred thousand patients spend close to $10 billion yearly to come from around the world seeking treatment

> ...the "root cause" of the US healthcare problem is not quality nor cost, but rather the administrative friction that drives up cost and ultimately impacts quality.

in US hospitals from US healthcare professionals.[10] The reason these patients come to the US has nothing to do with the lower cost of healthcare, since they will pay commercial uninsured rates in cash transactions for the world's most expensive healthcare system. Instead, it has everything to do with the quality of care, innovative therapies, and the greater likelihood of a successful outcome.

Equally telling is the fact that, on the other hand, a nearly identical number of US residents are turning to medical tourism,[11] where they travel to countries outside of the US, not for higher quality, but specifically to find lower-cost healthcare.

This is admittedly a controversial point. In fact, I'm sure that many people who read this will instantly react negatively to the way I'm portraying the quality of US healthcare. But the statistics used to denigrate the US healthcare systems often have little, if anything, to do with the actual quality of healthcare.

For example, an extensive article in the online magazine *Quartz* quoted a UN study as ranking US healthcare 28th in the world. That sounds atrocious until you look at the UN report, funded by the Bill & Melinda Gates Foundation, that the article was based on.[12] In fact, the UN report had very little to do with the quality of healthcare itself, and much more to do with the general state of diseases, injuries, and risk factors in 188 countries. It looked at things such as levels of pollution, suicide rates, vehicular accidents, and rates of intimate partner violence. It's highly unlikely any of these would be impacted by the quality of healthcare or the availability of some sort of universal healthcare.

Other studies have shown mixed results among the world's largest and wealthiest countries. A 2019 report by the Peterson Center for Healthcare and the Kaiser Family Foundation[13] measured a variety of factors in nine countries including the Netherlands, Germany, Australia, the UK,

France, Sweden, Switzerland, Canada, and the US.

Although the US lagged in some categories such as same-day access to a doctor or nurse (sixth), it was third for mortality rates from cancer, and below the nine-country average for thirty-day mortality following heart attacks and strokes.

...the statistics used to denigrate the US healthcare systems often have little, if anything, to do with the actual quality of healthcare.

Although the use of rankings provides important insights, it's also important to keep in mind that the differences among the top ranked countries amount to only a few people per hundred thousand. In other words, bridging these differences and bringing the US into a position of preeminence in healthcare is not something that is outside of our reach. That's not to say that there isn't more than ample room for improvement in many areas of the US healthcare systems.

An Old Story

What is clear is that whatever the current rate of friction, which impedes quality delivery of healthcare, may be, it is being amplified by the much more demanding needs of an aging population. Currently, half of all medical care is provided by emergency rooms.[14] The US is second only to Canada in the use of emergency room visits in place of regular doctor visits, and the trend has been steadily increasing over the last twenty years. (Illustration 1.1.) Of those ER visits, 25 percent are for people sixty-five and over.[15]

Hospital Emergency Department Visits per 1000 Persons 1995-2016

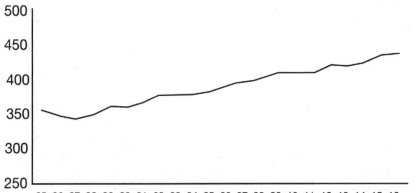

Source: Analysis of American Hospital Association Annual Survey for 2016 for community hospitals and US Census Bureau National and StatePopulation Estimates, July 1, 2016
https://www.aha.org/guidesreports/2018-05-23-trendwatch-chartbook-2018-chapter-3- utilization-and-volume

Illustration 1.1 Visits to the ER (Emergency Department) have been increasing steadily over the past twenty years.

As we'll see in chapter 3, demographic shifts in the US population will radically change the complexity of healthcare. According to Jonathan Vespa of the US census bureau:

> the year 2030 marks an important demographic turning point in US history according to the US Census Bureau's 2017 National Population Projections. By 2030, all baby boomers will be older than age sixty-five. This will expand the size of the older population so that one in every five residents will be retirement age.
>
> The aging of baby boomers means that within just a couple decades, older people are projected to outnumber children for the first time in US

history. By 2035, there will be 78 million people 65 years and older compared to 76.7 million under the age of 18.

To compound the effect of this on healthcare even further, according to the Association of American Medical Colleges, the shortfall of doctors will grow to over 121,300 by 2030.[16] Moreover, fewer doctors wish to pursue a primary care career, and fewer still geriatric medicine, favoring instead the more lucrative and less-intruded-upon practices of specialization.

This is not a challenge we can address by putting more beds in hospitals in the same way that we did during the twentieth century. In fact, admissions to hospitals have been dropping steadily as walk-in clinics, ambulatory care facilities, and home care are increasingly becoming the less-costly alternatives. Beds per thousand persons fell by nearly 30 percent, from 3.5 in 1995 to 2.5 in 2016. (Illustration 1.2)

Number of Beds and Number of Beds per 1000 Persons 1995-2016

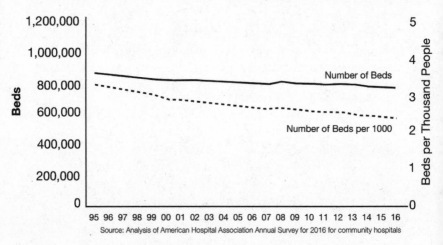

Source: Analysis of American Hospital Association Annual Survey for 2016 for community hospitals

Illustration 1.2[17] Admissions to hospitals have been dropping with the advent of less-costly alternatives. Beds per 1000 persons fell by nearly 30 percent, from 3.5 in 1995 to 2.5 in 2016.

This aligns with the emphasis in healthcare on reducing reliance on hospitals by shifting the focus to keeping people well rather than delivering in-hospital episodic care for preventable illnesses. (As we'll see, this doesn't mean that hospitals go away, but that their role will change.)

There are already economic incentives to move away from hospital admissions provided by Medicare as well as commercial payers. However, the challenge is that many health insurance plans often discourage patients from seeking adequate care to begin with by shifting more of the costs—in the form of high copayments and deductibles—directly onto consumers.

The bottom line is that any attempt to scale the current system to meet a very different set of demands without a fundamental change in how both healthcare providers and payers operate is a recipe for not only the economic collapse of healthcare, but also the incalculable loss of opportunity in realizing the promise and innovation of healthcare.

If healthcare providers and payers were able to shed the administrative albatross, they would have the latitude, resources, and capital to innovate entirely new ways of managing the transition to more effective healthcare business models that incentivize patients, providers, and payers to achieve the best possible healthcare outcomes.

The bottom line is that any attempt to scale the current system to meet a very different set of demands without a fundamental change in how both healthcare providers and payers operate is a recipe for not only the economic collapse of healthcare, but also the incalculable loss of opportunity in realizing the promise and innovation of healthcare.

When all is said and done, that is the ambitious objective of the chapters that follow: to provide a path forward which delivers on that promise.

ON THE PRECIPICE, CHAPTER 1 RECAP AND LESSONS LEARNED

The forces shaping the future of healthcare are: an aging demographic with more complex health issues, the increasing sophistication and volume of diagnostic tools, new therapies and pharmaceuticals, and the exponential rate at which digital technology is advancing.

These trends hold both the promise of longer and healthier lives as well as the challenge of a far more complex and costly health system.

The Ten Culprits that undermine affordable, quality healthcare are:

1. The Anonymous Patient
2. The Asymmetry between Costs and Outcomes
3. The Episodic Care Conundrum
4. The Complexity Crisis
5. The Missing Link
6. Drifting from the Core
7. The Tragedy of the Commons
8. Defensive Medicine
9. The Primary Care Crisis
10. The Aging of America

All of these Ten Culprits generate friction, which restricts the innovation of new business models through which to deliver better healthcare outcomes. We showed that by many measures, US healthcare providers are among the best in the world; the problem is not the quality of care but the administrative friction that hinders access and affordability of healthcare.

The existing shortfall of PCP doctors, which will grow to over 121,300 by 2030, will put enormous strain on an already strained healthcare system.

Scaling the current system to meet a very different set of demands in the future, without a fundamental change in how both healthcare providers and payers operate, is a recipe for not only the economic collapse of healthcare, but also the incalculable loss of opportunity in realizing the promise and innovation of healthcare.

CHAPTER 2
HIDDEN IN PLAIN SIGHT

Seventeen-year-old Nataline Sarkisyan desperately needed a new liver. She had already beaten leukemia, but the intensive regimen of chemotherapy that was used to battle her cancer had caused her liver to fail.[1]

A new liver would give Nataline a 65 percent chance of living a normal life. Without a transplant, doctors speculated that she had only a few days to live at best. Luckily, Nataline matched for the perfect liver. There was one problem: her insurance would not cover it because it was considered "experimental" and unproven in the specific set of circumstances surrounding her particular form of cancer.

Nataline's family protested and created such a large public relations scandal for her healthcare insurer, Cigna, that they finally approved the liver transplant.

Unfortunately, the approval came just a few hours too late for Nataline, who passed away days before the transplant was scheduled.

Nataline's situation is anything but exceptional, and it speaks to how inept our healthcare system has become at fulfilling the needs of patients as individuals. This is not because the healthcare system is filled with unfeeling people, but because they are shackled by outdated processes.

The current state of healthcare is the result of a century of well-intentioned policies meant to preserve the sanctity of the relationship between doctor and patient and to manage the increasing volume of options to both. The majority of these polices were put in place during the industrial era, following the well-understood principles of scaling markets through an assembly line and factory automation model that served the average needs of average people (Culprit #1, The Anonymous Patient). By and large, they were instated in order to keep pace with a fast-growing population. It's important to keep that in mind, since it is tempting to blame everyone and everything involved in the development of our healthcare system.

Despite all good intentions, these policies have inadvertently created a system riddled with friction that often brings the entire objective of healthcare—the well-being of the patient—to a grinding halt. For Nataline, it wasn't the inability of the healthcare provider to perform the liver transplant that she needed, but rather a process with so much inherent friction on the part of the payers that it could not respond to her needs in time. Clearly, payers need to develop criteria that will allow them to make hard choices about coverage. I'm not proposing that payers should try every experimental treatment available for every patient.

No matter what sort of healthcare system is in place, from universal government-funded healthcare to private insurance self-funded by an employer, someone still needs to make these difficult decisions. In Nataline's case, the survival rates for a seventeen-year-old range from 80 percent to 60 percent over one to twenty years, respectively,[2] this compared with 86 and 53 percent overall for all liver transplants. So it's hard to call her payer's initial decision to deny coverage clear-cut; far too many variables are involved beyond these simple percentages. Although we are not in the position to guess what the outcome of a liver transplant would have been, it certainly did not help that the decision took as long as it did.

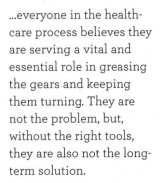

Ironically, most of the friction that slows healthcare is hidden in plain sight. We knowingly experience it as patients, providers, and payers, but we accept it since it is all we have known. What's worse is that this friction supports 25 to 30 percent of an industry that forms the single largest part of our economy. It's foolish to expect that any change to a system that supports the economics of an industry so vast will be welcome by the many who profit from its waste, inefficiency, and friction.

> ...everyone in the healthcare process believes they are serving a vital and essential role in greasing the gears and keeping them turning. They are not the problem, but, without the right tools, they are also not the long-term solution.

Good People Stuck in a Bad Process

You'd be hard-pressed to find anyone who works in healthcare as a clinician, doctor, nurse, administrator, or insurer who has not, in some significant measure, dedicated himself or herself to the goal of helping patients. And yet, the overall process has somehow lost its ability to deliver on that same objective. That's the nature of complex systems; they take on a life of their own and are shaped organically through incremental measures that all conspire to make large-scale change nearly impossible.

The overwhelming majority of people who have chosen to work in healthcare believe they are serving an essential role in delivering quality care. With very few exceptions, hospitals, health systems, clinics, doctors, nurses, clinicians, insurers, and administrators are doing everything they can to keep the gears of the healthcare systems turning to best serve patients. It is easy to vilify any one party, as is often the case in much of the media coverage of healthcare, but healthcare workers are not the central problem. However, without the right tools, they are also not the long-term solution.

The real problem we need to face is the convoluted nature of the healthcare process: a process that pits providers of healthcare against those who pay for it, creates silos of information and caregivers rather than integrated healthcare, lacks price transparency, and puts the patient on the periphery of the healthcare system. The collateral damage of this process is the deprioritization of patients' well-being. Rather than put the patient at the center, they end up putting the patient somewhere inside of a vast maze with an overwhelming number of paths—with little, if any, direction as to which may be the best one out.

It is far easier to point the finger of blame at the people, the hospitals, the insurers, or even the patients than it is to look at the dauntingly convoluted process of healthcare.

The immense Gordian knot complicating all aspects of how we deliver and pay for healthcare is woven of threads from well-intentioned participants doing the best they can with the tools they've inherited, and yet, like a hapless Charlie Chaplin lost in the gears of an enormous industrial engine, they are all losing the battle to keep the gears turning faster and faster.

> ...since 1970, there has been a negligible rise in the number of healthcare providers, doctors, and clinicians. Yet, the number of administrators has increased by nearly 2500 percent.

The accelerating needs of an aging population, an ever-increasing array of new illnesses along with a commensurate increase in therapies and pharmaceuticals, and the tremendous burden on primary care doctors to handle growing patient loads all serve to accelerate the complexity crisis in healthcare (Culprit #4).

While every player involved in the delivery of healthcare needs to be held to the highest standards, continuing to vilify healthcare providers and insurers ignores and, in many ways, distracts us from the more treacherous and pervasive problem of dealing with the underlying causes of the dysfunction.

Out of Control

Providers and payers, as well as those responsible for public policy, have built fortresses of administrative procedures that make navigating healthcare akin to running an obstacle course blindfolded. Many of these are well-intentioned processes. For example, HIPAA, which was designed to make patient data portable and private across the healthcare ecosystem, resulted in one of the steepest increases ever seen in administrative overhead and documentation. (Illustration 2.1)

Consider that since 1970, the number of administrators has increased by nearly 2500 percent. Almost all of the increase in administrative burden has been due to one overwhelming factor: the

> While every player involved in the delivery of healthcare needs to be held to the highest standards, continuing to vilify healthcare providers and insurers ignores and, in many ways, distracts us from the more treacherous and pervasive problem of dealing with the underlying causes of the dysfunction.

increasing complexity of how we document and determine the justification for medical procedures and bill for healthcare services.

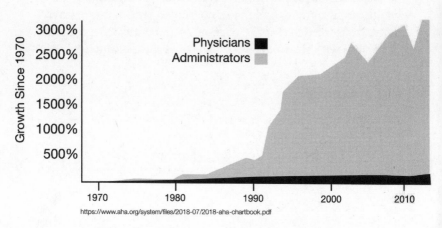

Illustration 2.1 The increase in healthcare administrators since 1970 has been extraordinary, while the number of physicians has remained relatively static.

For healthcare to become more focused on the patient over the process, the healthcare industry needs to drastically reduce, or even shed, these administrative costs. Providers and payers need to reallocate their precious resources to focus on their respective core competencies of improving patient outcomes and providing patients and clinicians with the ability to make informed decisions about healthcare, its value, and its costs. In today's healthcare system, the latter is nearly impossible for the patient to do on their own. (The reasons for that will become obvious as we delve into the case studies later in the book.)

What's equally alarming about the recent trend in the increase of administrative personnel is that the number of physicians has remained relatively flat. The burden this puts on doctors has severe consequences for both doctors and their patients. Being a doctor has always been an incredibly stressful profession. It's been known for over ten years that doctors have a higher rate of suicide than the average population. Even in medical school, the second leading cause of death among students, after accidents, is suicide. It's estimated that the equivalent of an entire class of a medium-sized medical school is lost to suicide each year.[3] Although we could argue that those individuals who make it through the demands and rigors of medical school and residency are the ones most able to take on that burden, there is clearly a point at which the demands of the job exceed the capabilities of even the most superhuman among us.

In a 2018 survey of 6,695 physicians conducted by the Mayo Clinic, 54.3 percent reported symptoms of burnout, 32 percent reported excessive fatigue, and 6.5 percent reported recent suicidal thoughts. And all of this ultimately trickles down to the quality of care the patient receives. Physicians reporting errors were more likely to have symptoms of burnout, fatigue, and recent suicidal ideation.[4]

Driving Ms. Ivy

To better understand the degree of convolution in the current process of navigating a simple healthcare situation, I'd like you to imagine the following scenario. As absurd as it may appear to be at times, follow along because there's a surprise ending to this story.

Ivy Austin's pride and joy was her fifty-nine-year-old antique Cadillac Series 62 drop top, a luxurious land yacht painted Antoinette blue, complete with massive bulging fenders, steel slab sides, and art deco-inspired gray leather interior.

While she had the car officially appraised at $94,000, to Ivy it was priceless, having been handed down to her as a birthday gift from her parents. To keep it in pristine condition, Ivy had purchased a rather expensive warranty from an antique auto club that cost her $500 per year. The warranty did have a deductible of $2,250, but it capped her out-of-pocket costs for repairs to $7,150 per year, and it was from one of the largest, oldest, and most trusted brand names in the auto warranty business. Besides, Ivy wasn't much worried about the deductible since her parents had had the car fully restored to a pristine condition in 1996 and had barely driven it. The warranty was a small price to pay for peace of mind.

Shortly after she bought her warranty, Ivy noticed that the car's headlights started to exhibit an odd flickering behavior. Ivy checked her warranty and chose a well-known and reputable nearby repair shop—the only one close by that was covered by the plan.

The repair shop ran a series of tests on Ivy's car that turned up nothing wrong save for a small spot in the rear of one of the headlights. The shop clerk directed her to one of their specialist mechanics who worked on headlight problems. When Ivy saw the specialist, he commented that he wasn't really a headlight specialist but more of an exhaust specialist who sometimes looked at headlights. Nonetheless, Ivy had already taken the time off to have the car checked out, so she went along with the exam.

The "specialist" quickly looked at the problem and told Ivy that everything was fine. She didn't need to worry at all about the spot on the headlight, but to be safe, she should really schedule time to see an antique headlight specialist the next time she came in. The whole episode only took a few minutes.

Ivy went home with her headlights still flickering but assumed the mechanic knew what he was doing.

A few days later she got a bill for $820 directly from the exhaust specialist rather than the repair shop. On the bill was a note that Ivy had seen him for an "extended" time. Ivy called the shop to find out how she could have been billed for an extended visit when she only saw the mechanic for a few minutes. She was told that the mechanic wasn't an employee, but that he just rented out a bay for his private clients. If Ivy wanted to dispute the bill, she'd need to take it up with the mechanic directly.

Ivy considered it but didn't want to make waves with a repair shop conveniently located so close to home. Besides, since everyone at the repair shop had said her headlights were fine, she was relieved and figured she might as well just go ahead and pay the bill. After all, she assumed it would be applied toward her warranty's deductible and she knew she had to go back for more tests.

Ivy then dutifully made an appointment with an antique headlight specialist to get everything thoroughly checked out as she'd been told to do. At that appointment, many of the same tests were repeated, and again nothing was found except for a small spot on the back of her headlamp which she was told was totally normal for a car of this vintage.

The shop then conducted a diagnostic test to make sure that the glass lenses used in the headlights were in fact correct for that particular vintage Cadillac. Sure enough, Ivy was told she needed new headlight lenses and was given a note with a code for the type of lenses she needed to get. The mechanic doing that test also told Ivy that, just to be safe, they really should redo another of the tests done during her first visit to check out her electrical wiring harness, battery, and alternator. Finally, Ivy pushed back, telling him that she'd just done those tests a few weeks ago.

The mechanic smiled and just said that he understood but it wouldn't hurt to repeat the tests. If Ivy didn't want to do them now, she should make another appointment to come back soon.

Ivy soon received another bill, this time for $900. Luckily, that was covered by her warranty plan, so she assumed that there was no need to dispute its high cost—until she was notified that while her claim for the $900 was covered, she had not yet met her deductible since the previous bill of $820 was because the exhaust specialist was an independent contractor and not part of the covered repair shop. Ivy was frustrated, but mostly at herself for not asking more questions of the shop. Reluctantly she paid, knowing that, at least this time, it was applied to her deductible.

When Ivy went to buy the new headlight lenses, she realized that she'd left the note with the lens part numbers at the repair shop. Embarrassed, she called the shop. The very kind lady who answered found the note and told Ivy that the headlights she'd been told to buy were absolutely not the right ones. She went on to say that the mechanic who had written the note wasn't actually a mechanic yet, but a student mechanic. She told Ivy that, after thirteen years in the auto repair business, she knew with complete confidence that the headlight lens recommendation made by the mechanic was not right. Ivy was irritated that the shop had still billed her for $900 but wasn't in the mood to pursue the issue since she'd already applied it to her deductible. Besides, the nice lady had taken care of the error and provided Ivy with the information she needed.

Unfortunately, it turned out that Ivy's car troubles were not yet over. During a regular oil change the next week, at a drive-in lube shop, the technician noted that the Cadillac was in great shape for its age except that its undercarriage hadn't been treated with an anti-rust coating, so it was now showing signs of surface corrosion and was in need of a restorative treatment, something only a qualified specialty shop that dealt with older automobiles could provide.

Although there were other repair shops near her that he recommended, none of them were covered under her warranty. So Ivy went back the same shop she'd visited for her headlight problem.

The shop told Ivy that she had two options. She could come in twice a year for a quick fifteen-minute treatment to remove the rust and spray on a light protective coating, or they could provide her with a self-applied compound called Forteo that Ivy could periodically spray on at home.

There was one problem; her warranty didn't cover the Forteo, which cost $4,206 for each ninety-day supply. Since that was out of the question, Ivy asked about the price of the twice-yearly in-shop service. The shop couldn't tell her the cost, since that was done at a separate specialty repair shop they worked with and that shop didn't disclose pricing until after the procedure was done. Ivy called the specialty repair shop herself, but she was passed around from person to person until she was finally told she'd be called back. Nobody ever called.

> After another twenty-one phone calls, she finally reached someone who offered to help.

After another twenty-one phone calls, she finally reached someone who offered to help. However, all she could tell Ivy was that while they could not tell her the price, they would try to bill the warranty company in a way that ensured the treatment was covered under Ivy's plan. However, it was up to her warranty company to decide if the treatment was, in fact, covered.

Ivy tried to get the cost from her warranty company. After another six calls, she finally got the answer that the actual compound used in the procedure was only about $60–$100, but each twice-yearly application would cost $9,735, and she would be responsible for her $7,150 deductible yearly.

Frustrated and exhausted, Ivy decided to forgo the treatment, avoid driving through puddles or in the rain, and take her chances.

I'm sure you've figured out by now that the story you just read has nothing to do with antique automobiles or auto repair warranties. If you substitute Ivy's eyes for her headlights, her disconnected clinics and doctors for the repair shops and mechanics, and her diagnosed osteoporosis for her aging car frame, everything else is pretty much exactly as it happened to Ivy Austin when she went into NewYork-Presbyterian Hospital with her Empire Blue Cross Blue Shield health insurance.

Like Ivy, the majority of patients today are being asked to navigate a healthcare system that was built to be anything but consumer friendly or patient centered. Trying to obtain satisfactory outcomes that make economic sense from treatments that are masked in opaqueness is almost impossible (Culprit #4, The Complexity Crisis, and Culprit #2, The Asymmetry between Costs and Outcomes).

Patients are handed from one healthcare employee to another with little or no understanding of their diagnostic or treatment process, and, as with Ivy's mechanics, doctors who aren't aware of a patient's history are put into situations where they order redundant tests to be on the safe side or to protect themselves against future outcomes (Culprits #3, The Episodic Care Conundrum, and #8, Defensive Medicine).

Most of this handling is performed by administrative staff, who may themselves have little understanding of the overall process, and even less understanding of the patient's medical history and context, resulting in higher costs that are often masked from the patient. (Culprits #1, The Anonymous Patient, #5, The Missing Link, and #7, The Tragedy of The Commons.) And the real value of many services has little to do with their costs but rather the arrangement between provider and payer (Culprit #2, The Asymmetry between Costs and Outcomes). And in all of this, the providers of services spend far too much time trying to manage the administrative process over the actual care being delivered (Culprit #6, Drifting from the Core).

It's Complicated

The automobile analogy illustrates the absurdity of the healthcare patient-provider-payer relationship. This level of dysfunction is something we would not put up with in any other context as consumers. The reason we won't put up with it is because we've actually figured out how to deal with this level of complexity in pretty much every other consumer interaction we have.

For example, think about the many varied disconnects in managing a patient's care and compare them to the assembly of an automobile. A modern assembly line extends well beyond the factory floor, from the tens of thousands of suppliers of parts to the data collected from subsequent use of the automobile by the buyer. This warrants the creation of a vast and complex digital ecosystem in which the behaviors of customers translate into the way the suppliers are orchestrated in order to deliver the best experience to future customers. Some companies are

...the US spends 30 percent of every healthcare dollar on administrative costs, more than any other country in the world.

using this approach to create innovation on demand before customers even know to ask for it.

A notable example of on-demand innovation is Tesla's response to customers trying to evacuate Florida during the devastation of hurricane Irma in 2017, nicknamed Irmageddon by many due to its category-four winds.

At the time, Tesla used to offer its Model S with 75 kWh batteries that could be locked by software to limit battery access to just 60 kWh. A buyer choosing the lower sixty-kWh capacity would pay less for the car. This limited the effective range of the car to two hundred miles, about a thirty-to-forty-miles lower range than the 75 kWh option.

A Model S owner trying to evacuate and get out of Irma's path, called Tesla to ask if they would unlock his extra 15 kWh to provide added range for his evacuation. Tesla gladly complied, but then went on to do something unprecedented. It geofenced the perimeter of Irma's path, identified every Tesla owner with a battery limited to 60 kWh within that area, and unlocked their battery and notified them of the added range—even though only a handful of Tesla owners even knew to ask for it.

In the case of a typical automotive manufacturing process, while each worker for each supplier, on the assembly line and in the dealerships, performs his or her own specialized task, there is always a system-wide awareness of how every part of the process impacts the efficiency of every other part.

The roots of this approach to managing complex processes are in large part due to the work of Taiichi Ohno, a Japanese engineer at Toyota, during the mid-twentieth century, whose "just in time" method revolutionized modern automobile manufacturing. The evolution of this approach resulted in what we now call digital control towers: software algorithms that hover over a digital marketplace like a virtual version of Adam Smith's[ii] invisible hand of commerce, which drives free markets, to orchestrate and optimize entire systems in real-time. (We'll talk more about the role of a digital control tower in how healthcare services providers, HSPs, operate in chapter 6.)

But nothing even remotely like this approach exists in healthcare. In some cases, a patient's health history can't even follow him or her through a single provider's health-care system. This is the Missing Link (Culprit #5) that is so desperately needed to provide some level of overarching awareness for patient care.

The result of this oversight is a lack of overall process awareness, visibility, and transparency, and the inability to take actions that could reduce friction throughout the process. In short, it's why the US spends $1.1 trillion, or approximately 30 percent of every healthcare dollar on administrative costs,[5] more than any other country in the world. By way of contrast, that amount is about 16 percent in England and 12 percent in Canada.[6] Coincidentally it's also how much the US federal government spent in total for healthcare in 2018.

And yet, the cost of healthcare is only the most obvious symptom of a dysfunctional process. There is the very real

---

ii It should be pointed out, so as not to take this analogy too literally, that Adam Smith was looking for solutions through an 18th century lens. Although I appreciate his democratic intent of liberating the economy from monarchical constraints, it was within the context of a different world in all aspects. Smith actually valued the role of government and regulation within an economy to an extent not many people recognize. He did not have blind faith in the market. He preached the role of government in endeavors private enterprises couldn't or wouldn't (e.g., public works and other shared, common goods), promoted pro-labor regulation such as increased wages for workers, and even supported progressive taxation (e.g., the rich should pay more: "...not only in proportion to their revenue, but something more than in that proportion."—Adam Smith) toll that friction takes on the quality of the care that patients receive as the result of administrative delays and denied claims for life-saving procedures, diagnostics, pharmaceuticals, and therapies (Culprit #4, The Complexity Crisis).

That disconnectedness manifests, in part, as runaway costs that often have little apparent rationale. In 2018, a *Wall Street Journal* report on Wisconsin-based Gundersen Lutheran Medical Center described Gundersen's recent review of the cost of a knee-replacement procedure in its hospital.[7] They discovered that the procedure had been increasing at a 3 percent annual rate. The result was a $50,000 price tag. Knee replacement surgery is the second most frequently preformed surgical procedure in US hospitals, second only to surgical procedures related to childbirth.

According to the *Wall Street Journal* article, the price charged for the procedure was arrived at through "a combination of educated guesswork and a canny assessment of market opportunity." To translate, this means that it was not based on the actual resources, clinician value, components, and services needed to perform the procedure. When Gundersen considered these factors, they found that the actual cost of the procedure was just $10,550, 20 percent of the listed price (Culprit #2, The Asymmetry between Costs and Outcomes).

To Gundersen's credit, they took on the task of doing this analysis on their own. Interestingly enough, it was started by a Gundersen employee, Lisa Wied, who had previously worked in manufacturing. Ms. Wied conducted diligent time-motion studies and inventoried every step of each task and the resources used—something that you would expect every organization with complex processes to do, especially one which, in this case, is performed by Gundersen four hundred times a year.

Much of that $50,000 price tag is likely due to costs incurred from providing care to indigent people or to those without insurance. However, that doesn't mean that hospitals are just passing on those costs to patients who can afford to pay. Research from the Kellogg School of Management at Northwestern University concluded that hospitals end up absorbing a majority of the cost of care for uninsured patients.

It may seem that with such outrageous pricing, hospitals should be incredibly profitable. They aren't. According to Christopher Kerns, executive director of the Advisory Board, hospitals had a median operating margin of just 1.7 percent in 2018. Kerns calls a 2.5 percent margin sustainable, but stated, "That's still an anemic margin overall."

> The unemployed mother of two was looking at nearly $500,000 in unpaid medical bills.
> An amount that would bankrupt 90 percent of American households.

One reason that hospital margins are so low is due to the Emergency Medical Treatment and Active Labor Act (EMTALA), passed in 1985. The act requires hospitals to treat anyone who needs emergency care no matter what their insurance status is. Although there is some government reimbursement to hospitals for these uninsured patients, it is far from adequate to offset the costs of treating those patients to the hospital. The result, according to the Kellogg School's research, is that "ultimately, hospitals are left to absorb at least two-thirds of the cost of all of uncompensated care."[8] While that may be easier to absorb for a large conglomerate healthcare system, it is driving community hospitals and smaller providers to the brink.

A Decision Nobody Wants to Make

A dramatic case is that of Wanda Wickizer, who in 2013 was forced to make a decision that no one would want to make. After her husband died, Wanda had to stop working to care for her children. Although that meant her children were covered under Medicaid and Children's Health Insurance Program (CHIP), Wanda was unable to afford the $800 monthly payment she needed to also receive health insurance for herself due to a pre-existing condition. So, she did what many people in her position do, and chose to roll the dice.

On Christmas Day of 2013, an otherwise-healthy fifty-one-year-old Wanda began vomiting and experiencing excruciating headaches.[9] Her son called 911 and Wanda was rushed to Sentara Norfolk General Hospital in coastal Virginia, where she was diagnosed with a subarachnoid hemorrhage that left her in a semi-comatose state. However, the care Wanda needed required her to be airlifted to the University of Virginia Medical Center in Charlottesville.

The specific sort of cranial hemorrhage that Wanda had caused the accumulation of fluid at the top of her brain, pushing it down into the spinal cord, where the pressure on vital nerves and the spinal column can be lethal.

Wanda was lucky. The care she received in Charlottesville was exceptional, and after more than three weeks in the hospital, she went home. Unfortunately, Wanda's ordeal was far from over.

While still suffering from many of the aftereffects of the episode, and at a time when most people would expect to be recuperating peacefully, Wanda began to receive bills from the various healthcare providers who had been involved in her treatment. There was a bill from the first hospital for $16,000, then the air ambulance for $50,000, followed by two separate bills from physicians' organizations for $24,000 and $50,000. Finally, a bill for $356,884.42 from the University of Virginia Medical Center in Charlottesville arrived. The unemployed mother of two was looking at nearly $500,000 in unpaid medical bills—an amount that would bankrupt well over 90 percent of American households.

When she contacted the hospital and requested the bill be itemized, she received sixty pages of indecipherable and inconsistent items (Culprit #4, The Complexity Crisis). In an effort to just make it go away and get back to her life, Wanda offered to pay the hospital $100,000, the entirety of her retirement funds, which had come from her husband's life insurance, and which she had hoped to use to fund her children's education. The response arrived six months later, when Wanda came home to a sheriff's summons taped to her door. It was the University of Virginia suing her for nonpayment.

Without an insurance company to advocate for her and nowhere else to turn, Wanda landed on a Facebook group called "Paying Till It Hurts." There she found volunteers who helped her to decipher the various codes used to itemize her bill (We'll come back to these codes later in Chapter 3).

> Our current system almost conspires to create the greatest risk for the most vulnerable of the population.

The result was that the total cost to the medical center for Wanda's bills was less than $60,000, which was ironically $40,000 less than Wanda had been willing to settle with the hospital for initially. To be clear, the $60,000 was what a billing expert working with Wanda had estimated that the hospital had spent on her healthcare. And the $500,000 that the hospital was seeking from Wanda was the price for an uninsured individual, not the price it would have contracted with an insurer to pay. The latter would very likely have been significantly less than $500,000 (Culprit #2, The Asymmetry between Costs and Outcomes).

After another two years of battling with hospital administrators, the case was settled the evening before it was to go to trial. Likely, in no small part, due to the fact that a prominent *New York Times* reporter had become involved and announced that she would be at the trial.

Although the terms of the settlement were sealed, Wanda still had to deal with the long-term implications of a two-hundred-point drop in her credit score (the result of her doctors, not the hospital, reporting her nonpayment).

Wanda's experience is far from isolated. One of the most insidious aspects of today's healthcare system is that it disincentivizes patients for seeking medical care—the same patients who are in the worst economic position to afford the implications of longer-term catastrophic health conditions.

Consider that, according to a Gallup poll, "Among US adults of both genders, nationally, about three in ten (29 percent) report that they or a household member put off medical treatment because of cost in the past year. This figure has been stable over the past decade, ranging from 29 percent to 33 percent since 2006. The percentage of adults who put off medical treatment had been lower before that, including 22 percent in 1991 and 19 percent in 2001."[10]

Lest you look at this and come to the conclusion that it's just patient bills in the hundreds of thousands of dollars that are the issue, the challenge is just as pronounced for those who are dealing with far smaller amounts and have healthcare coverage. For many patients, any out-of-pocket cost is simply impossible to cover.

The Jordan family, Carla and John, had healthcare insurance that they were paying $501 for each month. So, when a rash of unexpected and unfortunate medical problems rippled through the family, they assumed insurance would cover it for them.

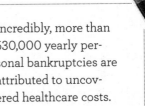

Carla needed a gall-bladder operation, then John had a seizure and came down with an infection. Just on the heels of John's recovery, Carla was diagnosed with diabetes.

Despite the insurance they had with Anthem, they owed eighteen different providers a total of $8,000. Although they were insured, insurance covered only a small portion of their medical bills before the $2,000 deductible was reached. The family ended up filing bankruptcy for the second time in four years because they couldn't afford their medical debt—even while covered by insurance.[11] Our current system almost conspires to create the greatest risk for the most vulnerable of the population.

Amplifying the problem is the fact that many smaller hospitals and hospital systems, which would once write off these smaller amounts as bad debt, are now much more likely to pursue collection actions against patients. Hackensack Meridian Health, New Jersey's largest health network with eight hospitals, had been allowing patients to make payments over time that stretched out over ten and even twenty years. Eventually these bills were written off as bad debt, according to Marilyn Koczan, senior vice president of revenue cycle operations for the network. However, as Hackensack has grown with more hospital acquisitions, it has become far less tolerant of outstanding amounts owed by patients. In 2019, the network entered an agreement with a third party to arrange payment plans with patients that spanned no more than two years. Hackensack would receive amounts owed upfront and the third party would then make payment arrangements with the patient.[12]

> Incredibly, more than 530,000 yearly personal bankruptcies are attributed to uncovered healthcare costs.

These sorts of arrangements are becoming more prevalent and can be devastating for patients who simply cannot pay. Uncovered healthcare costs are considered a contributing factor in more than 530,000 personal bankruptcies each year.[13]

They are also devastating to smaller community hospitals and hospital systems that are increasingly relying on third-party debt collection. According to a 2014 study by the Consumer Financial Protection Bureau, 52.1 percent of all reported collections that have been assigned to an agency for collection are associated with medical providers.[14]

It's easy to look at these situations and paint the providers as the culprits. Although no reasonable person would offer absolution to the hospital or the doctors for these egregious billing practices, the fundamental challenge is that these institutions need to make the economics of their business models work in order to be sustainable.

As even the greenest of CEOs knows, a failing business model can only be fixed by either decreasing costs or increasing revenues. However, in the case of healthcare, the costs have become so embedded within the system that they are no longer visible to any one person. In fact, administrative friction actually masks the clarity needed for the individuals involved to apply common sense to the process (Culprit #7, The Tragedy of the Commons). Because the costs are hidden, we see providers trying desperately to increase revenues any way they can. According to a 2017 article in *Forbes*:

> *The problem isn't declining revenue. Since 2009, hospitals have accounted for half of the $240 billion spending increase among private U.S. insurers. It's not that increased competition is driving price wars, either. On the contrary, 1,412 hospitals have merged since 1998, primarily to increase their clout with insurers and raise prices.*[15]

This is a systemic problem baked into the healthcare system. Consider that if you could replace all of the people in Wanda's story with an entirely new set of players, you'd likely still get the exact same results. Blaming the people, or even the organizations, makes little sense

> The result of all of this complexity is that we often buy into the false premise that healthcare is so broken that only extreme measures, such as switching to a single-payer system, will save it.

when the process itself is wired to be ineffective. The very nature of coding, accounting, and billing is shrouded in layers of indecipherable administrative processes that make any sort of straightforward analysis nearly impossible.

Like the fat in a pound of ground beef, you could say that the process friction, which is pervasive within healthcare, is 90 percent lean meat, but the fat is inextricably part of the package and cannot be reduced to 5 percent fat in any practical manner.

To extend that analogy, it's worth asking, "How much fat exists in nonclinical operations for many providers?" Consider that, according to health economist David Cutler, Duke University Hospital has 900 hospital beds and 1,300 billing clerks.[16]

A 2009 Health Affairs study found that "when time is converted to dollars, [doctors'] practices spent an average of $68,274 per physician per year interacting with health plans."[17]

Clearly, we're not dealing with anything close to an FDA "lean" equivalent! In fact, it appears that the fat is the predominant part of the equation.

The result of all of this complexity is that we often buy into the false premise that healthcare is so broken that only extreme measures, such as switching to a single-payer system, will save it.

What we'll see is that in the same way that the problem is hidden in plain sight, so is the solution. There are precise and surgical ways to apply many of the approaches used in other industries—some that have already been implemented by specific healthcare providers—to create significant increases in efficiency and equally significant reductions in costs. These methods will reduce friction and improve the patient experience, all without radically changing the current clinical model of healthcare.

> ...there is a precise and surgical way to take many of the approaches already used in other industries to create quantum increases in the efficiency and costs of healthcare while also reducing friction and improving the patient experience.

Here is where smartsourcing, which we describe in chapter 6, can play a significant role: by offloading and innovating administrative distractions while refocusing healthcare providers and payers on their core competencies rather than the administrative processes that detract valuable resources from their core (Culprit #6, Drifting from the Core).

This sounds straightforward, but it's clear that the challenge of actually implementing these changes has proven to be anything but easy. If it was, you wouldn't be reading this.

On the Razor's Edge

Most smaller and mid-tier community hospitals are running on incredibly slim margins of single percentage points.

Their administrative staffing has evolved and has grown organically over many years to handle the increase in the complexity of their administrative systems. This gives each hospital the illusion that nobody else could ever understand, much less manage, their administrative tasks, such as billing and claims processing. Although there are definite differences in the way some hospitals deliver what's termed "local care," which is tailored to the local demographics of the community, each hospital is far from unique in how they go about their business.

What's worse is that the current trend of hospital mergers, which is intended to reduce overhead and administrative costs in order to harness economies of scale is, by some measures, further eroding the quality of healthcare. Studies show that having one dominant healthcare system in a region can result in prices that are 40–50 percent higher.[18]

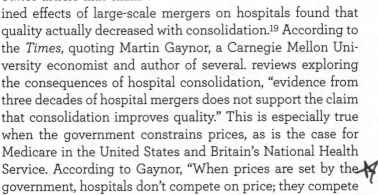

...evidence from three decades of hospital mergers does not support the claim that consolidation improves quality.

A 2019 *New York Times* article that examined effects of large-scale mergers on hospitals found that quality actually decreased with consolidation.[19] According to the *Times*, quoting Martin Gaynor, a Carnegie Mellon University economist and author of several. reviews exploring the consequences of hospital consolidation, "evidence from three decades of hospital mergers does not support the claim that consolidation improves quality." This is especially true when the government constrains prices, as is the case for Medicare in the United States and Britain's National Health Service. According to Gaynor, "When prices are set by the government, hospitals don't compete on price; they compete on quality." But this doesn't happen in highly consolidated healthcare markets since the options for care are diminished, also reducing the pressure for quality differentiation (Culprit #2, The Asymmetry between Costs and Outcomes).

If you doubt that, just think of the state of quality in the cable industry, where government-controlled markets severely restrict the number of cable providers in a given region. In these cases, the need to innovate and compete based on quality is significantly reduced. The rationale often used to create these government-controlled markets is that the enormous investment required on the part of a telecom provider justifies protecting their longer-term interests in monetizing that marketplace. This artificially protects pricing and limits choice.

Numerous studies have uncovered the obvious, that hospital competition increases the quality of outcomes.[20] From decreased heart attack mortality to lower rates of pneumonia, a free-market healthcare system is significantly better at delivering higher-quality outcomes than one that limits choice and encourages protectionism.

On the other side of the equation, health insurers are in a constant battle to manage insurance plans that seem to have more variations than the flora of a rainforest. Of course, much of that is due to the need to develop plans that meet the demands of varied market segments and largely self-insured employer clients. These are companies that take on some of the risk for paying insurance claims while using larger insurers to cover what are referred to as stop-losses or claims above a certain threshold. This has become an increasingly popular alternative for employers to minimize insurance costs. In 2018 61 percent of all covered workers were part of a self-funded plan, an increase from 44 percent in 1999.[21] Additionally, 91 percent of companies with more than five thousand employees are self-funded. This shifts the burden of risk onto the employer, since they now pay directly for healthcare costs.

However, the risk to insurers is increasing rapidly as the number of large-seven-figure claims also increases, the result of new therapies for catastrophic illness, such as cancer. Million-dollar claims have risen 87 percent in the past four years, according to Sun Life Financial's "2018 High-Cost Claims Report."[22]

...we could be spending as much on the over-sixty-five population in 2060 as we are on all of healthcare today!

This challenge is further complicated by the rapidly growing base of older insured members who are increasing the volume and size of claims, as well as the range of simultaneous services needed—a situation called comorbidity[iii] in the vernacular of healthcare professionals (Culprit #10, The Aging of America).

Today, over one-third of all healthcare expenditure is for the sixty-five-or-older demographic, although they only represent 16 percent of the population.[23] However, the sixty-five-and-older population will double by 2060,[24] meaning that we could be spending as much on the over-sixty-five population in 2060 as we are on all of healthcare today! If we look at just one disease category, Alzheimer's and other dementias cost the US $290 billion in 2019. By 2050, these costs could rise to as high as $1.1 trillion.[25]

---

iii   Comorbidity is the presence of one or more additional health conditions co-occurring with a primary condition.

Whose Risk Is It Anyway?

It is important to note that we haven't arrived at this predicament suddenly; the healthcare crisis has been coming for some time. Much of the friction in healthcare stems from the fact that the industry has operated under a "fee for service" model for the past five decades. Fee-for-service (FFS) simply means that doctors, clinicians, and healthcare providers get paid based on the volume of the services they deliver. A 2017 study by Deloitte found that 86 percent of physicians are still paid under an FFS model.[26]

Under an FFS model, the provider carries relatively little risk since they are paid for all the services they deliver. (This is an admitted oversimplification, but, for now, it helps to illustrate that the inability to determine risk drives the economics of healthcare.)

One of the most significant shifts away from FFS was the evolution of health maintenance organizations (HMOs). HMOs were often operated under a capitated model,[27] in which a contracted group of healthcare providers is paid a set amount for the number of enrolled patients. HMOs increased dramatically in the 1970s as the result of the US government's 1973 HMO Act, which required employers with over twenty-five employees to offer HMOs along with traditional indemnity insurance.

HMOs were intended to move away from the FFS model to what's been called a value-based approach to healthcare. This meant increasing the value of healthcare by shifting the burden of consumption onto providers, who were incentivized to deliver just the right amount of healthcare. Too little care and the patient could develop more serious longer-term health issues. Too much care and the provider lost money on the services delivered. The thinking was that HMOs would deliver more cost-effective healthcare since providers would have to determine how to best treat patients within the contractual confines of the HMO.

The idea was sound, but the flaw was that shifting risk to the HMOs also required better access to data across the entire healthcare ecosystem in order to fully understand the patient's current and future healthcare needs. Until recently, this access was not available, which is partly why HMOs fell out of favor. (We'll see that a new type of HMO model is coming back into favor as a result of more readily available patient data with which to better measure outcomes.)

The other flaw of the HMO model was that patients tended to change insurers and healthcare providers as they moved from employer to employer or geographically relocated their household. The incentive to balance risk was therefore almost always artificial. If a patient has an average tenure of eight years with a primary care physician (PCP), they will move through about ten PCPs during their lifetime. The same rate of turnover would likely apply to their HMO. Amplifying this trend is the fact that millennials and Gen Z are increasingly shunning the notion of PCPs. A US poll of 1,200 adults conducted by the Kaiser Family Foundation[28] concluded that 45 percent of eighteen- to twenty-nine-year-olds did not have a PCP, compared with 18 percent of fifty- to sixty-four-year-olds, and 12 percent of those above age sixty-five (Culprit #9, The Primary Care Crisis).

As data about patient care has become more readily available through EHRs, the focus has shifted from traditional HMO capitated models to value-based care, or VBC. The difference between HMOs and VBC is that VBC pays the provider based on health outcomes, rather than patient load. However, again, the challenge here is that an outcome is not always tied to the same providers who are delivering the care that leads to those outcomes.

Returning to our auto-industry analogy, a fundamental premise of the revolution that took place in manufacturing was that each task and part must be measured and monitored constantly to ensure the utmost quality and value.

The obvious difference is that in manufacturing, we can not only agree on the basic metrics and outcomes that define quality, but we also relentlessly track any variables that constitute risk across an ecosystem of providers, designers, and engineers.

There is a reason that auto manufacturers can offer warranties that increasingly provide greater coverage for longer and longer periods of time; they have a high degree of visibility into every aspect of the manufacturing process, the quality of the automobile, and the risk of repairing it. By the way, it's worth pointing out here that another reason extended warranties have become such a standard for the automotive industry is the increasing cost of automobiles and the resulting trend toward leasing. This means that it is in the best interests of the manufacturers and dealers to maintain the cars they sell, since they will ultimately be dealing with the longer-term life cycle value of the automobile.

For especially complex manufacturing processes, such as those used to build a jet engine, the entire life cycle of every part can be traced to determine where quality adjustments need to be made in the event of an unacceptable outcome. And, once again, the reason for the relentless tracking of parts and outcomes is that the engine you see strapped onto the wing of a commercial aircraft is being paid for by "time on wing,"[29] meaning that the manufacturer is responsible for its lifetime performance, maintenance, and outcomes. Unless you've diligently compiled a record of every medical procedure, doctor's comment, imagery, pharmaceutical, and therapeutic result over the course of your lifetime, there is no such single source of truth for your medical history.

Of course, as I pointed out at the very outset of the book, humans are not machines. Different people have different biological predispositions to disease and exposures to environmental risks, not to mention the impact of differing lifestyles and socioeconomic context.

While these biological and cultural differences make it impossible to standardize patient treatment with the precision and predictability of maintaining a jet engine, the larger point of using outcomes as the final arbiter of quality is still elusive in healthcare, since nobody owns the patient outcomes over a lifetime—other than the patient (Culprits #3, The Episodic Care Conundrum and #5, The Missing Link). This is not because there is no way to measure the quality or value of care, but rather because the system itself is so inherently disjointed, and data so scattered in various subsystems (many of them still in paper) that we are simply unable to link the many points of healthcare delivery to the quality of outcomes in any consistent or continuous way. In fact, despite digitization, many providers still rely on fax transmissions to share data. Just think of the last time you showed up at a doctor's office, perhaps one that's part of a provider network you've already used, and have been handed a clipboard with six different forms to fill out, each of which asks for your name, address, and birthdate.

Contrast that to a jet engine manufactured by GE or Rolls Royce, which is relentlessly tracked through every single step of its manufacture and use, from raw materials to "time on wing." All maintenance, resources, diagnostics, and failures are accounted for and can be tracked to what may appear to be absurd levels of precision. This not only helps to analyze engine failures, but also to predict them.

We all have countless healthcare providers and payers scattered about throughout our lifetime, and the vast majority have no idea that the others even exist—much less the

> For most patients, there is no single source of truth. We all have myriad healthcare providers and payers scattered throughout our lifetime, and the vast majority have no idea that the others even exist, much less the ability to share data and measure the quality or value of outcomes.

ability to share data and measure the quality or value of outcomes from healthcare that extends beyond each provider and payer system. This isn't solved with the use of EHRs, which are still not universal in how they are shared among providers and insurers. In fact, even if they were, the following question would still remain: How can we measure the risk and value of any given healthcare service across a population of patients extending well beyond any single provider's or payer's purview?

Healthcare outcomes are dependent partly on the patient's history and context and partly on the analysis of larger populations with a similar history and context. Achieving that level of scale and scope in the data available to any single provider has been challenging at best. In the case of anything other than a handful of large teaching hospitals, it is simply not possible at all. The risk this creates is that when algorithms are run against too small of a population, they can create unintended consequences.

We've seen the bias of algorithms surface in many areas where algorithms are being trained to make what would otherwise be human decisions. The challenge is that algorithms use large volumes of data to identify patterns. If the data contains bias, then the decisions made by the algorithm will incorporate these biases. For example, predictive policing algorithms used in law enforcement have been the subject of controversy because they may reinforce deep seated racial and socioeconomic biases.[30]

By the way, I want to be careful not to hold out FFS as an inherently flawed model, as it's often made out to be. There are many nonhealthcare-related instances where a service is provided for a fee based on the volume of use without a guaranteed tie to outcomes.

For example, a lawyer representing a client will in most cases be paid an hourly rate for work they perform regardless of the outcome. However, in most other cases where a service is rendered for a fee, there is a level of transparency that allows renegotiation of the actual work being done, and both the provider of the service and the consumer are relatively well informed of the risks.

This is not true of healthcare, where there are numerous administrative personnel involved in every clinical activity, with no responsibility for, or investment in, the outcome.

When you're working with a lawyer, automobile mechanic, or financial analyst within a free market, you are also constantly evaluating the value you receive for the product or service you are purchasing. And you have the option at any point in time to switch providers if that value, perceived or actual, does not meet your expectations. However, even in these industries, there is a movement away from FFS arrangements. Consumer legal services, such as LegalZoom, charge fixed fees for a set of services that can be covered by a membership fee.

Fixed-fee models are made possible through the collection of vast amounts of data that are run through statistical algorithms to more precisely predict how the risk and outcomes of a set of services will impact the resources required to deliver the service.

However, in the case of healthcare, the data required to accurately assess impact are scattered, and the conversation about delivering value occurs almost entirely between intermediaries such as insurers, employers, and administrators. Healthcare administrators determine the value, risk, and costs of services based on relatively primitive metrics, especially when compared with other less-complex services used to calculate risk and resources.

Another aspect to consider is that very often, the decision behind what an insurer is willing to pay for seems to occur in a black box. Take, for example, the case of Joseph Pero, detailed in a 2019 *LA Times* article.[31]

It Shouldn't Be This Hard

According to *LA Times* reporter David Lazarus, Joseph found himself in what he called a very "dark place" after a recent divorce and trying financial issues.

Not seeing any way out, Joseph took his loaded Glock 17 handgun, pointed it at his chest, and pulled the trigger. But rather than hitting the intended target, his heart, the bullet punctured Joseph's lung and shattered six of his ribs.

Joseph's insurance paid for the initial emergency surgery. However, after a year, his ribs had still not healed. Enduring excruciating pain, Joseph was told by his doctor that there was a way to repair the ribs by using metal plates and screws to fuse them back together. Joseph's insurance company, Aetna, denied approval for the procedure because the use of screws and plates to fuse the broken ribs back together was considered experimental. They also indicated that the procedure could only be approved if the patient could not get off of a ventilator, which Joseph was never on.

A letter of appeal from Joseph's doctor claiming medical necessity did nothing to change the insurer's decision.

After months of agonizing pain and emergency room admissions for difficulty breathing, Joseph decided that he desperately needed the procedure. But, without insurance covering it, he would have to pay $30,000 out of pocket after receiving a 75 percent discount from the hospital.

Joseph agreed to the hospital's requirement that he pay $8,000 up front, and they scheduled the procedure.

However, before the procedure was due to be performed, Joseph reached out to *LA Times* reporter David Lazarus, mostly just to vent about what he considered to be a ludicrous decision on the part of his insurer, who would rather pay for a lifetime of ER visits than permanently fix the problem.

When Lazarus called Aetna for comment, the insurer told him that the decision had been reversed and the procedure was now approved. In his article, Lazarus makes a convincing case for the highly suspect timing of Aetna's reversal, as nothing had changed about Joseph's case other than media involvement. All Lazarus could think was, "[It] shouldn't be this hard."

Indeed, the mantra "it shouldn't be this hard" is the common thread in every case of an insurer denying a claim until the patient has been forced to resort to extraordinary means of exerting pressure on the insurer.

These sorts of black-box decisions by insurers are based on a variety of factors, which they put in place to ensure that standardized and consistent decisions are made about healthcare coverage. Insurers are, after all, businesses that need to make a profit. However, what is also clear through the study of dozens of similar cases is that understanding the context of each patient's case and

> ...while healthcare is increasingly moving toward personalized medicine...insurers are still pursuing the notion of the average patient to determine coverage.

projecting the long-term cost of their healthcare plays less of a role in decision-making than applying these standardized metrics. This is why Culprit #3, The Episodic Care Conundrum, undermines so much of the healthcare system. Decisions about care made without context will rarely be as effective, from both the standpoint of lifetime costs and overall outcomes.

The irony in the episodic approach is that while providers are increasingly moving toward personalized medicine, which takes into account the specifics of each patient down to matching therapies for a patient's unique genome, insurers are still pursuing the industrial-era notion of the "average patient" to determine coverage. Ultimately, this increases the overall cost of an FFS model by ignoring the lifetime implications of personalized healthcare, which is optimized for each individual's long-term healthcare outcomes.

> The primary underlying flaw is not FFS, but rather the way it is currently implemented with near-zero transparency.

In addition, the FFS model is deeply embedded into the healthcare system. One healthcare industry analyst I spoke with stated,

> *"I love to hear high-paid consultants come in and say, 'Fee for services is going away. Everything is going to fee for value.' I will say ninety-eight percent of hospital administrators, directors, and leaders have no idea or are unwilling to take the risk of turning off that spigot on the volume-based model and to turn it all of a sudden to, 'I'm at risk*

for this entire population.' It's not going to happen. Again, it's a generation of leaders who understand the business model of volume through the door [FFS] versus managing a population—so, there's enormous risk aversion. [Their thinking is,] 'I know that I'm going to survive on a five percent margin at best, and anything I do that could potentially move that one point is something I can't take the risk to do.'"

The primary underlying flaw is not FFS, but rather the way it is currently being implemented with almost zero transparency. In many instances, conversations about coverage and cost are conducted without the patient having any knowledge of the underlying parameters that determine the cost or acceptability of the service (Culprit #2, The Asymmetry between Costs and Outcomes).

Think back to our earlier example of Wanda Wickizer and the difficulty she had in deciphering her sixty-page bill. Shifting risk to the consumer in these situations assumes that the patient understands the risk, which they invariably do not. They are not clinicians nor are they (or could they be) familiar with the tens of thousands of codes used to assign billing categories. This strategy also ignores that patients, without an insurer, have no bargaining power and cannot take advantage of the pre-negotiated rates of an insurer.

> Imagine telling the hypothetical median wage earner that he or she could get an instant $6,173 (or 30 percent) raise if healthcare was fixed. What sort of response do you think that would evoke?

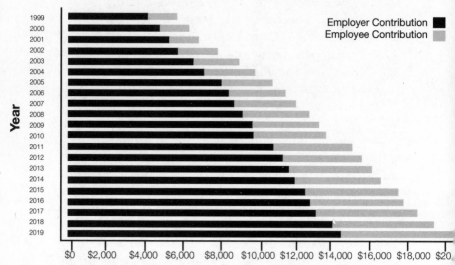

Average Annual Worker and Employer Contributions for Family Health Insurance Coverage 1999-2019

Source: KFF Employer Health Benefits Survey, 2018-2019 and
Kaiser/HRET Survey of Employer Sponsored Health Benefits 1997-2017

Illustration 2.2 According to the Kaiser Family Foundation, since 1999 the total average employee premium has increased by 355 percent. Although employees are contributing a slightly greater percentage of that (30 percent in 2019 versus 27 percent in 1999) the lion's share of the increase, which is not apparent to employees, is the 70 percent contribution by the employer.[32]

It's also worth noting an earlier point, which is key in understanding how risk is buried so that it is not apparent to the patient. Recall that in 80 percent of all employer-sponsored health plans, the employer, not the insurer, or the employee, is carrying the bulk of the risk. This figure is as high as it is due to the incredible increase in healthcare premiums over the past twenty years. According to the Kaiser

Family Foundation, the total average employee premium has increased by 355 percent since 1999. Although employees are contributing a slightly greater percentage of that (30 percent in 2019 versus 27 percent in 1999), the lion's share of the increase, which is not apparent to employees, is the 70 percent contribution by the employer.

To make this much more vivid, think of it this way. According to the US Bureau of Labor Statistics, the median wage in 2019 was $47,000. Imagine telling the hypothetical median wage earner that he or she could get an instant $6,173 (30 percent of their total healthcare contribution) raise if healthcare was fixed.[iv] What sort of response do you think that would evoke? The reason that most people fail to see it this way is that employer contributions mask the real cost of healthcare to the majority of workers (Culprit #2, The Asymmetry between Costs and Outcomes).

Lastly, FFS is artificially restricted in healthcare by the imposition of a no- or low-choice consumer model. The option of consumer choice in providers is limited or entirely unavailable to the patient. It's rarely the value of the service that determines who you select to perform a procedure, but rather the insurance plan you have access to and the agreement the insurance company has with selected providers, which determines who you have to work with.

In a popular blog dedicated to helping patients understand the way healthcare costs work, Dr. David Belk describes this in simple-to-understand terms:

> *Insurance companies will always pay whatever a medical provider bills up to the maximum amount they're willing to pay for*

---

iv   The $6,173 pay increase is based on multiplying the total 2019 contribution of the employer and employee by 30 percent, which is the assumed cost of unnecessary administrative overhead.

any service. So, if a doctor bills $100 for an office visit, and the insurance company is willing to pay $75, the doctor will get $75. If the doctor bills only $60 for that office visit then $60 is all he'll receive.

There is absolutely no penalty in health care for over billing, but any medical provider who under bills will short change themselves. This is why billing charges have exploded by so much in health care. This payment system is far too confusing for any health care provider to really understand, so the best strategy is to bill high for every service then take what they give us.

This creates a huge problem for anyone who is uninsured, but an even bigger problem for people who have insurance and had their claim denied for any reason. The uninsured will be forced to negotiate on their own behalf against billing charges that might be many times the value of a medical service. This puts the uninsured at a severe disadvantage. A person who uses their insurance, but has their claim denied is almost always expected to pay the full bill, though. They aren't even allowed to try to negotiate."[33]

This relationship between patient-provider-payer (think back to the example earlier in this chapter of Ivy Austin and her antique car) creates a black box that's impossible to work outside of and just as hard, if not outright impossible, for the patient to understand. Consider that the typical contract between a payer and a provider contains hundreds of pages of terms and conditions covering tens of thousands of different disease categories. These categories range from common ailments such as hypertension and vitamin D deficiency to obscure codes such as being injured at an opera house or sucked into jet engine (yes, there really is an ICD code for that: V97.33[v]).[34] Additionally, the "rules and instructions" for Medicare and Medicaid (CMS) contain over 130,000 pages. That's three times larger than the IRS code and its associated regulations![35]

When I learned about the enormous volume of rules and instructions for CMS, I was reminded of my first undergraduate degree in tax and accounting. Even with open-book tests, it was still incredibly challenging to try and figure out even moderately complex tax situations. Now multiply that threefold, add in the volume and immediacy of decisions that need to be made in a healthcare setting, and you start to get a sense for just how difficult it is to follow this bevy of rules and instruction.

Our healthcare system has simply become too complex and too sophisticated for humans to handle without the assistance of much more sophisticated technologies that use data analytics, predictive algorithms, natural language processing, AI, and machine learning to help interpret the uniqueness of each situation and map the available healthcare options (Culprit #4, The Complexity Crisis).

The result of this complexity is a sort of out-of-body experience in which patients become passive observers of a process that they cannot even begin to control or comprehend. It's like watching a game of chess without knowing the rules. You could spend hours, perhaps days, observing a chess match and still not know why the pieces are moving the way they are, much less who's winning. Only, in the case of healthcare, the stakes are infinitely higher.

---

v   We talk more about ICD codes in the next chapter under the section
     titled "Breaking the Code."

> Imagine for a moment that rather than the approximately twelve thousand prescription drugs available today, there are millions of variations custom built for each patient.

While all of this is going on, the complexity of healthcare continues to increase exponentially. Personalized medicine has approached the complexity problem by grouping patients based on genetic risk and response to treatments.[36] This method has taken advantage of the dramatic drop in the cost of sequencing the human genome to create diagnostic methods, therapies, and pharmaceuticals that are as variable as the patients they are used for. Imagine for a moment that rather than the approximately twelve thousand prescription drugs available today, there are millions of variations custom built for each patient.

We are increasingly able to diagnose more conditions through advances in imaging. The use of digital tomography, magnetic resonance imaging (MRI), and ultrasound have reduced the need for many exploratory surgeries, but they have also been able to identify opportunities for clinical intervention when a disease is identified much earlier than if the patient had waited for a symptomatic diagnosis.

Image diagnostics for x-rays, CT, and MRI scans that use AI algorithms are already able to outperform doctors and radiologists in many cases when diagnosing medical imaging for cardiac conditions and cancer. Since the US already leads the world in the volume of diagnostic imaging it performs,[37] the ability to use AI to diagnose scans will be a welcome assist to providers looking for ways to leverage their resources. The introduction of AI technology will also increase the volume of imaging, which can lead to early diagnosis of certain cancers, coronary artery atherosclerosis, early onset dementia, aneurisms, and many other conditions that can be entirely asymptomatic and not diagnosed otherwise.

As life expectancy continues to increase, the opportunity to uncover more medical conditions, which we would otherwise have died before encountering, will only add to the volume of healthcare services required throughout a patient's lifetime. The growth of an aging population directly translates into a much higher volume of individual healthcare needs and transactions (Culprit #10, The Aging of America).

The bottom line is that in order to create an economically sustainable healthcare system, we need to address the problem of how to best assess, share, and manage risk across providers and health services throughout a patient's lifetime while maintaining the option of choice for the patient.

All of this directly relates to how we collect, store, share, and analyze patient data in a way that makes it possible to follow individuals through all of their healthcare interactions (Culprits #1, The Anonymous Patient and #5, The Missing Link).

This will be especially important in managing care for younger generations who are moving away from PCPs, as well as older patients who require greater and more complex ongoing care management across a broad spectrum of healthcare providers.

Moreover, insurance companies must play their part in anticipating this change and the accelerating

> Hope can be found in the fact that there is ample precedent for solving similar challenges in many other industries. From manufacturing to banking, and transportation to commercial aviation we have already built systems that can... drive friction out of the processes...

increase in the volume and the complexity of their coverage. Payers' understanding of the patients they serve (as we'll see in our discussion about healthcare service providers in chapter 6) may end up playing one of the most significant roles in decreasing the friction caused by unnecessary procedures and therapies by using historical data about the individual, and the larger population, to predict healthcare needs in advance and to better anticipate their outcomes.

The good news in all of this—and it's very good news— is that the use of advanced technologies such as AI and machine learning, along with the evolution of large third-party healthcare service providers (HSPs[vi], which we'll talk about in chapter 6) helping to offload the administrative burden, are making it possible to assess risk for both individuals and large patient populations in ways that were simply unthinkable a decade ago.

As we'll see when we discuss HSPs further in chapter 5, while alleviating the administrative burden may be a short-term goal of a smartsourcing approach, data-driven risk modeling is a much more significant long-term benefit. By using smartsourcing, providers can create a trusted relationship with a third party that has the data, expertise, and resources to identify patterns within patient and population data. Mitigating risk through the use of predictive algorithms on large data sets that cut across enormous patient populations is something that no single provider or payer could ever do as well on their

> I wish I would have known. I would have said "no" to life support. We'll lose everything.

---

vi   Healthcare services provider (HSP) is a term that I've coined in this book to specifically call out the evolution of new for-profit enterprises that provide smartsourcing services in healthcare.

own and which may ultimately be one of the greatest benefits of smartsourcing. We'll come back to this in later chapters as we delve further into smartsourcing.

The Surprise Nobody Wants to Wake Up To

In virtually every healthcare decision, the driving factor is the assessment of risk, or, more specifically, how the cost of any treatment is justified relative to its value. At first, that may sound callous and unfeeling. After all, the primary purpose of healthcare is a healthy population, not profit. However, the process only becomes callous when we do not have the ability to make costs transparent and value evident. It is in these cases that the patient gets stuck in between providers and insurers. Without transparency, insurance against the risk of illness turns into nothing more than a false promise of security.

Take, for example, fifty-nine-year-old Debbie Moehnke, a cocktail waitress who suffered a heart attack while waiting to be seen by her PCP for her painfully swollen feet.[38]

Debbie was stabilized at her local hospital and then transferred to the Oregon Health & Science University (OHSU), across the river in Portland, for urgent cardiac valve replacement and bypass surgery. Unfortunately, shortly after the surgery, Debbie developed an infection that required IV antibiotics and a month-long hospital stay.

By now you're likely familiar with the trajectory of these cases and what comes next. Debbie received bills totaling $454,000, of which her insurance covered exactly half. The remaining $227,000 was Debbie's responsibility. In this case, Debbie's insurer, LifeWise Health Plan of Washington, paid what it considered to be fair.

Kaiser Health News quoted Debbie as saying what many others in her position have already thought when being brought back from the brink only to face the horror of financial ruin, "I wish I would have known. I would have said 'no' to life support. We'll lose everything."[39]

Known as "surprise" or "balance" billing, these situations have become a national epidemic. Nine states have comprehensive protection against surprise billing (another nine have partial protection), which forces providers and insurers to work out payment for the uncovered portion of a bill without involving the patient.

In Debbie's case, the back-and-forth reads like a third-grade playground drama over who's to blame. As reported by Kaiser:[40]

> *Debra Tomsen, OHSU's director of hospital billing and coding, said LifeWise officials should have notified the Moehnkes after receiving bills for nearly $250,000 halfway through her stay.*

> *"Insurance should tell them they're incurring out-of-pocket costs," she said.*

> *[Bo] Jungmayer, of LifeWise, said it was up to OHSU to let Debbie Moehnke know about the high bills—and about the option to transfer to another hospital.*

> *"Typically, we allow that conversation between the provider and the patient while they're there," he said. "I don't know why OHSU didn't ask them."*

When providers and payers try to protect themselves by pushing blame back onto each other it's the patient who pays the price. Culprit #7, The Tragedy of the Commons doesn't get much more vivid than that.

As a society, we seem to have succumbed to the illusion that a sustainable healthcare system requires shifting more and more of the burden of responsibility and risk onto patients through the use of high deductibles, copays, and restricted choice. We also expect healthcare providers and payers to make decisions about risk in the care of patients through capitated or value-based approaches. Neither approach is sustainable.

In theory, shifting risk to the patients, who have to live with the implications of their healthcare, and to providers, whose services determine healthcare outcomes, seems to make good sense. But it's not effective in practice. Patients do not typically have the knowledge or competency to weigh healthcare services against their short- and long-term health and economic consequences; of course, that's if they are even in a position to make a competent decision based on their physical, emotional, and mental state at the time that care is being delivered.

Take, for example, Scott Kohan, who in 2018 was violently attacked in Austin, TX, leaving his jaw broken in two places. With Scott unconscious, witnesses called 911, and an ambulance was dispatched to take him to the emergency room. Kohan underwent emergency surgery on his jaw, which was broken in two places.

Unsurprisingly, one of Scott's first thoughts coming out of surgery was the cost of his care. In fact, this was the first thing he googled after regaining consciousness. Initially, he wasn't concerned, since the hospital where he was seen was in-network. So you can imagine his surprise to later receive a $7,924 bill

> While much of the conversation about fixing healthcare ends up being on who pays the bill, that masks the much more important issue of... determining what the bill should be to begin with.

85

from the surgeon. It turns out that while the hospital was in-network, the surgeon who treated him was not—clearly not something Scott could have made any sort of decision about while unconscious and under general anesthesia.

Providers, as was the case with Scott, are most often dealing with patients in episodic care situations while having to make critical healthcare decisions that may involve life-and-death situations (Culprit #3, The Episodic Care Conundrum). This is in the absence of the patient's health-care context and in time frames that do not always allow for the luxury of a consult with the patient's insurer—if that insurer is even known.

You can see the inherent risk in that scenario, and it's all too typical given the current disjointed nature of the US healthcare system.

Risk is one of the most insidious and least understood aspects of the current healthcare crisis. While much of the conversation about fixing healthcare focuses on who pays the bill, that masks the much more important issue of managing the risk of determining what the bill should be to begin with.

Unlike many other products or services that we consume, healthcare requires an ability to understand the implications of many complex variables that are dependent on a level of expertise and an ability to balance short-term actions with long-term consequences. The information needed to make these decisions is often either unavailable to the consumer and the provider—due to unknown reimbursement rates from the insurer—or not supported by the healthcare system. For example, in the case of Scott Kohan, there was simply no means by which, in the current system, the hospital or the surgeon could have determined his history or medical coverage.

I should point out that the element of coverage should clearly not have been a factor in whether or not Scott, or Debbie in the prior case, received adequate care. Situations such as this one are specifically the objective of the 1985 EMTALA act, which mandates emergency access to health-care, and the state-by-state balance-billing policies described earlier. It's important to note, however, that EMTALA does not apply to doctors who can pick and choose the patients they attend to. To make sure that ERs have adequate coverage, hospitals will often contract with individual specialists to perform emergency procedures. However, depending on the specifics of the contract and insurance coverage, patients may be left with the sort of surprise bills from out-of-network clinicians that Scott encountered.

These same factors—the lack of understanding required to balance risk and costs—can have a long-term detrimental impact on a patient's choices. For example, a simple diagnostic procedure intended to provide early detection, if put off due to the near-term cost in the form of a deductible or a copayment, can result in extraordinary costs in the future, which could potentially bankrupt a patient. Recall the earlier statistic that showed at least three out of ten adults putting off medical assistance due to costs.[41]

Although health plans are increasingly covering many diagnostic procedures that fall under the rubric of "preventative medicine," such as mammograms or EKGs, this isn't always the case.

In my own experience, an ultrafast CT scan was suggested by my doctor several years ago as a way to double-check the results of a stress test, which showed a potentially serious cardiovascular condition. I was in excellent health otherwise, working out regularly and with no apparent symptoms of a problem. The concern, however, was that there might be an underlying asymptomatic condition. The CT was not covered by what I thought at the time was an already fairly comprehensive health plan. Regardless, I gladly paid out-of-pocket for the test, which fortunately reversed the earlier incorrect diagnosis and saved me a lifetime of medications as well as other ongoing procedures, most all of which would, ironically, have been covered by my health plan. These cumulative lifetime costs would very likely have been far more expensive for both my insurer and for me than the cost of that one CT scan.

I'll admit that in this particular case, I was much less concerned with the math of present versus future costs of my healthcare and much more concerned with simply knowing what was going on. However, given the high cost of the CT scan, it's clear that many patients would not have made a similar decision, resulting in far greater overall lifetime healthcare costs.

Hospitals, on the other hand, are increasingly working under what we've already described in this chapter as capitated or value-based payment models. There are many ways capitation models are implemented based on patient demographic groupings, preventive incentives, and specialty care that may be included. However, they all shift the burden of risk onto the provider. A capitated or value-based model simply won't work without significantly better leveraging of patient data, which is currently scattered throughout the system.

One of these models, which has been growing in its use of patient data, is that of accountable care organizations. Put in place by CMS, ACOs represent collections of physicians, hospitals, and other providers who have agreed to provide coordinated care to Medicare patients (Illustration 2.4).

The objective is to deliver care that recognizes and orchestrates the various specialty needs of a patient, while at the same time avoiding duplicate services, medical errors, and waste. CMS has established thirty-three metrics for ACOs that are used to determine quality levels and outcomes. When certain thresholds are achieved against these metrics, the ACO can share in the savings through Medicare Shared Savings Program (MSSP).

To be clear, risk-sharing scenarios are necessary for any complex ecosystem as the amount of data and the transparency of the system increase. For example, in the case of automotive insurance, the insurance company and the insured consumer share the risk through the adjustment of premiums and deductibles.

However, the reason companies such as Progressive, Allstate, and Geico are able to incentivize and

> If healthcare providers were able to shed the administrative albatross, they would have the latitude, resources, and capital to innovate entirely new ways to deliver healthcare to patients who will inherently require more ongoing services.

ACOs and Covered Lives Over Time

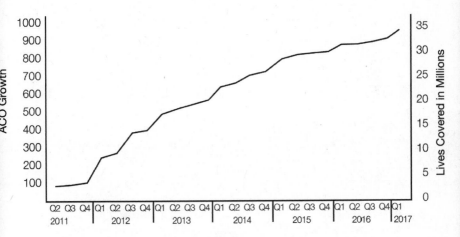

Illustration 2.3 The number of ACOs and the patients covered by them have increased steadily since 2011. This is one way that CMS is driving the change toward more outcome-driven healthcare.[42]

reward driver behaviors that lower risk is through the use of onboard sensors that track a customer's good driving habits and report them in real time, thereby providing the same level of coverage while also reducing premiums and the risk for the insurer. To be clear, the insurer still carries risk, but the technology and the data it has access to significantly mitigate that risk.

Simply continuing to jigger copays and deductibles, without addressing this underlying issue of managing risk through better access to data and analytics, is effectively applying bandages and tourniquets to healthcare. If the healthcare crisis seems overwhelming today, it will be infinitely worse if we continue to travel this path.

A Different Kind of Problem

It's important to stop here and think about why and how healthcare is uniquely different from other risk-sharing scenarios that involve insurance.

In the case of automobile insurance, property insurance, or life insurance, the variables to be considered are relatively few and can be handled without an abundance of data concerning the value, replacement cost, location, or age of the asset or person being insured. Although there may be some degree of inherent uncertainty in all insured risk, virtually every industry other than healthcare has access to enough data to make fairly accurate probabilistic assumptions that allow the insurer to take on the lion's share of the risk and still make a healthy profit.

Healthcare presents a very different problem. The degree of complexity that makes policy change so difficult was summarized well in the *Journal of the American College of Radiology*:[43]

Attempting to capture the almost infinite complexity of medical science and medical practice through laws having finite dimensions has clearly not worked as intended in many cases. Moreover, these laws are often largely crafted by people with limited knowledge of the health care system, an approach that has not worked in the past and will not work in the future.

The article goes on to review numerous well-meaning changes in policy, from the creation and incredible expansion of Medicare from its inception in 1965, to the implications on coverage for pre-existing conditions in the ACA (Obamacare) and on consumer behavior. (We'll look closer at the history of these and many other policy changes in the next chapter.)

Trying to fix healthcare through policy alone is a long, arduous, and socially divisive approach. That's not to say that we shouldn't continue to pursue legislative efforts, but rather, that we also need to look at ways to shore up healthcare that can significantly impact costs, quality, and access while we evaluate systemic policy changes.

Besides, if the track record of US healthcare policy is any indication of the impact future changes will have then they will likely continue to have the unintended consequence of increased costs. Consider that Medicare, which was less than 2 percent of federal spending in its first year of enactment, 1967, now accounts for 26 percent[vii] of the federal budget, nearly twice that of defense spending, which is 15 percent (Illustration 2.4).

---

vii   The 26 percent represents not just Medicare, but also federal contribution to Medicaid, ACA, and CHIP

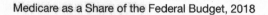

Medicare as a Share of the Federal Budget, 2018

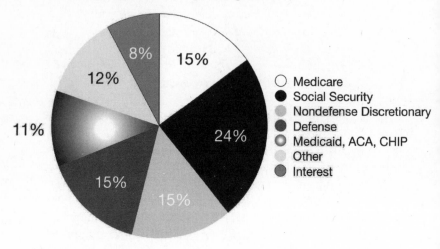

Illustration 2.4 Medicare, Medicaid, ACA, and CHIP are now 26 percent of the federal budget, nearly twice that of defense spending, which is 15 percent.

Policy acts as a safety net when a social or commercial system is unable to provide adequate value to society on its own within the forces imposed by a free market. But that does not mean that we cannot or should not continue to find ways to fix the system so that it operates better within the context of a free market that encourages innovation, competition, and most importantly, choice for the consumer.

In an article for the *Journal of the American Medical Association (JAMA)*, Harvard Medical School Professor of Medicine Lewis Lipsitz, MD, makes the point that unlike many industrial-age systems, healthcare is a complex system that behaves in nonlinear ways.[44] "In contrast to mechanical systems in which component parts interact linearly to produce a predictable output, the components of complex systems interact nonlinearly over multiple scales and produce unexpected results."

Think back to our discussion about why the clock analogy falls short of describing the healthcare system. The result is that any attempt to alter the direction of healthcare by pulling any one lever in the system through siloed policies results in unintended consequences. For example, Medicare and Medicaid are, as we've already said, now over 25 percent of all federal spending. Complex systems, Lipsitz argues, exhibit self-organizing behavior driven by simple rules. If that's the case, then chasing after grandiose architectural solutions may do more to create the illusion of progress, and unintended consequences, than to establish any meaningful long-term change.

Today, as patients, providers, and payers, we tend to accept this dysfunction as the norm. For many of us, it's what we've grown up with; we've only known a healthcare system that is at best opaque and riddled with administrative friction. In the short term, we could make the case that healthcare will continue to be an awkward and strained system that fails to serve its customers' needs particularly well as we await some unforeseen political wizardry to enact policy change.

It's equally clear that over the next five to ten years, the enormous complexity of healthcare and patient demands will grow dramatically, soon reaching a point of implosion. In fact, if the trend of the past twenty-six years continues, by 2050, healthcare spending will be approaching half of US GDP (Illustration 2.5). No one action, policy, or event got us to this point, but understanding the myriad forces that have shaped this trajectory is critical if we are to stand a chance of stemming it. And that's the next step in our journey.

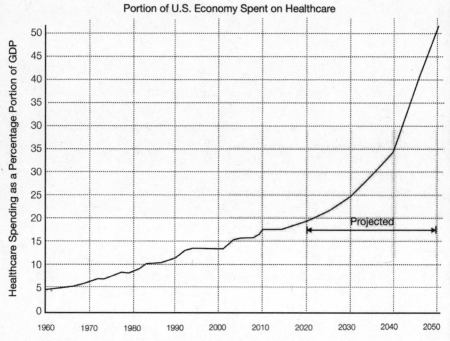

Portion of U.S. Economy Spent on Healthcare

Source:
Average U.S. GDP annual growth rate from 1961-2018 = 3.4%
https://www.macrotrends.net/countries/USA/united-states/gdp-growth-rate
2019 Healthcare growth rate is 5.5%. Authors projection is for an increase in that growth rate of 0.5% every five years after 2020

Illustration 2.5 Healthcare is the largest, fastest-growing industry in the US. Projections from the Bureau of Labor Statistics anticipate that it will add four million new jobs by 2026. By 2050, it will be approaching half of all US GDP (author's projection).

HIDDEN IN PLAIN SIGHT, CHAPTER 2:
RECAP AND LESSONS LEARNED

The current state of healthcare is the result of a century of well-intentioned policies like HIPAA, which resulted in one of the steepest increases ever seen in administrative overhead.

The story of Ivy Austin illustrates the ridiculousness of the healthcare system at present and how this level of dysfunction is something which we would not put up with in any other context as consumers.

Digital ecosystems are becoming the norm in industries such as manufacturing to coordinate, track, and ensure quality. However, nothing even remotely similar exists in healthcare to provide some level of overarching awareness of the patient's healthcare history.

The US is spending 30 percent of every healthcare dollar on administrative costs, more than any other country in the world.

Almost three out of ten people (29 percent) put off medical treatment for fear of the economic consequences. Yearly, more than 530,000 personal bankruptcies are at least partially attributed to uncovered healthcare costs.

Hospital consolidation and mergers increase the price of healthcare by driving up costs due to the ability of larger providers to negotiate higher reimbursement rates with payers as a result of their size and buying power.

Three decades of hospital mergers does not support the claim that consolidation improves quality.

The challenge for most smaller and mid-tier community hospitals, which are running on single-percentage-point margins, is administrative overhead.

An older demographic is amplifying the volume and size of claims as well as the range of simultaneous services needed.

The sixty-five-and-older population will double to 50 percent of the total US population by 2060, meaning that we will be spending as much on the over-sixty-five population in 2060 as we are on all of healthcare today!

Fee-for-service or FFS, is a historical model in which the provider carries relatively little risk since they are paid for all of the services they deliver.

Approaches to move toward value-based healthcare, such as the introduction of HMOs in the 1970s, required much better access than was available to data across the entire healthcare ecosystem in order to better understand the patient's current and future healthcare needs.

The lack of a single patient history is the Achilles' heel of healthcare since it results in episodic care in which nobody owns the patient outcomes over a lifetime—other than the patient. EHRs, which were meant to solve that, are still far too disjointed and varied to change this.

Healthcare service providers, or HSPs—a term we've coined in this book to create a new category of for-profit enterprises that deliver smartsourcing services—are emerging to offer smartsourcing partnerships that offload a hospital's administrative burden.

HSPs use advanced analytical technologies and AI to assess risk for both individuals and large patient populations in ways that were simply unthinkable a decade ago.

The fragmentation of patient data makes it impossible to adequately assess risk in the current healthcare system; although, in virtually every industry where insurance plays a role, there is enough data to make fairly accurate probabilistic assumptions that allow the insurer to take on the lion's share of the risk and still make a healthy profit.

National policy needs to be in place when a system is unable to provide adequate value to society on its own within the forces imposed by a free market. But that does not mean that we cannot or should not continue to find ways in which to fix the system so that it operates better within the context of a free market, which encourages innovation, competition, and most importantly, choice for the consumer.

CHAPTER 3
NOBODY'S AT FAULT BUT EVERYBODY'S TO BLAME

*"Civilization begins with order, grows with liberty,
and dies with chaos."*

—WILL DURANT

Marissett Tolentino was on vacation in the Dominican Republic with her husband and their two young children when her six-year-old daughter, Isabella, began to complain of stomach pains and developed a fever.[1] Before Marissett and her family left the US, she had thoroughly investigated her Blue Cross Blue Shield of Texas (BCBSTX) insurance plan to make sure that, in the event of an illness, there would be appropriate care in the DR, as well as options to come back home in the event of an emergency. She was reassured to learn that not only was a nearby hospital in the DR approved as an in-network provider, but her plan also covered emergency air transport in a medical plane back to the US in the event of a severe life-threatening emergency.

When the resort doctor told Marissett that they needed to go to the local hospital, there was some relief in not having to worry about coverage. However, the situation quickly escalated when Isabella was diagnosed with appendicitis and hospital doctors said surgery would be necessary.

The Tolentinos wanted the surgery to take place back home in America, which was only a short one-hour plane ride away. However, both the DR doctors and Isabella's pediatrician in the US cautioned against a commercial flight. Not a problem, thought Marissett; after all, they had

> The Tolentinos begged BCBSTX to arrange Isabella's medical air transfer, but BCBSTX refused to consider the request until they received a full written report from the DR clinic.

insurance coverage for private medical air transport, they were only one hour from Miami, and this was clearly an emergency that could become life-threatening. However, after reviewing the case, Blue Cross Blue Shield of Texas denied the request because it didn't consider Isabella's appendicitis an emergency.

Given the options they were presented with and the severity of the appendicitis, the decision was made to operate on Isabella locally.

What should have been a routine operation took a dramatic turn for the worse. After the procedure, Isabella did not come out of anesthesia as expected. Marissett, a nurse, also noticed that Isabella's oxygen levels were low. She was told by the staff not to worry, yet Isabella's condition worsened, and the Tolentinos were notified that she would be transferred to intensive care. This did not happen until midnight of the day after Isabella's surgery.

The Tolentinos begged BCBSTX to arrange Isabella's medical air transfer, but BCBSTX refused to consider the request until they received a full written report from the DR clinic. Another day passed.

On the third day, BCBSTX finally agreed to set up a transfer, however, the clinic would not allow the transfer until their bill was paid, something that BCBSTX should have handled given that the clinic was already confirmed to be in-network. Yet another day passed. The Tolentinos would later allege that during this time, BCBSTX was receiving updates on Isabella's worsening condition, and was fully aware of the situation.

Finally, after four days, a medical team and a private plane were arranged. Immediately, upon attempting to stabilize Isabella, the plane's medics determined that her vomit and blood were clogging an intubation tube that was meant for an infant and was far too small for Isabella. They found the tube had been blocked, likely since the surgery, and Isabella had been deprived of adequate oxygen for four days.

Isabella never woke up. After arriving at a US hospital, doctors examining Isabella declared her brain-dead from lack of oxygen. The family made the difficult decision to take her off life support.

What conspired against Isabella was a process that in total took far too long to resolve because each player was following processes that made sense to them but did nothing to provide coordinated care for Isabella.

Isabella's family filed a lawsuit against Blue Cross Blue Shield for their involvement in their daughter's passing. The suit was settled two years later under undisclosed terms.

Isabella's story is tragic, but—and I get tired of saying it—not unique. In my research for this book, I came across numerous heartbreaking accounts of patients who had encountered circumstances in which a painfully slow process of communication between insurers and providers created life-threatening delays and, in many cases, claims that were simply approved too late to impact the outcome.

It's easy to look at this case and point fingers at virtually everyone responsible for Isabella's medical care. From the insurer to the providers, there were numerous points at which decisions were made, or alleged to have been made, such as the intubation tube used, that increased the likelihood of this tragic outcome. But what most conspired against Isabella was a process that in total took far too long to resolve because each player was following processes and protocols that made sense to them without any coordinated effort to resolve the urgent decisions necessary to provide quality care (Culprit #7, The Tragedy of the Commons).

It's a situation where nobody is at fault, yet everybody is to blame. A process that is inherently disconnected, subject to miscommunication, poor management of risk, and delayed resolutions that compound the severity of what is, in many cases, a scenario requiring complex and timely decision-making.

While the stakes may be higher in healthcare, the challenges of miscommunication, poor management of risk, and delays due to process complexity are familiar territory to anyone who has had to navigate and manage complex systems in any industry.

But before we discuss how we're going to attempt to solve these challenges, we need to understand why the healthcare system has reached its breaking point.

From Bond and Benjamin to Baylor and Blue Cross

Hospitals have been around in one form or another for over 2,500 years.

The predecessors to the modern concept of a hospital were most often affiliated with spiritual sects or religious institutions. From the ancient Greek Temples of Asclepius—healing sites dedicated to their eponymous doctor-god—to the many religious hospitals throughout Europe spanning the thousand years from 500 to 1500 AD.

It wasn't until 1540, when King Henry VIII disbanded England's monasteries, that secular hospitals were first established. Institutions resembling the modern hospital funded by private benefactors first appeared in the mid-1700s in both Europe and the colonies.

The emergence of larger hospitals with the capacity to house thousands of patients didn't come about until the 1800s, stemming directly from Napoleon's efforts to provide care for the thousands of wounded soldiers who fought in his wars. Those were also the first teaching hospitals.[2]

Then, in 1859, Florence Nightingale established the first school of nursing at St. Thomas' Hospital in London.[3]

On the other side of the Atlantic, the first US hospital was established in Philadelphia in 1751 by Dr. Thomas Bond. One of Bond's early advisers, and ultimately one of his largest benefactors, was Benjamin Franklin. While there may have been many points of disagreement between England and the colonies, both Bond and

The conditions were far from the sort of sterile and well-organized settings we associate with a hospital today. To be blunt, you went there as a last resort, not as a first line of defense.

Franklin had seen firsthand, and were deeply impressed by, how England was instituting and managing its hospital system.

Shortly thereafter, in 1796, another local hospital was established as the Boston Dispensary,[viii] financed by a group of patriots including Paul Revere and John Adams. The Dispensary's founders funded tickets that enabled the city's poor to receive medical care; one of the original tickets signed by Revere can still be seen today at the Massachusetts Historical Society.[4]

Early US hospitals, such as Bond's and Revere's, were meant to care for the disadvantaged, poor, and mentally disabled in the community. These were institutions that would be shunned by anyone of means. The conditions were far from the sort of sterile and well-organized settings we associate with a hospital today. To be blunt, you went there as a last resort, not as a first line of defense.

A turning point for hospitals, and the way that medicine was practiced, came in 1847 with the formation of the American Medical Association (AMA), that provided physicians with a common voice with which to influence the practice

---

viii   The Boston Dispensary, now known as Tufts Medical Center, is in many ways accountable for the fact that you are reading this book, having quite literally saved my life when I was a ten-year-old with an undiagnosed case of Hepatitis A contracted during a trip overseas. After months of being shuttled from doctor to doctor and being misdiagnosed with a variety of illnesses from cancer to anemia, my father happened upon a local pediatrician, Dr. Lester Abelman. Dr. Abelman was affiliated with the Tufts Floating Hospital for Children—a pediatric hospital that was located on a ship in Boston Harbor from 1894 to 1927. While Hep A normally runs its course, I had developed a severe case and was a week away from liver failure. I was immediately admitted and spent the next month being treated at the Floating Hospital for Children, followed by another three months recovering at home. Not coincidentally, Tufts is where my current PCP practices.

Teddy Roosevelt ran for the US presidency in 1912 on a platform that proposed the first national health insurance. It was the start of a century-long political and social discourse that has followed nearly every politician seeking national or state office since then.

and policy of medicine. As we'll see, the AMA would also come to be one of the most influential organizations in both the evolution of the healthcare system and the role of healthcare insurance.

The rise of the hospital's role in delivering healthcare during the twentieth century is something that we take for granted today. From Bond's first hospital in 1796 to the turn of the twentieth century, nearly one thousand hospitals were built in the US. Today, there are just over six thousand hospitals.[5] What's especially telling, however, is the recent drop in the number of hospital beds nationwide. Rising from about 50,000[6] in the mid-1800s to over 1.4 million in 1946,[7] there are now just over 900,000 staffed beds today.[8] As we'll see later in the book, this points to the changing role of the hospital in healthcare.

The Evolution of Health Insurance

Unlike the long-standing history of the hospital, the concept of health insurance is a relatively recent phenomenon. The first general-purpose sickness insurance was issued in Massachusetts in 1847. A similar plan consisting of a community of preapproved physicians, much like today's HMOs, was established in San Francisco in 1853. There had been government-funded insurance for seamen and later for veterans as early as 1798, when John Adams signed a law that guaranteed care for sick or injured seamen.

US federally funded hospitals for disabled veterans were brought on by the enormous casualties of the Civil War. Lincoln's call to "bind up the nation's wounds" and "to care for him who shall have borne the battle and for his widow, and his orphan" was not simply a metaphor for the nation's healing, but a directive to care for the injured and their families. In 1865, this led to the creation of the National Asylum for Disabled Volunteer Soldiers, the precursor to today's Veterans Administration.

The earliest example of government-mandated health insurance for the general population appeared in 1883 when German Chancellor Otto von Bismarck introduced a law enacting compulsory health insurance in order to placate a socialist-leaning working class. Britain followed suit soon after, creating the National Insurance Act (NIA) in 1911 as the result of the Prime Minister's visit to Germany in 1908. Britain's approach was also intended to assist low-income citizens.

On the heels of Britain's NIA, Teddy Roosevelt's 1912 campaign for the US presidency ran on a platform proposing the first national health insurance program. It was the start of a century-long political and social discourse that has followed nearly every politician since.

The fledgling AMA, which was formed only sixty years prior, spent the next decade establishing its opposition to insurance programs that limited a patient's freedom of choice. In the words of the AMA, "The practice of medicine must remain a process of personal contact, invoking the patient's right of selection and the direct moral responsibility of the physician, with a sympathetic reaction between the two." While the rapport between doctor and patient should clearly be at the center of healthcare, this one-to-one relationship has increasingly given way to the mounting complexity of care, the constraint of choice, and the loss of continuity of care that comes from a long-term relationship with one physician.

In the early 1900s, US corporations began to provide healthcare to employees. In 1929, the archetype of most modern-day insurance was first established at Baylor University Hospital in Texas. It would later become the prototype for Blue Cross, which covered hospital charges but not private physicians.

Mining companies in California put in place medical service bureaus that were an early form of HMO. These collections of private physician practices were paid monthly fees to care for employees of member mining companies. This was the precursor to Blue Shield, which was later formed from these medical service bureaus in 1939.

By the election of Franklin Roosevelt in 1932, the Great Depression was in full force, with unemployment rates reaching 25 percent. FDR's enactment of social security included a provision for national healthcare; however, an outcry against universal healthcare ensued, spurred by concerns about socialism from groups such as the American Health Association. In a rush to get the bill through Congress, the provision was eliminated, and universal healthcare suffered its first in a long series of derailments over the next ninety years.

FDR continued to push an agenda for universal healthcare; however, with the onset of World War II, the effort was again sidelined and ultimately

> The unintended consequences of this single, well-meaning act, put in place by a wartime agency that rightfully should have had no control over a peacetime economy, created the unfortunate trajectory toward the current healthcare crisis.

passed off to Harry Truman, whose Fair Deal legislation also included a national health program. Truman's efforts were blocked repeatedly by the then-Republican-led Congress.

The Historical Quirk that Set the Trajectory for 100 Years of Healthcare

Still, private health insurance flourished in the post-WWII era due to a historical oddity which set in motion the foundation of healthcare for the next eighty years. Prior to WWII, individuals paid for healthcare out of pocket, while low-income workers relied on one of the few existing insurers, such as Blue Cross.

However, during WWII, the US government had sanctioned a series of price and wage controls to increase wartime production.[9] These stayed in place after the war in order to avoid the skyrocketing inflation rates seen in post-WWI Germany and the chaos predicted by many economists. Outraged, US labor unions threatened to cripple US industry with strikes in protest of continued wage controls.

As a compromise, the War Labor Board, which was originally intended to provide controls that would ensure the labor needed for the US war machine, instated a set-aside for healthcare benefits that exempted them from wage controls and taxation. The unintended consequences of this single, well-meaning act, put in place by a wartime agency that rightfully should have had no control over a peacetime economy, created the unfortunate trajectory toward the current healthcare crisis.

With wage controls in place, employers resorted to luring prospective employees with the promise of health insurance. What had been a minor leak in the foundation of a levy holding back healthcare costs soon burst into a flood of employee-earned benefits[ix] that not only drove up healthcare costs by pouring more money into benefit plans, but also masked the cost of healthcare from employees who had little reason to keep track of it. The decreasing contribution to increasing health insurance costs by employers over the past two decades has been an unwinding of the legacy that was established in the early, formative stages of US health insurance.

Compounding the problem was the fact that because employers were offering insurance benefits, most people didn't see the need for national health insurance. After all, by 1950, 57 percent of the US population had medical insurance coverage, in most cases had ample choice of where to receive treatment, and had little reason to concern themselves with the cost of healthcare. Employers, on the other hand, were able to take a tax deduction for employee health insurance costs. In the post-war boom, the system seemed to work—for most.

Still there was an ever-increasing segment of the population that did not have access to healthcare. In fact, until 1986, when the Emergency Medical Treatment and Active Labor Act (EMTALA) was passed guaranteeing access to emergency medical services, you could still (legally) be turned away from even emergency healthcare based on an inability to pay.

It took another twenty years after WWII for Lyndon Johnson to sign Medicare and Medicaid into law in 1965 as an amendment to FDR's Social Security Act, which had been proposed as part of a universal healthcare system thirty-three years prior in 1932.

President Nixon then followed suit by instating the HMO Act of 1973, which was intended to provide a vehicle that

---

ix   Note that I'm not calling these "entitlements" but "earned benefits," since that's what they were at the time.

enabled greater predictability and control of healthcare costs for insurers and the government. While HMOs where not structurally new—recall, for example, the mining companies mentioned earlier—the US government would now provide significant economic incentives and grants to establish HMOs. Again, this had unintended consequences by nearly eliminating the marketplace for individual health insurance policies.

Other changes followed, including the establishment of hospice care funded by Medicare, diagnosis-related groups (DRGs) that standardized hospital payments based on categories of illness, and COBRA, the Consolidated Omnibus Budget Reconciliation Act, which required partial subsidies from employers to terminated employees' health insurance coverage.

> At each point in the healthcare narrative, well-meaning people shaped the evolution of healthcare in ways that were intended to address the needs at the time.

Still, the push for universal healthcare continued. While President Clinton's Health Security Act of 1993 never made it through Congress, the Health Insurance Portability and Accountability Act (HIPAA) was put in place in 1996. In addition to protecting patient health information, this act made it easier to carry insurance over to a new employer. However, HIPAA was also one of the greatest contributors to increasing healthcare administrative costs. Whenever you look at a chart that shows increased spending and headcount for administrative services in healthcare, the elbow at which both begin to accelerate much faster is concurrent with HIPAA. (See Illustration 2.1 in the previous chapter.)

Finally, in 2010, the Affordable Care Act (ACA)—also known as Obamacare—was passed, making sweeping changes in coverage for preexisting conditions, removing lifetime limits on critical coverage, and establishing a means to appeal claims denials. Health insurance exchanges, which enabled individuals to purchase affordable coverage based on need and without an employer sponsor, were also put in place at both the federal and state level.

The impact of the ACA can't be overstated. Prior to its passing, insurance companies were not only able to deny coverage for individuals with preexisting conditions, they could even retroactively deny coverage. A horrifying example of retroactive cancellation of coverage is the case of four-year-old Selah Shaeffer. After Selah was diagnosed with a serious tumor and had racked up over $20,000 worth of medical bills, her parents, Steve and Leslie, were informed by Blue Cross that the company was terminating their coverage and would no longer pay for the previously authorized and completed surgery performed on Selah. Blue Cross cited the fact that they were not informed of the tumor when they agreed to cover Selah; however, the Shaeffers themselves were not aware of the tumor at the time. Only after receiving the coverage and receiving treatment was their attention brought to it. Along with the fear for their child, the Shaeffers found themselves drowning in $60,000 of medical bills and facing the threat of losing their home.

As you read through this admittedly brief history of healthcare's evolution,[x] you'll notice that there is no one point where we can say that the system took a turn for the worse. In fact, just the opposite seems to be true. At each point in the healthcare narrative, well-meaning people shaped the

---

[x]   To get a thorough history of how healthcare has evolved and the myriad decisions that have resulted in today's healthcare system, I suggest the book *Understanding Healthcare: A Historical Perspective* by Kenneth A. Fisher (Freedom in Health Care: Kalamazoo, 2016), Ebook.

evolution of healthcare in ways that were intended to address the needs at the time. In many cases, policy has helped, as with Medicare and the ACA. It's important to keep this in mind as we look deeper into how to solve the current challenges of healthcare's costs, quality, and accessibility. In many ways, the pieces of the healthcare system, from physicians to administrators,

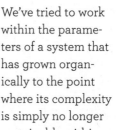

We've tried to work within the parameters of a system that has grown organically to the point where its complexity is simply no longer sustainable within the same confines...it [has] evolved within.

are all working diligently within the confines of the system to deliver the best service possible. Unfortunately, those constraints are making both the coordination and the affordable delivery of healthcare increasingly more difficult. And with each effort to shore up the system while working within those constraints, we only further complicated it.

The Healthcare Trinity

The century-long attempt to reach a national agreement on healthcare has always come down to three cornerstone principles: cost, quality, and access. First introduced by Dr. William Kissick in 1994,[10] the central premise of this "Iron Triangle" was that any attempt to shore up one angle was always at the expense of the other two. Just as geometry mandates that the angles of a triangle must tally up to 180 degrees, the Iron Triangle of healthcare is always a zero-sum proposition.

For example, if we look back to the hospital model described earlier, decreasing the number of beds would reduce cost but also decrease the quality and accessibility of healthcare. However, that's not the case as new models of healthcare delivery are created that—among other advances—increase early diagnosis and intervention, incorporate telemedicine, establish remote ambulatory clinics, and develop faster, less invasive surgical techniques.

Constructs such as the Iron Triangle are an artifact of an industrial age intended to help scale healthcare to the masses. That type of healthcare worked in accommodating the needs of a nineteenth- and twentieth-century America in which life expectancies where much shorter, medicine and a knowledge of diseases was much less complex, and societal pressure to deliver high-quality healthcare to every citizen was far less prevalent than it is today. However, it also created a wasteful model in which costs were directly tied to the practice of medicine in hospital settings where patients could be observed for extended periods of time, resulting in the rise of the hospital's role through the 1970s. The problem is that we are still stuck with the infrastructure of that same healthcare system. Breaking free of that model is going require transitioning into a new post-industrial-age version of healthcare: Healthcare 2.0.

Healthcare 2.0

So far, we've looked at many of the individual pieces of the healthcare system that are in need of reimagining, rethinking, and reforming. It's time to start narrowing our focus to those areas that represent the greatest areas of friction that we need to take on in order to create a vision of what Healthcare 2.0 will need to look like over the next hundred years.

When trying to focus on a starting point for solving very complex problems, there's always the risk that you will either be drawn into a quagmire of details and tangents or that the scope of your focus will exclude areas that some consider to be just as, or more, important as starting points. There's no doubt that there are many areas that need to be addressed in order to create a truly sustainable model for the future of healthcare. But there are also some fundamental issues that absolutely must be addressed if we are going to stand a chance of even starting on that journey. The four that we need to cover in more detail before moving on to the solution are denials, diagnostic coding, the consumer patient, and demographics. Of necessity, we are going to have to get a bit into the weeds of how these currently work and the challenges they represent in the current model of healthcare and in creating a vision for the future of Healthcare 2.0.

Denied

When I work with senior executives in identifying impediments to success, I'm fond of asking them, "What's the problem that most keeps you up at night because you just can't figure out a way to fix it?" In the case of healthcare, there may seem to be an abundance of likely answers to that question, but the most frequent answer is getting claims paid. That's because the greatest single point of friction, contention, and revenue leakage for providers is that of submitting claims.[xi]

Insurance claims are denied for a variety of reasons, from simple coding errors to the determination of medical necessity (recall the case of Isabella in chapter 2), to differences in how a provider and payer account for limits on covered services such as doctor's visits. Not every denied claim ends up being paid for directly by the patient. In many cases, the patient never knows that the claim was denied. In other cases,

---

xi   Revenue leakage is a term that applies to revenues that an organization believes it is due but which it cannot collect. In the case of healthcare, the process most often resulting in revenue leakage is unpaid or uncollectable claims.

as with Debbie Moehnke in chapter 2, the denial could result in very high costs to the consumer.

Providers also expend valuable resources disputing claims that have initially been denied. For each claim, they spend an average of $118 to recover funds from payers.[11] Extrapolated nationwide, that amounts to as much as $8.6 billion in administrative costs.[12, 13]

The most recent AMA national health insurer report card found that major payers such as Aetna, Anthem, Cigna, Humana, and UnitedHealth Group kept overall claim denials down to well under 5 percent.[14]

At first blush, that sounds pretty good. That is, until you consider that the total cost of all denied claims to hospitals comes in at $262 billion per year.[15] To put that in context, keep in mind that total profit for all US hospitals in 2017 was just under $90 billion.[16] Two-thirds of all hospitals are losing money according to Gary Young, director of the Center for Health Policy and Healthcare Research at Northeastern University.[17] Even some of the largest hospital systems are losing millions. According to the Harvard Business Review, MD Anderson Cancer Center lost $266 million in FY 2016; Boston-based Partners HealthCare lost $108 million in FY 2016, its second operating loss in four years; and Providence St. Joseph Health, the second-largest Catholic health system in the US, saw operating income fall $512 million with a $252 million loss in FY 2016.[18] The overall denial rate for large payers also masks the high rate of variability among all payers, which ranges from 1 to 45 percent.[19]

...the total cost of denied claims...comes in at $262 billion per year. To put that in context, keep in mind that total profit for all US hospitals in 2017 was just under $90 billion.

However, even for those claims that are approved, the estimated costs of billing and insurance-related activities ranged from $20 for a primary care visit to $215 for an inpatient surgical procedure, representing up to 25 percent of revenue.[20]

Of course, this also doesn't take into account the amounts billable and payable to patients directly; according to research by TransUnion Healthcare, 68 percent of patients failed to fully pay off medical bill balances in 2016, up from 53 percent in 2015, and 49 percent in 2014. TransUnion researchers attributed that increase to higher deductibles and expect the number to climb to 95 percent by 2020.[21]

Denied claims present an especially challenging situation for self-insured employers, for whom claims management has been called the greatest threat to an organization's total cost of risk, a measure that represents the sum of all aspects of an organization's operations that relate to risk.

Patients are also experiencing greater pressure due to higher deductibles. Total hospital revenue attributable to patient financial responsibility after insurance increased by 88 percent between 2012 and 2017.[22, 23]

According to the National Academy of Medicine, billing and insurance related administrative costs (BIR) amounted to $361 billion in 2009, or 14.4 percent of total health expenditures. Another study pegs BIR costs at $471 billion in 2012, or 16.8 percent of total health expenditures (with 80 percent directly related to the US's multi-payer system).[24, 25] If we assume the same rate of increase

> ...the US spends more on billing and insurance-related administration than the combined total expenditure of Germany, Canada, and Australia for their entire healthcare systems.

115

in BIR through 2020, then by the time this book is published, the US will be spending 25 percent of total healthcare expenditures on BIR administrative costs. Do you recall the analogy I used in the Introduction of a giant clock with its gears grinding away while we pour copious amounts of lubricant into it, just to keep it running? Much of that 25 percent is the lubricant. Keep in mind that BIR costs still do not reflect total administrative overhead, which we've estimated at closer to 30 percent of total healthcare costs.

To put it into perspective, the US spends more on billing and insurance-related administration than the combined total expenditure of Germany, Canada, and Australia for their entire healthcare systems. Clearly, the combined population of those three countries is less than half of the US, but the comparison is the total of all healthcare spending to just the administrative part of US healthcare.

The bottom line is inescapable; we are overrun with friction in the administrative sector of healthcare. While we are trying to reform healthcare through policy and sociopolitical discourse, we must also begin to address the root cause of so much of our national healthcare crisis by restructuring this one critical aspect of our healthcare system.

Breaking the Code

Another cornerstone of the healthcare system which generates enormous administrative overhead, for clinicians as well as administrators, is coding. We introduced the process of coding in the case of Wanda Wickizer in chapter 2. Coding is the means by which a specific medical procedure or diagnosis is uniquely identified. Each disease, injury, and medical condition has a unique code referred to as its ICD-10, or International Statistical Classification of Diseases and Related Health Problems, 10th Revision. The codes are developed and copywritten by the World Health Organization. A version of each ICD-10-CM (the CM stands for clinical modification) is used under license by the US National Center for Health Statistics.

Our focus will be on the use of the codes for submitting insurance claims. However, it's important to note that these codes are also used for tracking diseases, epidemics, and various health statistics, as well as supporting a value-based approach to healthcare. In many ways, the extensive and intricate taxonomy of the many types of codes we'll discuss provides a critically important language for healthcare researchers, public health services, and healthcare providers to precisely track and communicate vital information to better understand diseases and treat illnesses. So pervasive is the use of these codes that an ICD code will even appear on a death certificate to indicate the cause of death.

All of this sounds relatively straightforward until you find out that there are over 70,000 ICD-10-PCS procedure codes and 69,000 ICD-10-CM diagnosis codes. The only way a provider will be reimbursed by an insurer is to submit the codes consistent with the patient's visit and reflective of the patient's condition and necessary treatment during the encounter.

To complicate matters further, ICD is just one of several coding mechanisms used in healthcare. DRGs are used for Medicare billing. Current procedural terminology (CPT) codes have been developed by the AMA to identify the procedures used by a clinician to deliver services. Healthcare Common Procedure Coding System (HCPCS) codes were developed by CMS. Few things epitomize Culprit #4, The Complexity Crisis, better than this extraordinarily vast (and growing) collection of codes. Additionally, in Medicare Advantage capitated plans, there is a new level of coding that's needed, a Hierarchical Condition Category (HCC), which is a risk adjustment model that calculates risk scores to predict future healthcare costs.

The reason coding is an important topic for our conversation is that the accuracy with which codes are entered by a provider has direct implications on the amount and the timing of reimbursement for their services. Incorrectly coded claims are either denied or sent back for clarification and correction. This adds to the administrative burden of both provider and payer, but it also creates the potential that the unpaid claim might ultimately become the financial burden of the patient.

To quantify that, let's go back to the claims process we were discussing earlier in this chapter. If the additional administrative cost of recovering denied claims is $8.6 billion, the cost for each appealed claim would be roughly $118 per appealed claim. That may seem relatively insignificant, but it works out to an average of $5 million of provider revenue that is at risk per hospital. For smaller and mid-sized hospitals, that alone is likely to be the difference between profit and loss.

While any clinician involved in patient care can code a diagnosis or procedure, to mitigate and offset the risk of coding errors, both providers and insurers have coders on staff who have been trained, and in most cases certified and degreed, to code claims and (in the case of insurers) to evaluate the coding of submitted claims. There's even an American Association of Professional Coders with over 190,000 members!

However, to fully understand the challenge of coding, we need to take a step back and think about its purpose. Healthcare is an inherently complex process that requires a deep knowledge of many factors. Doctors spend years developing an understanding of illness and treatments that depends on not only an expert grasp of the science of healing but also an intuitive ability to diagnose and treat patients. I recall one doc I interviewed years ago telling me that he was well aware of how he drove nurses and other clinicians crazy because he would identify a patient's specific condition well before lab results had inevitably confirmed his diagnosis. Coding is ultimately about trying to translate this level of complexity in human judgment into a set of alphanumeric codes. That's a challenge not only from a clinical standpoint, but also from an administrative standpoint.

Coders working for a provider are tasked with having to interpret documentation, charts, doctor's notes, lab results, and lab notes, and then reduce this all into a set of codes that adequately represent the patient's condition and the procedures used to treat it. The payer's coders then have to deconstruct those same codes into a meaningful representation of the patient's condition and treatments to determine if they will cover the diagnosis or treatment based on the contract with the provider. When they can't approve a claim, their options are to deny the claim or to request additional documentation and explanation. Both cases result in additional effort for the provider as well as the payer.

All this complexity, and the high financial stakes involved, leads to what has often been called "the battle of the coders." However, that term portrays what would appear to be a win-lose scenario. In fact, coders are extraordinarily disciplined and focus obsessively on accuracy since their task represents the foundation of a provider's or payer's financial performance.

The problem in the overwhelming number of cases is not the coders but rather the complexity and friction of this process, which creates an inherent tension and conflict between providers and payers. That friction undermines, slows, and increases the costs for the entire process of reimbursements with a vicious cycle:

1. Providers spend time determining how to code each procedure

2. Insurers deny claims that providers consider valid

3. Providers lose money-fighting decision by payers

4. Providers upcode in order to make up for antici-pated denials or downcode and forgo revenues in order to speed claims processing

5. Insurers become more skeptical and spend more time scrutinizing claims

In her book, *An American Sickness*, Elisabeth Rosenthal goes to great lengths in describing the somewhat dubious practice of awarding productivity bonuses to doctors. This gives the impression that the system is being somehow abused by providers. The reality is far less sinister.

Although it would be naive to not recognize the risk of abuse by providers, the overwhelming majority are simply trying to streamline the claims system by doing what they can to take the low-friction route shown in Illustration 3.0. This usually takes the form of two scenarios, upcoding and downcoding.

Upcoding is basically performing or documenting added procedures and using a corresponding code for the diagno-sis that represents a higher reimbursement level. Although these practices are outliers, insurers who have had to deal with upcoding will more readily deny claims that they feel are not justified or adequately documented.

Downcoding, on the other hand, is more common and speaks to the dysfunction of the current system. In order to avoid the risk of extended back-and-forth with a payer result-ing from codes that require higher reimbursements, doctors

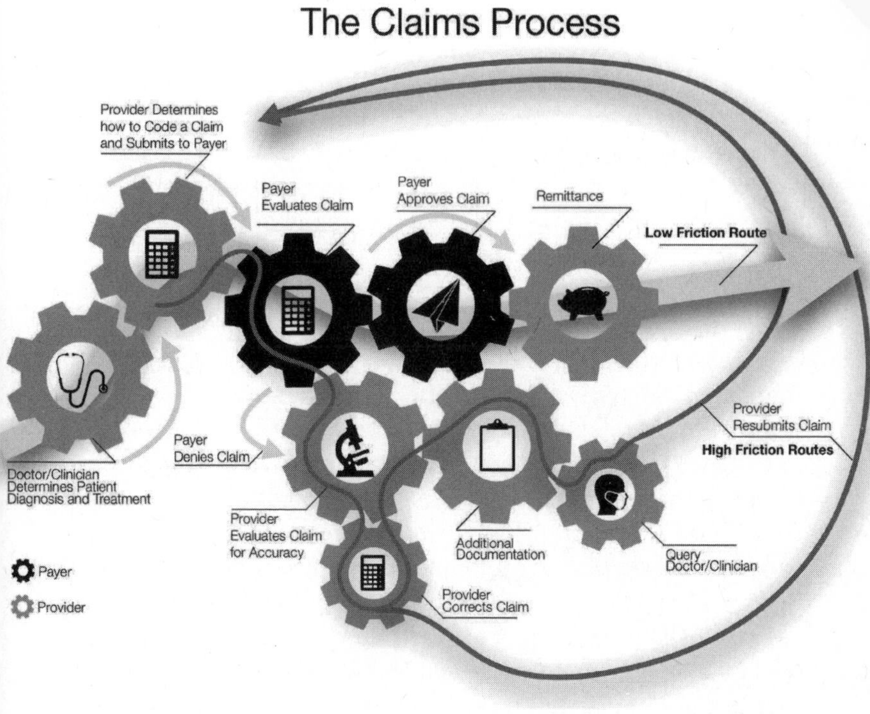

The Claims Process

Illustration 3.0 The least costly and fastest route for a claim to take is the path shown with the broad arrow labeled "Low-Friction Route." If a claim is denied by the payer, it is because of incorrect coding, an uncovered diagnosis or treatment, or lack of adequate supporting documentation. In these cases, the provider needs to decide if they will correct and resubmit the claim, submit the claim (as a bill) to the patient, or do additional research and resubmit the claim. These are labeled the High-Friction Routes. Keep in mind that this is a very high-level view of the process which does not also consider the various steps that may be taken to determine coverage prior to seeing the patient or which may occur during the billing of a patient after a claim is denied.

and coders will submit a code that represents a less severe condition or a less expensive service than what was actually provided. The thinking behind downcoding is that a lower reimbursement, which is more likely to go through, is more cost

a more expensive one that is likely to be rejected
r. That's due to the fact that denied claims simply
ional resources and time, which may exceed the
value of the claim, to be approved. This also happens when
a payer decides to downcode a submitted claim with the
expectation that the provider will just accept the lower reimbursement without appealing it because the appeal is costly.

There's another aspect to coding that is important to
our conversation. Since coding provides a means of tracking
diseases, illnesses, and treatments within a structured set of
categories, it is also being used by payers and providers to
implement value-based care (VBC). Recall that VBC is something we first talked about in chapter 2 when we looked at
how new payment models that paid providers set amounts
based on their meeting certain outcomes. Hospitals have tied
the bonuses of salaried doctors to relative value units (RVUs).
RVUs are based on a combination of factors such as the time
or task performed by a doctor, additional facilities charges
or overhead, what it costs to learn how to perform a task or
deliver a service, and malpractice costs. The link between
this and coding is that one of the best ways to consistently
account for RVUs accurately is through coding, which aligns
them with the VBC model put in place by the payer.

The bottom line is that coding is a critical and complex
process that is essential to many aspects of an efficient healthcare system. If the services provided are documented, follow
prescribed protocols, and are considered to be within the
scope of what the providing clinician deems necessary, the
claim is valid and, if needed, outcomes can be consistently
measured. However, if the claim uses codes that are not consistent with the diagnosis and the services provided, it will
not only be denied but it will also undermine a value-based
approach to the healthcare process.

The burden this creates is not just shouldered by coders. Doctors and clinicians often have to be brought back into the process to provide clarification, documentation, and other information needed by the coder to make sure the correct codes have been entered. That back-and forth-is costly, time consuming, and a contributor to doctor burnout.

Since coders are the linchpin for the success of the coding process, the only way to address the challenge of accurate and consistent coding is by helping coders do their job better. Today that means throwing more coders at the process. The challenge is that there just aren't enough coders. According to the US Bureau of Labor Statistics, the anticipated growth in jobs for coders over the next ten years will be 50 percent greater than that for doctors and surgeons.[26] This is where the smartsourcing approach, which we'll talk about later in the book, can yield significant results. By using AI and natural language processing, much of the more common coding can be done by algorithms. These algorithms are not only able to interpret doctor's notes, documentation, patient charts, and lab results, but they can also identify problematic patterns in large collections of prior claims that create unnecessary friction and denials.

What I've just described is for the coding alone. There is another aspect to this that puts enormous strain on doctors and clinicians, which is the documentation that has to be submitted to support the coding. We'll talk more about that in chapter 4 when we delve into the time doctors spend on EHRs.

The enormous amount of effort that it takes to support this sort of system is a direct consequence of the current FFS model that we talked about in chapter 1. FFS undermines trust between payer and provider, introduces ongoing systemic friction, and puts an enormous burden on the clinician to keep pace with changes in coding. Imagine any other system where nearly every transaction is suspect and needs to go through this sort of verification.

Notice that I called out FFS and not coding. That's because the solution here is not to eliminate the need for a medical lingua franca, which provides a necessary way to deal with the ever-increasing complexity of healthcare diagnostics and services, and which supports a value-based approach. Instead, coding is one of the areas that actually requires even more sophistication to support a sustainable healthcare system. As we delve into the revenue cycle in chapter 6, we'll take a closer look at how smartsourcing can have a dramatic impact on coding.

The Customer Patient

Since so much of the administrative burden we have been and will be describing ends up impacting the patient (for example, denied claims), it's important to touch on the discussion about treating patients as customers or consumers—something that inevitably opens up a Pandora's box for healthcare providers.

The controversy stems from something that we brought up at the very beginning of the book, that the doctor-patient relationship is the cornerstone of medicine and one of the most important determinants of quality healthcare outcomes. It's logical that anything that prevents, erodes, or otherwise impairs this relationship would decrease the quality of care.

I should point out that some primary care physicians see the notion of a patient-customer as potentially harmful to the doctor/patient relationship. Dr. KrisEmily McCrory, a primary care doctor who is affiliated with multiple hospitals in the Schenectady, New York area, describes the notion of the patient-customer as something that profoundly changes the physician-patient relationship. According to Dr. McCrory,

The individuals I take care of on a daily basis are my patients. They are neither my clients nor customers. For several years, I have been mortified at the implication that I provide a service akin to selling a car. Referring to patients as customers shifts the focus solely onto customer service and the transactional nature of exchanging goods for money. When administrators with their business training subtly adjust the language, it profoundly changes the physician-patient relationship. As a physician, I feel it demeans the actual time and effort I take in caring for my patients.

Within the very nature of a physician-patient relationship there is an undeniable level of inequality. Referring to patients as clients does not remove that imbalance of power. Rather, it only serves to gloss over it. Patients are ill or injured, sometimes gravely. Patients are exposed. Patients are often alone. Patients are vulnerable. Service providers have a commitment to profits first and customers second. Physicians, however, have a responsibility to their patients."[27]

Few of us would argue that the level of dedication and focus required to perform the responsibilities of a physician may not always come across as being customer focused. The delivery of unwanted test results, the diagnosis of a severe illness, or directives to follow a therapeutic or pharmaceutical regimen that the patient doesn't agree with or which is not convenient all run the risk of being perceived as not customer friendly.

Enhancing the customer experience cannot happen by simply trying to refocus clinicians on being more customer friendly. Any effort to fix healthcare without easing the burden on the PCP, enhancing access to primary care, and easing the challenge of navigating the administrative disjointedness of the current healthcare system is a setup for failure.

A Johns Hopkins Bloomberg School of Public Health study showed that a PCP reduces the odds of premature death by 19 percent over patients who only see specialists.[28] In addition, patients with a PCP save 33 percent on healthcare over their peers who only see specialists.[29] In fact, a study published in the *Annals of Family Medicine* estimated that the US healthcare system would save $67 billion every year if everyone used a PCP.[30]

Yet, 28 percent of males and 17 percent of women in the US do not have a PCP.[31] In addition, we've already mentioned that 45 percent of millennials and Gen Z[32] are shunning primary care relationships as being too time-consuming and too expensive. Add to that the preference for 60 percent of doctors to choose specialty fields over family or internal medicine, along with the projected primary care deficit of doctors, and you have a perfect storm that undermines any effort at creating a customer experience that is at least not frustrating and more likely to encourage adherence to a doctor's instruction (Culprit #9, The Primary Care Crisis).

The reason for this is that patients are most often frustrated by navigating aspects of healthcare that either do not have a PCP at the helm coordinating the healthcare system for the patient, or in which the patient is lost in the administrative quagmire that falls well outside of the purview of the PCP—or, for that matter, any clinician.

The bottom line is that illnesses are not treated or cured through better customer service. Instead, a model that promotes better engagement between clinician and patient is needed. And that starts by giving clinicians, most impor-tantly PCPs, less administrative overhead and more time to be with the patient. A more accessible and attentive physi-cian spending a longer period of time with a patient is much more likely to be perceived as focused on the patient-cus-tomer than a more "customer friendly" physician who spends less time with patients. And this will only become more of an issue as the population ages.

According to Matthew Lee Smith, lead author of a study conducted by the University of Georgia's College of Public Health and the National Council on Aging:[33]

"Approximately half of adults in the United States have a chronic condition, while one in four adults have multiple chronic diseases, and this number is expected to increase in coming years. Frustrations experienced by [these] patients are really symptoms of larger problems within our health care system."

The study found that 70 percent of patients with chronic conditions reported having at least two of six noted frustra-tions: feeling tired of describing the same condition over and over; wishing the doctor had more time to speak with them during visits; leaving the provider feeling confused; feeling alone when it comes to managing their health; feeling their doctor doesn't understand what it's like to manage their condition at home; and wishing they had a friend or family member who could go to the doctor with them.

Perhaps the most telling conclusion of the study is Smith's comment: "There are opportunities to make the system more productive, which can alleviate patients' frustra-tions—we need to improve patient-provider communication, but we also need to shift focus to what we can do outside of health care interactions."

When we look at the combination of the inevitable facts of fewer PCPs, less time for each PCP interaction, more interactions with specialists, and more administrative burden—especially for an older, more medically complex population—the issue of customer experience will only become more of a problem over time. To improve outcomes, providers need to focus on both the clinical experience and the nonclinical interactions that patients have. Otherwise, patients will only seek treatment when it is much too late for preventative measures.

Providers are not oblivious to the importance of a frictionless customer experience, and yet they are ill-equipped to do much about it. A Kaufman Hall study on consumerism showed that although 87 percent of providers are making consumer-centrism a priority, only 11 percent have high capabilities in this regard (Illustration 3.1). Although that may be an undesired but tolerable disparity today, the importance of adopting a new mindset that considers the value of treating patients like customers will be crucial as the demographics of the population shift radically to older patients with far more complex conditions requiring the coordination of more and more healthcare services and specialists. That's the final thing that we need to look at before we begin to delve into solutions for the many challenges we've described—Culprit #10, The Aging of America.

The Demographics of Bankrupting Global Healthcare

If I had to pick one thing that will most stress, change, and challenge the current healthcare system, it is the changing nature of age demographics in the US and across the globe. I'm taking a global look at this since all of the national healthcare systems that are often held out as role models for a nationalized healthcare program will be put at significant

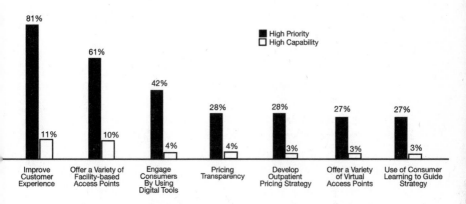

Illustration 3.1 Although 81 percent of providers rank improving the customer experience as a priority, only 11 percent rank their capabilities as high in achieving that goal.

risk as this phenomenon sweeps the planet over the coming decades.

The year 2080 will be remarkable. Not for the advances in medicine, which will no doubt be lightyears ahead of where we are today, but because it will mark the first time in recorded history that every five-year age band, from newborns to sixty-five-year-olds, will account for almost exactly the same percentage of the world's population: 6 percent.[34]

This nearly perfect symmetrical demographic distribution—what I

> ...changing demographics will make virtually every form of national healthcare unsustainable without changes to the underlying healthcare systems...

129

call the skyscraper—is without precedent and will exist in stark contrast to the pyramid-shaped global population distribution that has been pervasive for the majority of recorded human history.

Pyramid structures are so deeply embedded in not only healthcare but all of our social institutions—from education to economics to politics—that it's no surprise we cannot think outside this intuitive demographic metaphor. It's as though, over the past five thousand years, the pyramid has become an instinctive framework for thinking about the way the world works and how we solve many of our socioeconomic challenges. It's hard to imagine how to even begin to break free of this entrenched model of society. Yet the underlying shift in global demographics is on a trajectory leading to a radical change and ultimately the elimination of the demographic pyramid—whether we are prepared for it or not. The implications this has for healthcare, not just in the US but globally, need to be considered as part of any long-term sustainable healthcare strategy. This also has implications for other national healthcare systems, which use universal healthcare as an alternative to the US healthcare model. I suggest that these changing demographics will make virtually every national healthcare system unsustainable without changes to the underlying healthcare systems in place to deal with many of the Ten Culprits.

The End of the Population Pyramid

Over the past sixty years, we have seen the formation of a perfect global population storm that includes a dramatic drop in infant mortality; better access to healthcare, clean water and food; and increasing life expectancy. Although all of these started to take root in developed countries, they are increasingly reflected in nearly every major global geography.

The result is a global population pyramid that, although still growing in terms of overall population, has been growing more slowly at the base and expanding toward the top in relative terms.

Now do a simple thought experiment and picture what that population pyramid would look like over time as we move toward 2050. What do you see?

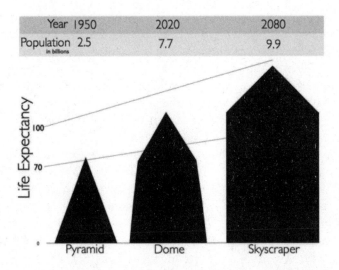

Illustration 3.2 The traditional global population pyramid, which existed until 1950, has changed considerably. In its place has evolved a dome with a much broader midsection and a more subtle tapering as it progresses up through generations. But the dome is only a transitional shape as we head into the defining permanent structure of the future: a world with ten billion fully educated and completely connected human beings. How we navigate that transition will likely define society for the next millennium. (The relative size of each shape—pyramid, dome, and skyscraper—represents relative growth in population.)

On a global scale, the result is astonishingly nonintuitive. During the next sixty years, we will see the global population pyramid reshaping itself into a nearly perfect skyscraper (Illustration 3.2).

If you stop to consider the long-term implications of this phenomenon, it's cause for serious concern in the case of healthcare. For example, how does the well-established notion of social welfare in which healthcare providers rely on the under-sixty-five demographic to fund lower reimbursement by Medicare for the sixty-five-and-over top third of the pyramid? What does it mean for national healthcare systems where all healthcare is funded entirely by government?

The previously unassailable assumption that many social welfare systems, such as healthcare, have made is that a growing middle class will always be able to support an increasing but significantly smaller population of elderly and retired people. The very simple economic consequence of that flaw in our generational system of funding healthcare is entrenched in myriad other social implications of a redistributed global population. By the way, while today many people look to the universal healthcare approach taken by other countries as a role model, it will ultimately begin to exert incredible—I'd claim unsustainable—pressure on those healthcare systems as global demographics shift to an older population.

Medicare, which accounts for the overwhelming majority of healthcare coverage costs for those sixty-five and over, is already projected to become inadequate to cover all of the needs of this aging population in the next ten years.[35] According to a Medicare trustee report, Medicare Part A will run out of sufficient funds to cover all of its projected obligation in eight years (Illustration 3.3).[36] I should point out that while Part A, which covers hospital insurance, is projected to fall about 20–30 percent short of meeting projected obligations, Part B (physician and outpatient services) and Part D (pharmaceuticals) are structured in such a way that they can never fall short of their obligations.

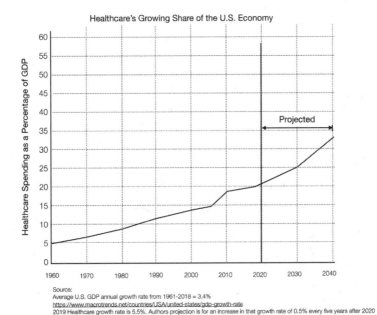

Illustration 3.3 According to a Medicare trustee report, Medicare Part A will run out of sufficient funds to cover all of its projected obligation in eight years.[37]

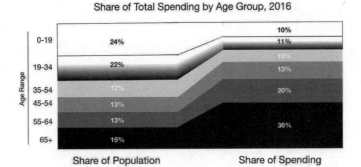

Illustration 3.4 People age fifty-five and over account for only 29 percent of the population but 56 percent of total health spending.

133

There is simply no way around the fact that America is graying. The nation's sixty-five-and-older population is projected to nearly double in size in the coming decades, from 49 million today to 95 million people in 2060. Overall, people age fifty-five and over made up 29 percent of the population but accounted for 56 percent of all health spending in 2016. In contrast, people under age thirty-five made up 46 percent of the population but accounted for less than a quarter of health spending (Illustration 3.4).

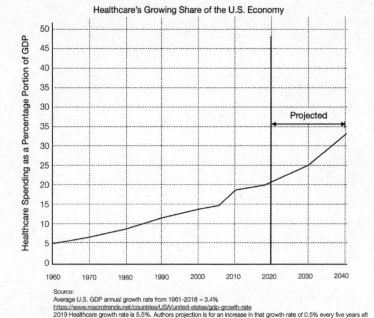

Illustration 3.5 At its current rate of increase, healthcare spending will account for nearly 35 percent of GDP by 2040.

As a result, overall healthcare costs are projected to grow from 20 percent to nearly 35 percent of US GDP by 2040 (Illustration 3.5).

Consider that when Medicare began paying benefits in 1966, there were 5.5 Americans in their primary working years (aged twenty to sixty-four) for every American aged sixty-five or older. By 2016, this ratio had declined to 4.0, or by 28 percent.[38,39] As the baby-boomer generation matures and projected life expectancy increases, the Social Security Administration projects that the ratio of people in their primary working years to Medicare benefit recipients will decline to 2.3 by 2030, or by 49 percent from 1966 to 2030.[40] The bottom line is that there is a systemic flaw in the approach of nearly every healthcare policy that relies on the notion of a population pyramid as its foundation. Policy change will not alter this trajectory; in fact, short of a catastrophic global event that alters demographics, nothing will. What's needed now are foundational changes to the way in which we not only fund healthcare, but more importantly, to how we create a healthcare system that can defuse this demographic time bomb by changing the way in which we manage the most fundamental aspects of healthcare delivery and management.

And that is the next stop in our journey.

NOBODY'S AT FAULT BUT EVERYBODY'S TO BLAME, CHAPTER 3: RECAP AND LESSONS LEARNED

Early US hospitals were shunned by anyone of means and were meant instead to care for the disadvantaged, poor, and mentally disabled in the community.

A turning point for hospitals, and the way in which medicine was practiced, came in 1847 with the formation of the American Medical Association (AMA), which gave physicians a common voice with which to influence the practice and policy of medicine. The AMA has become one of the most influential organizations in the evolution of the healthcare system and the role of healthcare insurance.

The first general-purpose sickness insurance was issued in Massachusetts in 1847 to the 1929 archetype of most modern-day insurance at Baylor University Hospital in Texas, which would later become the prototype for Blue Cross.

In the post-WWII era, the War Labor Board created a set-aside for healthcare benefits that exempted them from wage controls and taxation. The unintended consequences of that single, well-meaning act created the unfortunate trajectory of the system we have in place today by forcing employers to resort to the use of health insurance as a lure for prospective employees.

Since employers were generously offering insurance benefits, most people didn't see the need for national health insurance.

We discussed the genesis of Medicare and Medicaid in 1965, as an amendment to FDR's Social Security Act; President Nixon's HMO Act of 1973; the 1996 Health Insurance Portability and Accountability Act (HIPAA); and finally, the 2010 Affordable Care Act (ACA), also known as Obamacare.

The high cost of denied claims comes in at $262 billion per year and billing and insurance related administrative costs (BIR) amount to 25 percent of total healthcare expenditures—more than the combined total expenditure of Germany, Canada, and Australia for their entire healthcare systems.

The various codes used in medical documentation, such as ICD-10, create an enormous burden, room for error, and a gaming of the claims submission and approval process.

Although use of the term customer or consumer is something that creates controversy among healthcare providers, it will increasingly need to be part of not only the vernacular but also a focal point of process that will require increasingly more complex navigation and coordination by patients.

The changing demographics of healthcare will burden all national healthcare systems, not just US healthcare.

PART TWO:
THE SOLUTION

"Wisdom is given equally to everybody. The point is whether one can exercise it."

—Taiichi Ohno, *from his Ten Precepts*

CHAPTER 4
FOCUSING ON THE CORE: CREATING A DIGITAL HEALTHCARE ECOSYSTEM

Picture a healthcare system. What do you see—a hospital, a doctor's office, medical devices such as CAT scanners or MRI machines? Whatever image first springs to mind, it's unlikely to include the many administrators that make up the backbone of healthcare, obscure processes like the revenue cycle (which is how your bill gets paid), the reams of contractual agreements between providers of healthcare and insurers, the enormous volumes of data used to identify public health risks, electronic health records, or the sophisticated technology infrastructure that goes into deciding how much healthcare costs. And yet these invisible systems make up over two-thirds of every healthcare dollar spent in the US.

> We can rearrange the deck chairs and play "God Save the Queen" to distract the passengers of this ill-fated ship, or we can take on the much harder task of patching the hull.

It's a story that sounds dire. What we've described so far is a system riddled with: inefficiencies, friction, and disjointed processes; costs spiraling out of control; Medicare costs rising faster than GDP and projected to run out of adequate funds within the decade; an aging population with increasingly complex healthcare needs; and the only system in the world where individual healthcare costs are bankrupting individuals and families.

So, how is it possible to write a book that claims there's room for hope in all of this convolution?

The hope can be found in the fact that there is ample precedent for solving similar challenges in many other industries. From manufacturing to banking, and transportation to commercial aviation, we have already built systems that can precisely identify risk, drive administrative friction out of the processes, and focus on outcomes. The bold claim made here is that these approaches are directly applicable to the reengineering of healthcare.

Understanding the problem, which is what we've focused on so far, is half the challenge at best. We know why the healthcare ship is sinking, we've located the gaping holes through which water is pouring into the hull, and we can project the inevitability of the crisis to come if we do nothing. We can rearrange the deck chairs and play "God Save the Queen" to distract the passengers of this ill-fated ship, or we can take on the much harder task of patching the hull. This is our task for the second half of the book: to look at the ways in which we create a sustainable future for healthcare. We'll begin by revisiting the Ten Culprits.

Taking on the Ten Culprits

At the start of this book, I described what I termed the Ten Culprits. We've seen how the Ten Culprits have become embedded into the US healthcare system and the damage they are doing to the cost of healthcare and its outcomes. It's now time to take these on one by one in order to put together a strategy for fixing each of them. We'll identify how approaches such as smartsourcing, the preservation of community hospitals and local healthcare, and the use of healthcare service providers can address the challenges we now know so well.

It's important to keep in mind that what I'm suggesting is not a tumultuous change that requires radical shifts in national healthcare policy or extended political debate. Instead, what's needed is the application of sound business process changes that can be enabled by any provider or payer and can be supported by common-sense approaches that have worked in many other industries.

> ...using the uniqueness of healthcare as a way to insulate it from tried and tested approaches to applying technology and process-improvement methods only serves to confine the creativity with which we can make changes...

Yes, we've already agreed that healthcare is unique in that it is not, and should not, be driven solely by the same dynamics of a free market that dictate how we build and sell most other services and products. Healthcare doesn't follow the unyielding rules that govern the production of airplanes and automobiles, nor is it subject to the callousness of single-minded, profit-driven motives.

However, giving ourselves a pass by using the uniqueness of healthcare as a way to insulate it from tried and tested approaches to applying technology and process-improvement methods only serves to confine the creativity with which we can make changes—changes that set a course for a sustainable healthcare system and a future for healthcare that lives up to our hopes and expectations as individuals and as a society.

In every case where I suggest a way to improve the health-care system, I'll also attempt to describe how these changes increase quality for the primary beneficiary of these changes: the patient. The goal is—simply put in the 2500-year-old ver-nacular of the Hippocratic physician—to not only "first do no harm," but to go beyond this to extricate all of the many parts of the current system that create the potential for harm.

To start, let's begin by reviewing the Ten Culprits I set out at the beginning of the book (The descriptions below are summaries of the full descriptions found in chapter 1):

1. **The Anonymous Patient.** Despite all of the effort to create medical records that are portable and share-able, there is still no single continuous repository of patient data that can be used to adequately provide a reliable context for the treatment of patients and the projection of their outcomes.

2. **The Asymmetry between Costs and Outcomes.** A lack of visibility into the relationship between costs and outcomes of a healthcare procedure, treatment, or therapy prevents doctors from treating patients in a way that effectively balances cost and risk.

3. **The Episodic Care Conundrum.** A disconnected healthcare life cycle creates vast opportunity for errors, redundancy, suboptimal treatments, and diagnostic failures.

4. **The Complexity Crisis.** Our healthcare system has simply become too complex and sophisticated for

144

humans to handle on their own without the use of much more sophisticated technologies such as data analytics, artificial intelligence, and machine learning, which can quickly interpret the uniqueness of each patient's situation and handle the enormity of administrative work required for each patient.

5. **The Missing Link.** There is no single interorganizational entity to coordinate all the pieces of the healthcare system that need to be synchronized among patients, payers, and providers to coordinate care that both minimizes costs and optimizes outcomes.

6. **Drifting from the Core.** Healthcare providers have been forced to take on the responsibility of many administrative aspects of care, such as documentation, coding, and the billing process, which detract them from their core competency of caring for the patient.

7. **The Tragedy of the Commons.** Healthcare is an inherently complex process that has evolved organically over decades without a clear and well-thought-out overarching architecture. The result is often that patients get caught in the middle of a process that seems to have anything but their best interests in mind.

8. **Defensive Medicine.** The practice of physicians ordering unnecessary tests and procedures to protect themselves from the potential of malpractice accusations, although it has no beneficial impact on the patient, results in up to 25 percent of all healthcare costs.

9. **The Primary Care Crisis.** There is a growing short-age of primary care physicians.

10. **The Aging of America**. An aging demographic will multiply the consequences of all of the above culprits dramatically over the next two decades, ultimately making today's healthcare models economically unsustainable.

Focusing on the Core

The first step in fixing healthcare is finding ways to help providers focus on what should be their fundamental core competency, the care of the patient. That's easily said, but it needs to be more than a mantra. We need specific tools with which to alleviate the administrative burden that most often stands in the way of quality healthcare.

At the heart of that solution is the notion of smartsourcing, which I've mentioned throughout part one of the book. In its simplest terms, smartsourcing is a means of shifting toward partnerships that focus an organization on its core competency and core mission, and to then shed everything else that is not core to the organization's mission to a partner. The processes that are "shed" become the responsibility of another organization for which, in turn, these processes are core. The objective is to make sure that every task in a value chain of activities is ultimately performed by an organization for which it is a core competency.

This was the essence of *Smartsourcing*, a book that I wrote in 2006. Since that time, I've spoken with countless organizations across a variety of industries and I've been consistently amazed by the degree to which a simple concept such as core competency was nearly absent from their collective vernacular. In many cases, that was because it was just assumed. But

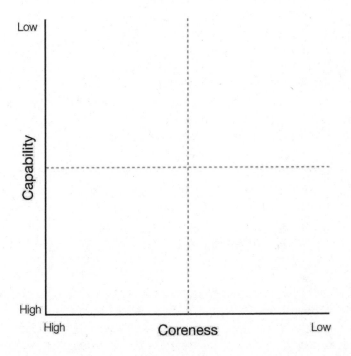

Illustration 4.1 Every organization can look at the spectrum of its activities and processes and identify the degree to which each is core to the organization and the degree to which they have the capability to perform the activity or process. Those activities which end up in the lower left-hand quadrant should be the focus of the organization. As activities drift to the upper right, the organization should consider partnering with another organization for which those activities are core.

core competencies are often much harder to define than any single product or service. They are also necessarily different from one organization to another since they form the competitive bedrock for their respective owners.

We can argue that in the case of healthcare providers, each one could rightfully claim that their core competency is caring for the patient. That's true in part, but it does not mean that there isn't also some aspect of that provider that is unique to their culture, heritage, and history.

One example of how important culture is to defining core competency is the Mayo Clinic. Ranked as one of the top three hospitals in 2019 by *US News & World Report* in fifteen out of seventeen ranked categories,[1] the two-hundred-year history of the Mayo Clinic is steeped in a culture of team-based integrated medicine. If you visit Mayo today, you can't help but be struck by the way their culture seeps into every aspect of the patient experience. Mayo is a microcosm of what the healthcare system should look like.

The Mayo Clinic focuses on the most complex health cases, which require an integrated, highly responsive model of healthcare. Their approach is the complete opposite of the episodic care that is so pervasive in healthcare (Culprit #3). Mayo's core competency is its ability to seamlessly integrate care around the patient experience. Patients who go to Mayo are typically there for four to seven days. During that time, all tests, referrals to specialists, and diagnostics are completed in-house. With 1.3 million people from all fifty US states and 138 countries coming to Mayo for care each year, you can imagine the amount of data involved. Although all of that patient data is now managed digitally, that wasn't always the case.

Long before digital technology allowed electronic records and images to be transmitted instantly, Mayo used a novel and sophisticated underground network of pneumatic tubes. Mayo doctors would transmit patient records from one clinician to another as patients made their way through the various parts of the hospital. I recall marveling at the ingenuity of that solution during a visit to Mayo in the early 1990s. As patients made their way from one specialist to another, their records, complete with notes from each prior doctor, followed them through the process.

Regardless of the technology being used, Mayo's culture has made it the place to go if you need coordinated and integrated care for complex medical situations. Whether it was using pneumatic tubes or digital networks, in a few days, their team of doctors, specialists, and clinicians could do what would otherwise take months within a typical system. In this way, Mayo acts as a microcosm of what the healthcare system should look like. Mayo is a role model for what exceptional patient-centered care should be. Unfortunately, it's a model that rarely follows the patient back home.

Even though today's technology has far surpassed that of pneumatic tubes, it's still exceptionally rare to go from one provider to another—sometimes even within the same healthcare organization—and have all of a patient's medical history available.

This is about more than just the electronic portability of a patient's health records or where the records reside. If a patient has been within the same medical institution throughout their life, it's likely that his or her records are intact and relatively easy to access on short notice. However, that is most often not the case because of two reasons. First, as patients move and change providers, insurers, and employers, their medical history becomes scattered about in isolated data silos. Second, the average hospital has sixteen separate electronic health record (EHR) systems.[2] Without the full context of an individual's health history, any treatment is, or ought to be, suspect. This lack of information results in unnecessary or redundant tests and treatments, misdiagnosed conditions, and, in the worst cases, outright medical errors.

To be clear, running a network of underground pneumatic tubes is hardly what you'd consider a hospital's core competency. However, Mayo is in a somewhat unique situation. Since they focus on patients with complex health conditions who come to Mayo for a finite period of time to see multiple specialists and receive numerous diagnostic tests, handling patient records in a way that creates a seamless, fast, integrated experience is essential to clinical outcomes. In fact, Dr. Henry Plummer, who joined Mayo in 1901, developed the original patient management that was the foundation of Mayo's patient-centered approach to medicine.[3] It's no coincidence that Mayo's most recent EHR, valued at $1.5 billion, is one of the largest EHRs ever deployed.

Time and time again, what I see in organizations that have an ability to focus their resources on innovating their core, as is the case with Mayo, is that they have a deeply embedded culture that weaves the core mission of the organization into nearly every decision, from the tactical to the strategic. Anything that distracts the organization and its employees from that core is immediately identified as nonessential and deprioritized. We'll see this again in chapter 6 as we delve into the case study of John Muir Health.

In healthcare, the notion of core competency is easier to understand when you think of providers such as the Mayo Clinic, MD Anderson, or Dana-Farber. Each has an obvious brand built around their culture, expertise, and core competency. It may be as general as Mayo's approach to integrated care or as specific as MD Anderson's and Dana-Farber's focus on cancer.

This is where the conversation about fixing healthcare takes an interesting and unanticipated turn.

During my research for this book, I spoke with dozens of administrators and clinicians across a broad spectrum of healthcare providers and payers. Initially, my focus was on how a method such as smartsourcing could help large healthcare systems better focus on their core. What I found was unexpected.

Large healthcare systems naturally want to achieve internal economies of scale and have a tendency to outsource very

little outside of a small set of activities that are entirely peripheral to patient care and patient experience (what we later in this chapter call the Dangerous Diversions). These include food service, security personnel, valet parking, and janitorial services.

...healthcare is indeed different than virtually any other free market industry, since the consumer ends up paying more for economies of scale rather than less.

In retrospect, the reason for this may be self-evident: large organizations that serve a network of smaller providers build their own solutions to maintain control over every aspect of their processes. The reasoning is that their scale gives them leverage in terms of buying power, repeatable use of various processes and technology systems, an interest in coordinating all of their resources across the organization and its members, and standardization of policies, procedures, and practices.

Although that all makes sense, even these large institutions are increasingly considering ways to smartsource many of their noncore activities as technology allows the same, if not better, levels of coordination with partners at lower costs and with better outcomes.

However, outside of these peripheral activities, most of these behemoth healthcare providers have not yet reached an economic tipping point adequate to drive smartsourcing. They can still absorb greater inefficiency due to their size and the higher fees that they typically charge to cover a larger investment in facilities. It's also critical to point out that the economies of scale promised through large consolidated providers, especially those with a thousand beds or more, create a perverse economic outcome.

The purpose of an economy of scale is basically twofold: to better leverage resources across a large organization by

increasing the buying power and leverage that a larger organization can exert on suppliers and creators; and to create
shared services that the various business units within the
larger organization can leverage.

On the point of bargaining power, consider Walmart as
an example. Walmart is able to dictate terms to its suppliers and partners through its immense size. This means lower
costs for the consumer. Although we can criticize Walmart's
ability to strongarm suppliers and drive smaller competitors
out of business, its ruthless demands on suppliers and its
ability to put pressure on low costs clearly result in benefits
to the consumer.

It doesn't work that way with healthcare. Although
"diseconomies of scale,"[4] which result from the friction in
coordinating large systems and workforces, are typical in
many larger organizations, something else occurs with very
large healthcare providers. Because of their size and buying
power, they are able to negotiate higher reimbursement
rates (as permitted by state regulations), attract higher-cost
doctors and clinicians, and ultimately drive higher costs for
healthcare. In that respect, healthcare is indeed different than
virtually any other free market industry, since the consumer
ends up paying more for economies of scale rather than less.

In addition, and more disturbing in the case of healthcare,
the quality of outcomes does not necessarily improve with
scale. This makes little sense on the surface. But what we'll see
later in this chapter is that scale makes the patient experience
more tedious, less personal, and far less customer focused.

In addition, since large providers are trying to leverage
shared services inside of their organization, there is far less
interest in considering outside partnerships. The irony here
is that the primary reason these shared services can be justified in house over partnerships is because the fees charged
for healthcare by a much larger provider allow it to absorb
higher costs.

I anticipated that smartsourcing would have a positive impact on these large providers and that their primary objection to it would be the simple one of "not invented here." What I found instead was that these large provider health systems often drive up costs by using the leverage of their size to negotiate higher reimbursements from payers rather than to drive out many of the more intractable costs we've described.[5]

Again, none of this is born of malice. Yes, fraud exists, but the vast majority of what I just described is simply a way to use the existing rules to maximize the provider's contracted reimbursement for its services. It's a simple tenet of commerce that the larger any organization gets, the more likely it is to find ways to bend the market to its economic benefit, regardless of the collateral damage along the way (Culprit #7, The Tragedy of the Commons).

In addition, whether it's Facebook, ExxonMobil, Starbucks, Walmart, or Partners HealthCare, large organizations insulate themselves from the market implications of their actions on the consumer. It simply becomes too difficult, if not impossible, to message values that support using personal judgement to assess each consumer's situation over standardized policies and procedures. And yet, nowhere is that more important than in healthcare, where every interaction involves a patient with personalized needs. This leads us to a central theme that you will hear echoed through the second half of the book: the critical role of the community hospital in creating a sustainable and affordable healthcare system.

It Takes a Community

What I did not expect to find in my research was the critical role that smartsourcing plays as not only a means for local providers to focus on their core competency, but also as an outright mandate for the survival of these community institutions. According to Moody's, "We expect small rural and community hospitals to seek capital partners as competition increases, and revenue and expense challenges intensify."[6]

The reason is utterly straightforward; these smaller institutions cannot reach the economies of scale necessary to negotiate favorable contracts to achieve higher reimbursement rates and therefore compete with large providers.

This was not always the case.

Community hospitals started to take up a significant part of the healthcare landscape during the mid-1900s due to the 1946 Hill-Burton Act, which provided federal funding to build rural and community hospitals. The law gave hospitals, nursing homes, and other health facilities grants and loans for construction and modernization. The quid pro quo was that Hill-Burton-funded institutions agreed to provide care for people unable to pay and to make their services available to all persons residing in the facility's area. Hill-Burton stopped funding in 1997; however, 140 healthcare facilities nationwide are still obligated to provide free or reduced-cost care.[7]

The Hill-Burton Act was intended to provide access to quality healthcare for all Americans, especially those who were economically disadvantaged and located in rural areas. However, with the cessation of funding and cutbacks to Medicare payments when fixed-cost reimbursements were put in place in the early 1980s, community hospitals began to struggle. To try and stem the exodus of these rural providers, government payers shifted to a reasonable-cost basis for reimbursements to community hospitals in 1997. This

> ...over 25 percent of all community and rural hospitals are on the brink of closure.

worked as a stopgap measure until the economy slid into recession during 2008.

Community hospital closures have steadily increased over the past decade. By some estimates, over 25 percent of all community and rural hospitals are on the brink of closure. According to Stroudwater, a leading consulting organization that focuses exclusively on healthcare, there have been 113 rural community hospital closures since 2010 and 155 since 2005.[8] Some estimates put the current number of closures at 30 per year.[9]

Percent of Community Hospitals Belonging to Health Systems 1999-2016

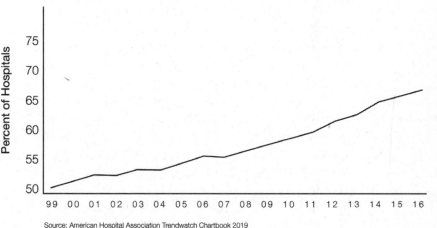

Source: American Hospital Association Trendwatch Chartbook 2019

Illustration 4.2 As pressures to achieve profitability mount, smaller hospitals are increasingly joining larger health systems in order to achieve economies of scale. Unfortunately, these mergers do not result in better healthcare outcomes.

These closures not only take away access to local emergency services, but also take with them an entire ecosystem of local doctors, clinicians, and medical services that relied on the hospital.

> What local providers need is a way to fundamentally change the economics of their business model as well as a means to invest in innovative technologies, facilities, and resources for patient care—in short, a way to refocus on their core.

As we'll see when we look at John Muir Health in chapter 6, the mission of community hospitals and the essential role they serve in keeping costs down and delivering high-quality outcomes is an essential part of a long-term solution to healthcare. While we could make the case that their social importance alone is enough to justify some policy-driven mechanism to keep them in place, we should also be careful to avoid stopgap measures that only hasten their decline. What local providers need is a way to fundamentally change the economics of their business model as well as a means to invest in innovative technologies, facilities, and resources for patient care—in short, a way to refocus on their core.

The other cornerstone (in addition to Hill-Burton) laid to support the community hospital model was the creation of Federally Qualified Health Centers (FQHCs), federally funded community health centers and clinics. FQHCs started as the result of efforts by a young doctor and civil rights activist, H. Jack Geiger, who had studied in South Africa. There, he'd noticed how effective a unique community-based healthcare model was for even the poorest citizens. Upon his return, he proposed the creation of a similar model to the federal Office of Economic Opportunity, part of President Lyndon B. Johnson's War on Poverty.[10]

His efforts resulted in the establishment of two Neighborhood Health Centers in Boston and Mound Bayou in

1965. Today 1,400 FQHCs provide primary care and medical services for more than twenty-eight million Americans,[11] making them the largest unified primary care network in the US.[12] To be clear, FQHCs are federally funded community health centers and clinics. However, their focus on local care and integrated medicine is consistent with the sort of community care model that we will be describing.

Before we go any further, we need to do two things. First, we must define what constitutes a community hospital; second, we'll provide a framework for the major functions where smartsourcing can have the most pronounced impact in a community hospital setting.

Defining Community

You would think that accounting for the total number of hospitals in the US would be a relatively easy task; however, it's not. According to the American Hospital Association, there are about 6,200 hospitals in the US.[13] However, Definitive Healthcare, an analytics and informatics company focusing on US healthcare, reports the number as 7,200.[14] If we break down the size of the 100 largest US hospitals by the number of active beds, approximately 20 hospitals have 1000 beds or more, another 40 have between 800–999 beds, and the remaining 40 have between 700–799.[15] The reason that there is such disparity among experts in defining what constitutes a community hospital is that it has as much to do with how the hospital operates as it does its size.

While the number of 1000 beds is a conventional way to define a community hospital, it's not meant to be the hard line of demarcation. When I speak with providers who consider themselves to be community hospitals, their focus is on the increased personalization of service that results from a better understanding of the patient and the local population's needs. In that regard, the ultimate measure of a community hospital is how it is perceived by the patient.

For example, think about the level of personalized service that you may receive from a smaller retailer who knows you over a large big-box store where you may be treated respectfully but as an anonymous customer.

What is a Community Health System?

Community Hospital*	Behemoth Health System
Under 1000 Beds	1000 Beds or More
Leverages External Economies of Scope	Leverages Internal Economies of Scale
Co-operative System	Consolidated System
Lower Patient Costs	Higher Patient Costs
Focus on Preventative Primary Care	Focus on Intensive Care of Complex Illnesses
Focus on Independence	Focus on Growth
Focus on Patient Understanding	Focus on Patient Throughput

Illustration 4.3 Defining what constitutes a community hospital or healthcare system is not black and white. Ultimately it speaks more to the mission of the hospital(s) and the focus on maintaining an independence which allows for greater flexibility in the personalization of healthcare, a focus on easier patient navigation of the healthcare systems, and the role of primary care in preventative medicine.

According to Cindy Matthews, executive vice president of Community Hospital Corporation, which owns, manages and consults with community hospitals across the country, "We look at [community hospitals] as governed by people who live in the community."[16] In other words, having local community leaders serving on their boards.

Keep in mind that there is wide variability within the many definitions used to identify community hospitals. Number of beds, governance, and leadership makeup are just a few easy ways to define a community hospital. For example, some definitions exclude teaching hospitals that use a standard residency model for incoming doctors.

...community hospitals do exactly what the name implies: serve local communities with an acute awareness of the needs of their population and highly personalized relationships with patients.

Dignity Health, which owns or operates more than forty hospitals and hundreds of care centers in California, Arizona, and Nevada, has a total of 9,000 beds across its system, but less than 400 beds in most of its hospitals, and is perceived by patients as a local community hospital.

For our purposes, a community hospital or hospital system is one that has under a thousand beds, identifies itself (and is identified by the community) as a community hospital, values its independence, believes in cooperative arrangements within its health network, leverages external economies of scope, and focuses on driving down healthcare costs that directly impact the patient.

I realize that cuts a broad swath, but as we'll see, absolute size is less important than the hospital's management, the role of leadership, and the willingness to invest in innovative means of healthcare delivery, accessibility, affordability, and new business models that directly benefit the local community and the patient.

The larger question is, "Why should community hospitals be the focal points of fixing US healthcare?" The short answer is that community hospitals do exactly what the name implies: serve local communities with an acute awareness of the needs of their population and highly personalized relationships with patients.

It would appear that the community hospital model is a role model for the future. Not so fast.

In a 2017 study, the Commonwealth Fund, a hundred-year-old endowment focused on healthcare for the disadvantaged, used thirty-three indicators of quality care across 306 community hospitals and found that only fourteen had advanced on a majority of the indicators. This points to a fundamental flaw in the local community hospital approach to healthcare, but not the one you might assume from taking that research at face value.

The reason community hospitals fare so badly in these sorts of metrics is that they are using their precious resources across far too wide of a spectrum of their operations. As a result, they are unable to keep down costs for the administrative aspects of healthcare. The spillover of administrative friction to the clinical operations (for example, poor implementation of the EHR or information technology) distracts clinicians from delivering the best healthcare, and, as an institution, these small hospitals are unable to focus on the innovation of either their administrative or clinical operations.

Not surprisingly, the reason many of these smaller hospitals are strapped for resources and capital is that they are attempting to keep healthcare as affordable as possible. In fact, the difference in cost and affordability between community hospitals and behemoth hospital systems is striking. For example, according to a 2017 report by the Massachusetts Health Policy Commission, in the Boston area, "Total health care spending per patient varies substantially by provider system, based on the affiliation of a patient's PCP. Annual spending per commercially-insured patient ranged from $5,393 per year (for patients with PCPs in the Boston Medical Center Health System—a community health system) to $7,668 per year (for patients with PCPs in the Partners HealthCare system—a large academic medical center), a 30 percent difference in 2017."[17]

I should take a moment here to point out the obvious inconsistency in how we've talked about economies of scale. Earlier, in the context of large hospitals, we saw the perverse economic effect that healthcare economies of scale have in driving up healthcare costs. Now, in the context of community hospitals, I have been implying that economies of scale are a good thing. The inconsistency is due to the fact that I'm using the same term, "economies of scale," to refer to two separate phenomena. I'll clarify this later in chapter 5, but for now the better term for a community hospital is an "economy of scope." Simply put, an economy of scope is one in which the community hospital relies on smartsourcing partnerships. Through these partnerships, they can create process efficiencies and greater innovation capability across all of their partners that equals and, in many cases, exceeds in-house economies of scale achieved by larger providers.

> ...to eliminate the community [hospital]...would be one of the greatest mistakes that we could make for the US healthcare system. Unfortunately, that's exactly the direction we are headed in without an intervention.

By the way, none of this is meant to imply that the trend toward local clinics, virtual medicine, and increased ambulatory care facilities (which do not provide overnight admittance) is in any way incompatible with community hospitals. These are all essential components of an integrated healthcare system. But to eliminate the community hub—which may be either the community hospital or the local physicians group—that provides for the continuity and integration of care patients need would be one of the greatest mistakes that we could make for the US healthcare system. Unfortunately, that's exactly the direction we are headed in without an intervention.

One more thing before we move on. One of the arguments made for consolidation is that it improves outcomes. The evidence doesn't support that. A study by PricewaterhouseCoopers (PwC), which analyzed data from more than 5,600 individual healthcare facilities and 526 healthcare systems across the US, found that "There is no correlation between quality and cost per encounter. Spending more money does not necessarily lead to better outcomes. Similarly, the data demonstrates no relationship between facility size and quality."[18] (Culprit #2, The Asymmetry between Costs and Outcomes)

According to Martin Gaynor, the Carnegie Mellon University professor I quoted earlier, "research evidence shows that providers in more concentrated markets charge higher prices to private payers, without accompanying gains in efficiency or quality. [This burden] falls on individuals, not insurers or employers."[19]

The National Bureau of Economic Research study on hospital supply chains found that acquisitions have resulted in only a 1.5 percent reduction in costs for the acquired hospitals through greater buying power.[20] Another study determined that in the highly concentrated healthcare markets where there are fewer providers, primary care costs were 23 percent higher than the national average.[21]

What all of this points to is that size does matter, but not in the conventional sense of the phrase. In healthcare, consolidation drives up the ultimate price paid by the insurer, employer, and ultimately the patient without an increase in the quality of outcomes.

The perverse free-market impact that large economies of scale have in driving up reimbursement rates from payers is one of the major problems in healthcare. If community hospitals were to somehow vanish from the healthcare landscape, one of the unforeseen, yet certain, consequences would be a sharp and sudden increase in healthcare costs. In that respect, community hospitals are an essential part of bringing healthcare costs down and are the closest thing we have to a free market lever to use in providing an element of healthy—pardon the pun—competition to the healthcare sector.

Framing the Challenge

If helping these community hospitals is the first key to the long-term sustainability of healthcare, then the second thing we need to identify is where it makes sense to smartsource aspects of these community hospitals. While virtually any aspect of a hospital's operations is a candidate for smartsourcing, we will focus on four areas that represent the lion's share of opportunities.

John Muir Health, which we will take a closer look at later in chapter 6, is a Northern California community hospital that has been consistently ranked as one of the nation's leading hospital systems. The organization recently embarked on a smartsourcing initiative that focuses on the four key areas they believe will be most likely to provide the benefits we've been describing throughout the book. These include the revenue cycle, information technology, analytics, and ambulatory care management. Don't get too hung up on the names of these areas; we will get into greater detail about each one later in chapter 6. For now, let's focus on *how* smartsourcing works and why it makes sense for community hospitals. We'll then come back to describe these four areas and see how smartsourcing can help in each of them.

...the greatest resistance to smartsourcing...isn't very sophisticated; it sounds something like this: "It would be impossible for anyone else outside of our organization to understand our process well enough."

It's important to acknowledge that the tendency for a hospital or hospital system to want to control all its processes is understandable given the economic pressures that most are already dealing with. The irony is that keeping tasks such as the revenue cycle in-house is often the least effective method since it diverts resources and funds that could be better invested in the core mission of the organization.

Additionally, providers don't necessarily have the capital to invest in the technologies and methods needed to optimize administrative functions. For example, advanced AI, machine learning, and natural language processing can significantly streamline much of the back-and-forth involved in managing insurance claims, coding, documentation, and the patient experience. Most importantly, these in-house systems are always at risk of failing under the stress of increased volume and complexity of healthcare. Add to this the struggle of every healthcare provider to better understand trends in their patient populations, and even if providers had the technology in place to do advanced data analytics on patient populations, no single provider (hospital or hospital systems) has a patient data set large enough to provide the depth and breadth needed to adequately fuel advanced pattern matching and predictive algorithms.

However, the greatest resistance to smartsourcing these processes isn't very sophisticated; it sounds something like this: "It would be impossible for anyone else outside of our organization to understand our process well enough." I've found this to be an ongoing theme in virtually every case where a company is evaluating shifting a critical and complex process from in-house control to a partner.

When I first started my career, I was working with a Boston tech startup developing and selling automated software accounting systems. This was in the early 1980s, when accountants still used green ledger paper to record transactions and balance their books. Serendipitously, I had two undergraduate degrees at the time, one in accounting and one in the nascent discipline of computer information systems. The startup I joined had decided to build automated accounting systems. It was a novel concept at a time when every accountant still used hand-held calculators. Writing the software code for these accounting applications was the easy part. Trying to convince accountants who'd built their careers on the premise that nobody but a CPA could possibly understand a general ledger or a chart of accounts was infinitely harder.

That's precisely what I've seen in healthcare when it comes to smartsourcing. Most providers have grown many of their processes organically over time. The bur-

> While the case is often made that a single-payer model... could be the superglue of a national healthcare system, it eliminates the option of choice—something which has never played well to the American psyche.

den of creating in-house systems to support the organization's administrative tasks has become so complex that they give off the illusion that nobody else could possibly understand the way that they fit into and support the core processes of the organization. This is a fatal flaw that only serves to further complicate these same processes, drive up costs, and eventually distract these organizations from focusing on their core mission.

And yet, so many hospitals continue to cling to the past when the option of smartsourcing many of their functions is clearly available. I'm reminded of an episode of the popular series *Downton Abbey* in which Cora, the lady of the house, is trying to convince the cook, Mrs. Patmore, to upgrade from an icebox to a refrigerator because it is more efficient than an icebox. She goes on to explain how food will be kept fresh longer, how the ice will not need to be delivered, and how Mrs. Patmore will be able to better focus on her job as cook. As Mrs. Patmore continues to insist that there could be no possible benefit to a refrigerator, Cora finally asks her, "Mrs. Patmore, is there any aspect of the present day that you can accept without resistance?"

At that, the cook pauses and then thoughtfully replies, "Well, me Lady, I wouldn't mind getting rid of me corset."

As is the case with Mrs. Patmore, the humor in how doggedly we cling to the past is obvious to everyone but those who refuse to be pulled out of it and into the future.

> If we could eliminate just half of the administrative burden that the EHR has on the physicians, we would free up 25 percent of the average physician's time.

The Healthcare Ecosystem

This is where I'd like to introduce a somewhat radical notion that is at the heart of how Healthcare 2.0 organizations will need to operate. What if, rather than looking at a hospital, doctor, or even a payer as a provider of a service, we thought of them all as part of a coordinated ecosystem that always conforms to the needs of the patient at the center? This may sound obtuse, but it's grounded in a fundamental shift that we are seeing in nearly every aspect of the economy: the move to the synchronization of large networks of partners in the production and delivery of any service or product. (Later, in chapter 7, we will extend this notion of the hospital as an orchestrator to what I'll term "The Hospital in the Cloud.")

The majority of diagrams depicting the healthcare ecosystem show the patient either as the hub of the ecosystem or as a peripheral participant. (Illustration 4.4) Depicting the patient at the center is visually appealing but it ignores the inability of the patient to advocate for his or her healthcare needs when their health is compromised, and it assumes the patient has adequate skills to coordinate their care and understand all of the risks involved. On the other hand, putting any single provider or commercial payer at the center assumes that they are incentivized to balance the objectives of the patient along with every other participant of the healthcare ecosystem. Notice I left out government payers. While the case is often made that a single-payer model, with CMS or some other government agency dictating terms, could be the superglue of a national healthcare system, it eliminates the option of choice—something which has never played well to the American psyche.

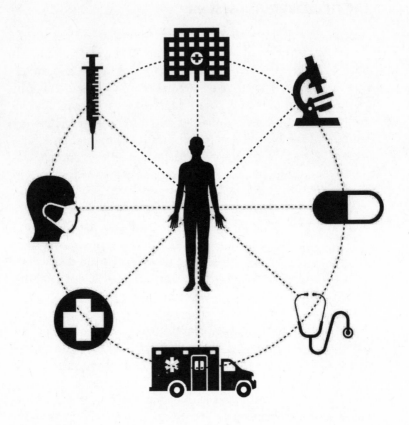

Illustration 4.4 Depictions of healthcare which show the patient at the center ignore the inability of the patient to advocate for his or her healthcare needs when their health is compromised, and it assumes the patient has adequate skills to coordinate their care and understand all of the risks involved.

The only way to correctly depict an effective healthcare model is to place the primary care provider as an intermediary between the patient and every other aspect of the healthcare system. The reason this can't be accomplished today is primarily due to the lack of PCP bandwidth. If we could eliminate just half of the administrative burden that the EHR has on physicians, we would free up 25 percent of the average physician's time.[i] And that's without offloading nonclinical aspects such as coding, the use of predictive care based on population health trends, and personalized medicine within the context of a patient's health history rather than episodic care.

To understand how we could both preserve choice and create a coordinated healthcare system with the patient not only at the center, but also fully informed, we need to go back to what I pointed out at the beginning of this chapter: that each activity required in the production and delivery of any service is ultimately best performed by an organization that has a deep core competency in that particular service.

For example, in automobile manufacturing, it has long been the case that there are tens of thousands of separate organizations involved in the manufacture and delivery of parts that make up an automobile. These networks of providers are referred to as supply chains. The brand owner of the automobile—Ford, GM, Daimler, Tesla—is ultimately just the orchestrator of these vast networks. Its role is to understand the customer's needs well enough to synchronize all of the parts into an automobile whose design and function will meet the needs of the market.

You may be thinking, "But coordinating care has always been the role of the primary care physician or the hospital." Yes, it has, but the ability to coordinate these resources has been hampered by an inability to work with a fully transparent system that allows the coordinator to actually have visibility into the costs associated with care. It's also crippled by Culprit #9, The Primary Care Crisis. There are simply

---

i   Author's estimate. This is conservatively based on the study cited in chapter 1, which found that a physician spends two hours of desk and EHR time for every hour of patient face-time.

> Unlike the trite saying that's often used to describe traditional outsourcing, "your mess for less," smartsourcing is about significantly ramping up the capacity to innovate and add value rather than simply cutting costs.

not enough PCPs, nor will there ever be, to take on the entirety of this burden. And a large part of coordinating care is helping the patient understand the economics of their choices before they have to make a decision about that care.[ii]

Going back to our car analogy, imagine walking into a dealership to buy a new Ford and having the dealer tell you that you won't know the cost of the vehicle until you've purchased it. And even then, only after you've put on a few thousand miles. The absurdity of that scenario is not lost on anyone. And yet, that's exactly what we do with our healthcare.

The challenge with almost all of these noncore in-house processes is that provider organizations are unable to invest in the level of technology, innovation, and staff needed to significantly improve the efficiency of these processes. So, instead, they plod along trying to do the best they can with incremental improvements. For a while that may continue to work, but as we've already said, the demands on healthcare will require that both providers and payers dedicate every dollar to their core operations. Unlike the trite saying that's often used to describe traditional outsourcing, "your mess for less," smartsourcing is about significantly ramping up the capacity to innovate and add value rather than simply cutting costs.

---

ii   This is of course referring to decisions that the patient is able to make in a nonemergency situations.

As an example of the difference, think of the other peripheral operations in a hospital, such as the cafeteria, janitorial services, and washing scrubs. It used to be that all of these functions were handled in-house under the assumption that it would be easier, cheaper, and more controllable than employing a third party do the same. The actual result was that each of these services was suboptimal. That's no longer the case. Partnering with a third party such as Aramark or Sodexo, which is constantly innovating food-service delivery, both helps to create a better overall experience for patients, staff, and visitors, and allows the hospital to avoid being distracted by something so far from its core. It's important, however, to point out that these partnerships are outsourcing relationships, not smartsourcing. The distinction is that in an outsourcing relationship, the partner not only takes over responsibility for the process, but also brings in all of their own personnel. The outsourcing partner relies on the standardization of its processes in order to create easily scalable capabilities and consistent outcomes.

The hospital cafeteria is a simple example of outsourcing, but it can just as easily be applied to many other straightforward processes. The challenge is trying to use the outsourcing model for more sophisticated processes, such as IT or ambulatory care management, where the tolerances and the demands of healthcare require a partnership model focused on innovation and core competency.

However, there's already a way to significantly improve outcomes without putting the additional burden of more administrative overhead on either the provider or the insurer.

This is where we need to stretch our creativity to rethink how Healthcare 2.0 *must* transform itself to take on the many challenges it faces and the many more which it will face.

FOCUSING ON THE CORE: CREATING A DIGITAL HEALTHCARE ECOSYSTEM, CHAPTER 4: RECAP AND LESSONS LEARNED

Community hospital-based health systems play a critical role in the delivery of healthcare. They are an essential part of bringing healthcare costs down and the closest thing we have to a free market lever to use in providing an element of healthy competition to the healthcare sector. However, they are struggling to survive.

The 1946 Hill-Burton Act was put in place to provide federal funding to build rural and community hospitals.

Still, over 25 percent of all community and rural hospitals are on the brink of closure, which not only takes away access to local emergency services but also takes an entire ecosystem of local doctors, clinicians, and medical services that relied on that hospital.

The reason community hospitals fare badly in many surveys that measure quality is not due to an inherent flaw in community healthcare, but rather because community hospitals are using their precious resources across far too wide of a spectrum of their operations. As a result, they are unable to keep down costs for the administrative aspects of healthcare. The spillover of administrative friction to the clinical operations distracts clinicians from delivering the best healthcare, and as an institution, they are unable to focus on innovation of either their administrative or clinical operations.

They can't compete against the larger systems since they don't have access to capital for innovation, nor the scale to negotiate higher reimbursement with payers.

Smartsourcing is a key strategy for the survival of community hospitals by helping them focus on and reinvest in their core.

CHAPTER 5
SMARTSOURCING

Smartsourcing is founded on a fundamental premise, that the cost and friction of maintaining a large vertically integrated infrastructure of noncore activities is greater, and less effective, than the cost of coordinating an external value chain with the same activities among partners who are core in these same areas.

This is key to understanding the shift that is occurring among community hospitals and hospital systems, physicians groups, and which will ultimately impact all healthcare providers.

Smartsourcing provides a lens you can use to look at the entire spectrum of an organization's capabilities and processes in order to determine how to best achieve the highest level of performance, cost, and innovation in each.

For community hospitals or hospital systems and physicians groups, that expect to survive into the next decade and beyond, there are only two viable options. One is to be acquired and become part of a behemoth healthcare provider system in which they have access to shared services and higher reimbursement rates that will provide economic headroom. As we've already seen, this does little to reduce costs in any significant way beyond just a few percentage points. The second is to smartsource everything that's not core and become a coordinator of your own ecosystem of core competency providers.

On the surface, that second option sounds like outsourcing. But outsourcing typically deals with shedding the extreme noncore activities. Even if a healthcare provider can define the extreme areas that constitute its high-performance core competencies—which it will keep—and its lowest-performing noncore activities—which it will shed—there remains a large collection of activities between those extremes. These activities are difficult if not impossible to outsource since they are tightly woven into many other aspects of the provider's business. For example, the revenue cycle, which we talk about later in this chapter, is a distinct activity but it has implications on everything from the patient experience, to the way in which services are determined and coded, to physician burnout.

We should also be clear that while smartsourcing is critical to the survival of community hospitals and physicians groups, it will undoubtedly trickle up to larger healthcare provider systems as the efficiencies it delivers start to be more widely publicized and recognized. That's because the shift to external economies of scope is accelerating across virtually every industry as technology delivers increasing capability to align partners into highly coordinated ecosystems. We'll look at this much closer later in this chapter.

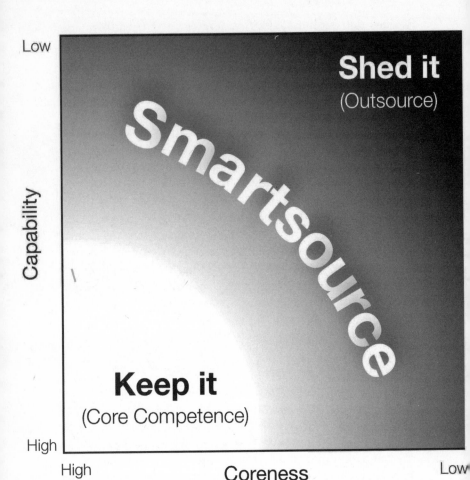

Illustration 5.1 While an organization may be able to define its core competencies—which it will keep in-house—and its extreme outliers—which it will outsource—the area between these two extremes is often difficult to outsource since it is still intimately linked to supporting the organization's core. This is where smartsourcing plays a critical role.

Smartsourcing provides a lens you can use to look at the entire spectrum of an organization's capabilities and processes in order to determine how to best achieve the highest level of performance, cost, and innovation in each.

But defining what smartsourcing is may be easier to do by first defining what it is not.

- **Smartsourcing is not about economies of scale; it is about economies of scope.** In healthcare, the economies of scale that come from in-house vertical integration by large providers create undue influence that drives up reimbursement costs from insurers, ultimately finding their way to higher out-of-pocket patient costs. An economy of scope relies on the coordination of external partnerships in what we will term a digital ecosystem.

- **Smartsourcing is not just about data and technology; it is about competency.** While much of what will drive innovation in healthcare is the use of data to better understand public health trends and the personal care of individual patients, providers need to identify and focus on their core to best leverage this data and technology in order to deliver patient-centered quality outcomes.

- **Smartsourcing is not about ownership; it is about partnership.** Moving away from organically grown in-house activities that are peripheral to patient care requires shedding the ownership model and adopting a trusted partner model for noncore activities.

- **Smartsourcing is not just about cost cutting; it is about innovation.** By focusing on and reinvesting in their core, providers can develop new innovative models for patient care.

- **Smartsourcing is not about cheap labor; it is about smart, educated, and motivated workers.** In-house administration of noncore activities rarely provides a career path or a means by which talented employees working on those processes can significantly enhance their position or knowledge. Smartsourcing provides this talent retention and growth opportunity by shifting employees in these areas to the core competency of the partner's organization.

- **Most importantly, smartsourcing is not a theory.** While it may be new to healthcare, it has been practiced by many organizations in reaction to the pressure to lower costs and increase innovation without sacrificing process excellence, innovation, or agility; these organizations recognize the opportunity smartsourcing offers to close the performance gap.

The objective of smartsourcing is to make sure that innovation is promoted across the entire value chain of clinical and nonclinical healthcare activities. For all of the reasons we've already discussed, accelerating complexity and increasing financial pressures will require providers to keep pace with a velocity of change that is simply unsustainable otherwise. We can't continue on the current trajectory and expect healthcare to somehow right itself. The only sustainable option is for providers to focus their bandwidth on their core areas and then partner with other organizations who can similarly focus on their respective cores.

Take, for example, the case of large employers that self-insure their employees rather than rely on third-party insurers. Even these organizations will use a third party to administer claims. This combination of accepting risk in one area (self-insurance) but shedding it in another closely related area (administration of the insurance) is an ideal example of smartsourcing where external economies of scope are optimized to better serve the consumer.

How Is Smartsourcing Different from Outsourcing?

The greatest risk in traditional outsourcing is focusing exclusively on costs and ignoring the importance of a concurrent innovation initiative. While outsourcing will often deliver reduced costs initially, the focus of outsourcing is too often on replicating the status quo, along with all of its inherent process flaws. Improving process excellence and promoting innovation are not prime objectives of the outsourcing process. As a result, in my experience, the short-term financial win looks good on paper when justifying the outsourcing arrangement, but rarely lasts more than a few years, since little has changed to provide long-term advantage or innovation.

It's worth pointing out that in some cases, this may be adequate, since outsourcing at least takes away the burden of managing additional resources. The cafeteria will have a greater selection of foods and the plants will no longer need watering without having to worry about maintaining the people and facilities involved in both. But these are outlier activities that have little or no impact on clinical outcomes.

Smartsourcing, on the other hand, is accompanied by a renewed attention on excellence and innovation among the organization's core process initiatives as well as other noncore but critical areas that do have direct impact on clinical outcomes. This sort of partnership not only achieves cost savings for the healthcare provider, but it also establishes preeminence and differentiation in the overall patient experience.

Outsourcing	Smartsourcing
CUT COSTS Focuses on cutting costs	CUT COSTS +INCREASE INNOVATION Combines cost cutting with increased innovation
STREAMLINE OPERATIONS Focuses on operational areas	STREAMLINE THE VALUE CHAIN Considers the entire value chain
PARTNER ON WHAT YOU KNOW Works well with defined processes	DIFFERENTIATE Innovates processes to increase differentiation
DISCONTINUOUS Changes in technologies and architecture are disruptive to the business process	CONTINUOUS Thought leadership combined with constant innovation buffer the business process from technology change
ARMS-LENGTH PARTNERSHIP Creates yet another enterprise silo	TRUST-BASED PARTNERSHIP Engenders trust and collaboration leading to greater value

Table 5.1

Many organizations that pursue an outsourcing relationship operate under the premise that there is a core group of distinct processes which can be fully separated from the rest of the organization. These are the prime candidates for outsourcing. The thinking is that since these processes are not directly connected to the organization's core activities, they can easily be handed off to a partner. This is classic outsourcing, or what's often referred to as "lift and shift." Although this can result in initial cost savings, I've rarely seen it work beyond a few years unless the areas being outsourced are indeed distinct from the rest of the organization (what we'll call the Dangerous Diversions later in this chapter).

> Providers that smartsource...shift from internal economies of scale to external economies of scope.

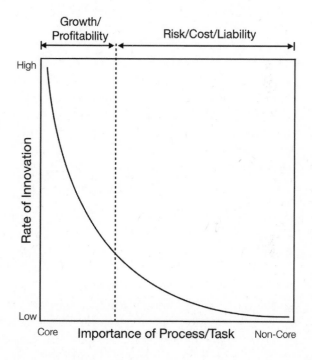

Illustration 5.2 Innovation in any organization will always be highest in those areas that represent the organization's core competency. These are also the areas that are most likely to deliver the greatest value to the organization and its customers. On the other hand, noncore activities create costs and liabilities that encumber the organization and are rarely where the organization has the ability or skills to innovate.

A smartsourcing strategy creates a much more intimate relationship between the organization and its partner than these sorts of arms-length outsourcing relationships. Smartsourcing increases innovation throughout the range of processes, from core to noncore, allowing organizations to focus on their most critical areas of differentiation and customer value, while also achieving high levels of innovation in noncore operations. This means increasing the differentiation, competency, and value across the spectrum of activities involved in delivering patient care. This is the precise opposite of the commodity label that is often placed on outsourcing services.

Providers that smartsource also shift from internal economies of scale to external economies of scope. An economy of scope, which we discuss in more detail later in this chapter, is one in which the benefits of a free market are best leveraged by the coordination of myriad resources, most of which are not owned by the organization but orchestrated by it, since they are owned by other core competency providers. But this requires an entirely new level of partnership transparency and trust.

This level of collaboration blurs the lines between provider and partner. In many ways, the smartsourcing partner becomes part of the organization. Think of this in the same way that you might think of the hiring process for new talent. When you hire someone, you are not thinking of them as an outsider or a contractor who is simply lending his or her talent to your organization, but rather as an insider who will become privy to many areas of sensitive data and processes that would be hidden from the view of anyone outside of the organization.

One of the best frameworks to use in understanding the sort of intimate relationship between a provider and its partners that's required to smartsource is that of the move from an ownership/product model to that of a strategy/service model, shown in Illustration 5.3.

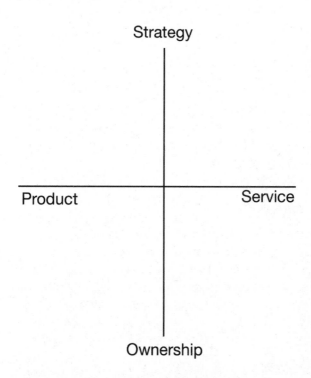

Illustration 5.3 Over the last century, industries have shifted from a vertical integration, in which they own all of the factors of production and provide standardize products, to a model in which vast ecosystems of partners are aligned by strategy to deliver highly customized services and experiences.

The lower left-hand quadrant of the model in Illustration 5.3 is where we'd place the highly vertically integrated industrial age model in which a single organization owned all of the factors of production and the resources to deliver a product. This is the prototypical model of Henry Ford's factory village, in which Ford owned everything from the rubber trees used to produce tires to the dealerships that sold automobiles. It's also the model that many larger providers have adopted in order to achieve control over large internal economies of scale.

The upper right-hand quadrant of the framework reflects the shift to highly coordinated models where everything becomes a service that is customized to the needs of the individual. The organizations formed in this upper-right quadrant are held together by aligned strategic objectives, much like an athletic all-star team where each player is world-class at his or her respective position but employed by a distinct organization.

The Value Chain

Smartsourcing didn't just appear on the scene recently. Although it's enabled by many recent advances in technology, its roots go back to organizational thinking that has shaped much of the movement toward partnerships in other industries as varied as manufacturing and retail.

In 1985, Harvard Business School Professor Michael Porter introduced the conceptual framework of the value chain. The value chain elegantly simplified and described all of the internal and external activities that are part of producing and delivering a product or service to the market.

Porter's premise was simple: by maximizing the efficiency of a value chain, costs go down and differentiation goes up, and from this movement, competitive advantage is created. Porter's work was rooted in the study of transaction cost economics, which looks at organizations as a series of activities, and sought to assess the relative costs of performing and coordinating these activities.

Porter's work followed that of earlier economists, such as R. H. Coase and later, Oliver Williamson, who focused heavily on the costs of performing activities internally versus partnering or outsourcing them. In their time, information technology was in its infancy, and as a result, the transaction costs involved in the coordination of a value chain's externalities were much higher than they are today. Coase and Williamson's conclusion was, in almost every case, to perform these tasks in-house. That was how economies of scale were realized. Although the value chain might have been interpreted by some as a manifesto to increase work mobility and allow greater partnership among businesses—along the lines of smartsourcing—it instead only increased the paranoia of most organizations that were already starting to lose control over their processes and what made their product or service unique. In many ways, that is precisely the path taken by large providers and provider systems that are acquiring local community hospitals and then providing them with in-house shared services that they own.

While Porter, who today is a staunch proponent of value-based healthcare, may not have intended for this outcome in healthcare, the appeal of economies of scale lead to the thinking behind vertical integration, where competitive advantage comes from total control

> Smartsourcing increases innovation throughout the range of processes, from core to noncore, allowing organizations to focus on their most critical areas of differentiation and customer value.

over every aspect of the value chain. Again, think of Henry Ford with his vision of the factory village, where iron ore would enter one end and a complete automobile would come out the other. It is this model of vertical integration that has defined the economies of the nineteenth century and the better part of the twentieth century—where everything fit on one balance sheet, from the sheep that produced the wool to fill car seats, to the steel foundries that created raw metal, to the stamping machines that formed it into car parts.

Other examples from the early twentieth century abound. For instance, the oil industry was built on a model where everything from exploration to retail delivery of oil products was controlled by large integrated suppliers, from J. D. Rockefeller's Standard Oil Company to present-day behemoths such as Chevron, Shell, and ExxonMobil. Even industries such as information technology have, at least early on, relied heavily on a model of vertical integration.

Think of the twentieth-century marvel of computing, the IBM mainframe, where every aspect of design and production was controlled and owned by IBM, from the internal components to the software that ran on it. Early competitors such as Honeywell, Unisys, and General Dynamics promoted the same Byzantine models, governed by the notion that "not invented here" was an anathema.

However, something started to change radically in this equation toward the end of the twentieth century. Advances in communication, network bandwidth, technology, the internet, and the economics of frictionless partnering started to make the cost of maintaining vertically integrated infrastructure greater than the cost of coordinating external value chains.

> Today, in virtually every industry other than healthcare, partnering across the value chain has become the norm.

One of the best examples that nearly everyone is now familiar with is that of ride-sharing services such as Lyft or Uber. These businesses exist entirely in the upper right-hand quadrant of Illustration 5.3 since all they do is align and coordinate resources, none of which they own. This is a market that is frictionless, purely digital, and entirely customer centered.

> As transaction costs move toward zero, the traditional notion of the corporation becomes far less relevant and the trident of success becomes that of partnership, core competency, and skillful sourcing.

Today, in virtually every industry other than healthcare, smartsourcing and partnering across the value chain has become the norm. Advances in information technology have drastically reduced the transaction costs that result from partnering, making integration a much more financially appealing proposition. Do not lose sight of just how important this point is. As transaction costs move toward zero, the traditional notion of the corporation becomes far less relevant and the trident of success becomes that of partnership, core competency, and skillful sourcing.

To look at this another way, Illustration 5.4 shows that today, the costs that an organization can control represent a minority of its total cost to build and deliver any product or service. Consider, for example, that in the automobile industry, nearly 75 percent of the cost in manufacturing and selling an automobile is cost that resides in the supply-and-demand chain of the organization. What is most striking about this analysis, however, is that even in industries where the costs may be under greater control of the product or service provider, an even smaller fraction of the costs for producing the product or service are attributable to the core competencies of the provider.

In healthcare, less than 80 percent of the cost to care for a patient is the cost of the healthcare,[iii] while the rest is attributable to managing the services required to administer and pay for the healthcare in the form of insurance, administration, facilities, and myriad other services that are essential but not core to a healthcare provider.

The result, as shown in Illustration 5.4, is that over time, we see a narrowing band within which providers will be able to control their own costs for their own core competencies. Although these core competencies may ultimately be the only area where an organization can fully control the level of cost and service, this is not a prognosis for higher costs, since the activities that the provider is shifting to a smartsourcing relationship are now being performed by a much more efficient organization for which these activities are core.

To be clear, however, the focus is not and should not be on cost reduction alone. Instead, as the provider shifts noncore activities to a smartsourcing partner, they can invest those savings in new innovations to their core—for example, the expansion into greater ambulatory care services, which we discuss in chapter 7.

---

iii   Earlier in chapter 3, we pointed out that the percentage of health-care costs attributed to administration (BIR) was 25 percent. The 80 percent quoted here is meant to be a conservative estimate. Various studies (see endnotes for this paragraph) attribute from 15 percent to 30 percent of healthcare spending to administrative costs.

The Shift from Non-core Activities Enables Providers to Reinvest in their Core

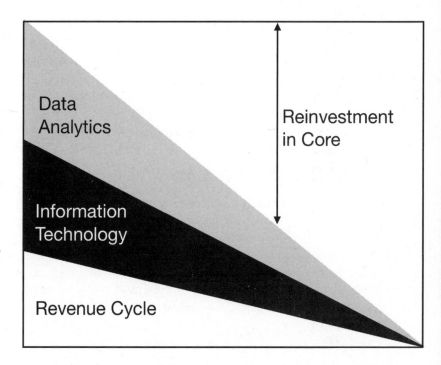

Illustration 5.4 As the focus of providers narrows on their core competency of patient care and sheds noncore activities, such as the revenue cycle, IT, and analytics, a greater percentage of providers' time and resources can be dedicated to new areas that enhance and innovate the core competencies of patient care and population health.

The point to be stressed is that in the absence of a smart-sourcing approach, costs will continue to rise, quality will suffer, innovation will be stifled, and patient satisfaction will continue to drop. In many ways, this is a foundational problem that we are already experiencing in the frustration associated with the healthcare industry.

Without the development of greater skills in how providers manage their relationships with partners, make the determinations as to what they should keep in house, and navigate efficiently through the sourcing maze, they will be unable to reduce their cost base in a way that permits them to stay in business, much less remain competitive.

Economies of Scale and Scope

Recall that the first thing said as I opened this chapter was that managing large, vertically integrated activities was becoming more expensive than coordinating an external value chain. This is what I call the shift from an industrial-era economy of scale to an economy of scope. Building economies of scale is one of the areas where healthcare not only lags behind most other industries, but also one which is at the heart of why healthcare has increasingly become more expensive.

During the first half of the last century, the notion of "economy of scale" dominated thinking on competitive advantage. The degree of competitiveness was measured in terms of how vertically integrated an organization could be and the degree of top-down control it could exert over individual value-creating activities. In simple terms, an economy of scale is the ability to derive greater value from one large entity than from a collection of smaller ones. This notion drove the design of value chains, and, in many cases, organizations themselves.

Nowhere is this more apparent than in the automobile industry, where organizations such as GM became the twentieth-century benchmark for what a vertical organization should be—or certainly what it should have been. It would have been inconceivable for anyone who grew up with the GM standard to imagine how an internal economy of scale could ever have made way for external economies of scope that would be more efficient.

This continues to be a difficult leap for us to make today. But while most businesspeople still acknowledge the value of vertical integration in many industries, they also appreciate the value of horizontal integration across the value chain in ways that would have seemed absurd at the apex of the automobile industry in the mid-1900s.

What happened in the automobile industry to finally bring it to terms with vertical disintegration was half a world removed from Detroit. It's also one of the best illustrations of a concept that is central to many smartsourcing strategies, that of the shared service.

Zaibatsu

The genesis of this change began in the pre-WWII era with the Japanese zaibatsu. Zaibatsu were large family-owned conglomerates that held enormous wealth and power over the Japanese market. For all intents, they were sanctioned monopolies. In the aftermath of WWII, the zaibatsu were disbanded in an effort to foster democratization and free trade within Japan. However, with increasing pressure on the United States to rebuild Japan and simultaneously fight the Korean War and the Cold War, restrictions on Japan's ability to impose anti-free-market policy relaxed and the zaibatsu morphed into what is today commonly referred to as a keiretsu.

Although the term keiretsu has become a popular euphuism for a partnership across horizontal structures, inside and outside of an organization, the original keiretsu was hardly exemplary of the way we use the term today.

Keiretsu were a way to create analogues to the zaibatsu that incorporated horizontal integration within large conglomerates with a central holding company. They epitomized the concept of shared services while also maintaining high levels of independence in their operations. By owning stock in each other's companies and by defining certain core services that would be provided through a central holding company, and in some cases through each other, they developed a very sophisticated manner of partnership that included both inter-reliance and interoperability.

But the model was far from a free-market poster child. A total of six conglomerates controlled large parts of the Japanese economy, what have popularly come to be known as the commanding heights of an economy, and were spurred by national policy against imports to Japan that might undermine their markets. Over time, these keiretsu took on one of the world's most successful and powerful industries, the US automobile manufacturers. And Japan's government, by using its own national buyers to subsidize low-cost imports to the United States, made it a priority to establish itself as the low-cost provider in the market.

With a foothold in the US market, the keiretsu began to accelerate its ability to respond to US market requirements well beyond what Detroit was

> ...increasing complexity will force providers to allocate all of their scare resources to their core competency of patient care, and to find trusted partners who will help them manage everything else.

able to achieve. Ultimately, however, it was not the low-cost appeal of the Japanese manufacturers, but rather the nimbleness of their keiretsu that won the market. By using this nimbleness, Japanese manufacturers were able to compress their time to market within whatever category they chose to compete.

While we could attribute some of their initial success to poor trade policy on the part of the United States and even poorer enforcement of the Potsdam principles that were at the heart of the postwar democratization of Japan, Japan's success was a bellwether for the sort of organizational structure that would be needed to compete in the twenty-first century. The reality is that the idea of keiretsu partnerships, intimate alliances, shared services, a focus on core competency, and horizontal integration have had a profound impact on our thinking about partnership and what ultimately defines an organization.

In the context of healthcare, instead of thinking in terms of keiretsu as large conglomerates, I suggest that you consider for a moment the notion of any size business not as a vertically integrated organization, but instead as an infinitely malleable and instantly responsive constellation of independently operating small businesses, each of which is exceptional at what they do. Although there may be a central or highly visible source of overall strategy, each of these businesses focuses on its own area of core competency, spends all its resources producing value in this same area in the most expedient manner possible, and expends very little effort in dealing with the politics and Byzantine organizational structure of a large organization. Now imagine the ability to address each opportunity by assembling the right combination of these small businesses and instantly being able to communicate, coordinate, and respond to the market appropriately. This is the vision of a smartsourced enterprise.

As we'll see when we look closer at the smartsourcing approach taken by providers such as John Muir Health, increasing complexity will force providers to allocate all of their scarce resources to their core competency of patient care and to find trusted partners who will help them manage everything else.

However, one of the best examples of how partnerships can help an industry manage increasing complexity and demand while both maintaining the benefits of a free market and aligning among the many independent organizations that make up the industry is one that we are all exposed to many times each day.

We've Been Here Before

The disjointed nature of healthcare is one of the primary causes of friction, high costs, patient frustration, and the resulting suboptimal quality of care. Yet, whenever conversation turns to creating a more integrated healthcare system, the most common objection raised is that there is simply no way to take the many disconnected and self-serving participants within the system and coordinate their efforts. However, although it is undeniably no small challenge, there is precedent for this type of integration in other industries. One of the more interesting examples that has had an impact on all our lives is that of banking and credit cards.

During the early- and mid-1950s, a variety of companies had developed a new method of payment then known as a charge card. Cards such as Diner's Club, the world's first independent credit card, and those for large corporations like Sears or Mobil, could be used by consumers to pay for purchases at specific retailers. However, the development of an all-purpose card that could be used across a large network of banks and merchants had proved to be incredibly complex due to the highly competitive nature of both retail and banking.

Bank of America stepped onto this stage by making the bold—some would say foolish—move of mailing sixty thousand BankAmericards to consumers. These were not the sorts of applications that you might receive in the mail today inviting you to open a credit card account, but rather actual operating cards that could be used immediately by the recipient.

The program was wildly successful at first, with over two million cards distributed in California alone. But it wasn't without its challenges, including high default rates of 22 percent, rampant fraud, and the inability of banks to expand into other states due to regulations at the time.

> Hock created an organization that...established a near-frictionless experience for both the customer and the bank, while still preserving the free-market element of competition, innovation, and choice.

From 1960 through 1966, only ten new brands of credit cards were introduced. Yet—in what can best be described as a credit card issuing orgy—from 1966 until 1968, over 440 credit cards were introduced in the US. The chaos that ensued created an enormous amount of friction and confusion for the industry. (While the 10 Culprits are intended for healthcare, we can clearly see Culprit #7, The Tragedy of the Commons, at play here.)

By 1968, the credit card industry was on the brink of self-destruction. At about the same time, Dee Hock, an enterprising young manager at a local bank, which was licensing the BankAmericard from Bank of America (BoA), happened to be present at a meeting of BoA's bank licensees. The meeting was intended to iron out the various differences between licensees in order to create a sustainable model for BankAmericard. However, the meeting quickly devolved into disarray. In an effort to keep the group together, Hock suggested a committee be formed. The group agreed. Hock was appointed to lead the committee and was tasked with the monumental job of figuring out a way forward.

Hock's approach, which was anathema at the time, has become legend in the annals of organizational theory. He boldly suggested that BankAmericard should not belong under the organizational umbrella of BoA but should instead exist as an independent entity.

That company, initially national BankAmericard, Inc., eventually became Visa International. It was a for-profit corporation in which banks were members with nontransferable rights of participation.

Member banks would still issue the cards and compete fiercely for market share while also sharing in supporting Visa, which would act as a clearing house for the benefit of all. Not only did this reduce the inherent friction in the industry, but it also made room for innovation in how Visa marketed its services and understood its customers. This was something any single bank could not accomplish, no matter its size.

Hock would later come to call what he orchestrated to establish Visa a chaordic organization, referring to the coordination of otherwise chaotic systems. The formation of a trusted intermediary, such as Visa, eliminates much of the friction in an industry by taking responsibility for the infrastructure needed to conduct transaction, acting as a clearing house, and also by resolving issues, such as fraud. The chaordic organization follows the principles of Adam Smith's "invisible hand of commerce" in that while each individual participant in the marketplace has selfish motives (such as profit and market share), they can still collectively create value for the entire marketplace. However, this should not be mistaken for altruism. As we've already said, payers are businesses just as banks are. They need to be profitable. For that matter, so do hospitals. While we can argue that profitability can be assisted through government programs, it is far more beneficial to first identify areas where the free market can best achieve the most efficient industry model before resorting to policies that take away, or outright prohibit, free market economics from playing their role.

Hock created an organization that, while still regulated by government, provided a near-frictionless experience for both the customer and the bank while still preserving the free-market element of competition, innovation, and choice.

The missing puzzle piece that made Visa possible was the introduction of an intermediary that had a core competency which allowed it to take on the administrative aspects of building an infrastructure that could scale to handle increasing industry demands.

Today, Visa processes approximately fifty billion transactions yearly on 3.5 billion issued cards, which account for an astounding $2 trillion in payment volume.

Knowing what we know about the importance of how credit cards support the health of the economy and how they enable frictionless transactions, it's hard, if even possible, to consider how commerce could possibly have grown in the way it has over the past fifty years without innovations such as Visa.

That's precisely the kind of progress that's possible in healthcare if we use the same sort of approach to offloading the administrative burden from providers and payers. These new entities, what we're calling HSPs, offload the administrative tasks that burden a provider and distract them from their core competency of delivering healthcare. HSPs bring a significant level of cost savings. In the case of John Muir

Health, a community-based health system in Northern California, which we profile in chapter 6, these projected savings amount to more than 10 percent of the provider's top-line revenues. At the same time, the HSP is able to create significant innovations in areas such as billing, information technology, data analytics, population health (using data to understand and respond to key trends in local populations), and the management of patient care. Long-term, we even see the HSP as being the final piece of the healthcare puzzle that creates the lifetime continuity of care, which we point to repeatedly as Culprits #1, The Anonymous patient, #3, The Episodic Care Conundrum, and #5, The Missing Link.

No doubt, however, that in the same way the banking industry resisted the formation of a central organization to take on what was once thought of as a highly proprietary process that imbued competitive advantage, providers and payers naturally push back on the idea of a third party HSP taking on the administrative aspects of their organizations. Challenging? Yes! But I never said it would be easy—at least not initially.

Evolution of the Healthcare Services Provider

We first mentioned HSPs in chapter 2, and we've discussed the role of the keiretsu and zaibatsu as entities that could hover over a marketplace to coordinate an ecosystem. The difference is that an HSP does not own or have an ownership interest in the members of the healthcare ecosystem. Instead it works with providers as a smartsourcing partner to take on many of the noncore aspects of the provider's business.

Although HSPs are a relatively new part of the healthcare ecosystem, 80 percent of hospitals surveyed by Blackbox Research indicated that they were vetting or considering a full revenue cycle partnership with an HSP. An amazing 98 percent were considering some sort of partnership that would allow them to better focus on their core.

HSPs also circumvent the risk of having to pick and choose the technology winners for every administrative system, since a large part of the HSP's role is to establish the technology platform. In these cases, the risk is taken off the partner and put onto the HSP.

For example, consider the confused and costly state of affairs in the capture and management of EHRs. The intent behind EHRs was simple and elegant: allow the instant transfer of patient data between healthcare providers. Over the past ten years (since President Obama signed a law accelerating the use of EHRs), the US government has put more than $36 billion into the adoption of EHRs,[1] $19 billion of which was invested through the American Recovery and Reinvestment Act of 2009.[2]

From one standpoint, the effort has worked, putting EHRs into 96 percent of all hospitals. However, there are still seven hundred separate EHR vendors who do not necessarily talk to each other's EHR systems. And, as we said earlier in chapter 4, the average hospital has sixteen separate EHR systems. And physicians groups working with hospitals, often have their own EHRs. Repeated efforts to "fix" the system have only created mounting cost and pressure on all sides of the equation, from patients and providers to insurers and payers. And this is just one example of a single healthcare point solution that still involves enormous hurdles.

A study by *Medical Economics* found that:[3]

- About 73 percent of the largest medical practices would not purchase their current EHR system. The data show that 66 percent of internal medicine specialists would not purchase their current system. About 60 percent of respondents in family medicine would also make another EHR choice.

- Two-thirds of physicians dislike the functionality of their EHR systems.

- Nearly half of physicians believe the cost of these systems is too high.

- As many as 45 percent of respondents say patient care is worse since implementing an EHR. Nearly 23 percent of internists say patient care is significantly worse.

- Almost two-thirds (65 percent) of respondents say their EHR systems result in financial losses for the practice. About 43 percent of internists and other specialists/subspecialists outside of primary care characterized the losses as significant.

- About 69 percent of respondents said that coordination of care with hospitals has not improved.

- Nearly 38 percent of respondents doubt their system will be viable in five years.

- Almost three-quarters (74 percent) of respondents believe their vendors will not be in business over the next five years.

A more recent study conducted by the Mayo Clinic gave EHRs an F grade for usability and found a strong correlation between EHR use and doctor burnout.[4] John Halamka, President of Mayo Clinical Platform where he leads digital health and strategy, who is also on the EHR standards committees for presidents Bush and Obama, put it succinctly:

Every single idea was well-meaning and potentially of societal benefit, but the combined burden of all of them hitting clinicians simultaneously made office practice basically impossible. In America, we have 11 minutes to see a patient, and, you know, you're going to be empathetic, make eye contact, enter about 100 pieces of data, and never commit malpractice. It's not possible![5]

There's another, uglier, side to EHRs that's rarely talked about. If a large hospital system standardizes on an EHR, then any doctor using that EHR will likely need to stay within that EHR in order to track a patient and all of his or her diagnostics and tests. In many cases, this means that a lab test submitted through the EHR will default to a laboratory integrated into the EHR by the hospital system. Effectively, this creates fortresses that separate health systems and isolate patients, rather than bridges with which to seamlessly navigate disparate healthcare providers. Ironically, something intended to address Culprit #1, The Anonymous Patient, has only made sharing data even harder.

An HSP has the potential to bridge this gap by providing a common EHR platform, or translation links between the most common EHR platforms (recall that the average hospital has sixteen EHRs),[6] that creates continuity of care for patients across providers and over their lifetimes.

In the last chapter, we'll look how the continuity of care that can be provided through an HSP may also become one of the most revolutionary forces in the future of patient-centered healthcare as we introduce the concept of the hospital in the cloud.

The other critical aspect of how HSPs deliver value is by investing in the administrative areas of a provider's business in a way no single provider ever could. For example, One HSP, Optum, invests over $3.5 billion annually on technology and innovation that focuses on AI, process automation, data and analytics. It holds over ninety patents across the entire healthcare value chain, and it has 240 million de-identified lives (anonymized patients) along with their clinically adjudicated claims. The value of all of this is an ability to look across the healthcare industry and patients in a way no single provider can.

It may well be (and after years of studying and researching the healthcare industry, it's my firm opinion) that the only way to "fix" healthcare is to take transformational risks through investments that no single provider, insurer, or payer would ever undertake on their own. Bridging that gap is ultimately the critical role of the HSP in addressing Culprit #5, The Missing Link.

But let's not be overly naive; there's a downside to the HSP model, too. The outcome of these efforts always involves a degree of risk, as does any partnership. Some of that risk is actually transferred to the HSP partner as they take on the responsibility for operating and innovating administrative systems. Smartsourcing partnerships also involve a level of transparency and intimate disclosure that can be perceived as being especially precarious if not well thought out. On the other hand, the payback is also considerable. In the case of John Muir Health, the yearly payback is anticipated to be close to $300 million, And that's on direct costs alone without factoring in the benefit of reinvesting those savings back into increased quality, new opportunities for care innovation, improved outcomes, and growth to allow for greater access to its healthcare services.

The HSP model may be the single most significant step forward for the evolution of healthcare. While a radical thought for many who have developed an in-house, vertically integrated view of healthcare, or for behemoth hospital systems that believe they need to own every aspect of the healthcare ecosystem, the idea of smartsourcing may be anathema. As HSPs become the driving force in determining the most cost-effective way to deliver quality healthcare outcomes to patients, these large vertically integrated providers are also the most likely to be pushed into a precarious situation of untenable and unjustifiable cost structures.

In 2008, the management of a St. Louis Medicare Advantage plan published what's come to be known as CPPM, the collaborative payer provider model. CPPM was a VBC blueprint for providers and payers. (In the case of CPPM, the provider refers to the primary care physician or team.) The idea behind CPPM is to align the incentives of payers and providers so the success of each is in part based on the success of the other. For example, in a typical CPPM contract, the payer would set aside 15 percent of revenues for its payer functions. Claims are then paid from the remaining 85 percent. If claims end up being less than 85 percent, the remainder is shared with the provider. The actual amount the provider receives might vary between 60 to 80 percent of the remainder based on pre-established metrics. These sorts of arrangements align performance of payers and providers.

Although these models have been tested successfully in Medicare Advantage plans, they still rely on the use of the same foundational systems that have been in place for both providers and payers. It may be more than a bit optimistic to expect that the otherwise contentious relationship between many payers and providers will support the sort of trust needed to scale CPPM. A better approach may be to have an independent third party, potentially the HSP, acting as an integrator to manage the aligned incentives and to develop claims processes that will concurrently streamline the submission and processing of claims.

The question now becomes, "What services and capabilities are most important to look for in an HSP?"

1. **The integration of process management as part of their sphere of core competencies:** The success of a smartsourcing approach is based on how well the complexity of tasks and activities are orchestrated, since it represents a previously unknown level of process integration. Think of the simplicity and process transparency of an online service such as ADP's payroll outsourcing, and then apply this notion to all the touchpoints across a provider's ecosystem.

2. **Letting providers share information from process to process:** HSPs assume the role of process aggregators, leveraging information across a much broader set of experiences than any provider or collection of providers could access otherwise.

3. **Best-practice management:** The HSP has deep visibility across the multitude of providers it serves, and therefore has greater insight for the development of new processes, new products, and new services. With this visibility, it can identify entirely new innovations that would otherwise be invisible to individual providers. It can also identify payer patterns for claim denials based on how payers process claims for multiple providers. That can help improve coding and claims processing.

4. **Providing broad data sets of patient populations:** An HSP should be able to provide large data collections which can be used to identify issues

relating to public health trends and demographics. The purpose of this is to cut across larger populations than those available to any single provider. In addition, the HSP should be able to use these data sets to map to the provider's patients and identify at-risk groups, segments of the provider's patient population (as we'll see in the case of John Muir's segmentation of high-risk patients for ambulatory care coordination), data analytics within the provider's patient population, and the ability to create predictive models for the needs of these segmented populations.

5. **The use of advanced technologies such as AI to eliminate denials and assist in coding and clinical support:** An HSP brings world-class technology competency and talent to a provider that would otherwise simply be inaccessible due to the provider's scale or their tight industry focus. For example, recall that in chapter 3, we talked about the enormous burden of claims denials on the healthcare system. Much of this is due to the complexity of coding as well as the back-and-forth of determining medical necessity (think back to the cases of Isabella and Wanda in chapter 2). Much of the back-and-forth that delays decision-making could be eliminated by using AI technology, such as clinically intelligent natural language processing (NLP)—a form of AI that works with clinicians to improve the speed of decision-making. This is key, since the point of most AI is to scale what may be a rarely used best practice (due to human resources constraints or the sheer complexity of the process) and apply it to every patient interaction,

EHR update, and claim. And all of this is done at the point of care in real-time, not as an afterthought.

Reimbursement is increasingly being tied to quality and outcomes that need to be accurately reported based on clinical documentation. The ratings and penalties not only have financial impact, but also impact the provider's brand in the community.

By using technologies such as NLP and AI, an HSP is able to offload the burden on clinicians, significantly reduce friction, and continuously innovate a provider's technology systems so that the provider can focus on patient care.

Another reason AI is becoming so much more important going forward is that new risk-based models have introduced intricate rules that impact documentation, coding, and reimbursement. Reimbursement is increasingly being tied to quality and outcomes that need to be accurately reported based on clinical documentation. The ratings and penalties not only have financial impact but also impact the provider's brand in the community. The ultimate objective of AI in these sorts of scenarios is to offload the clinicians so that they can focus on patient care, rather than being mired in the documentation of that care.

The greater long-term promise of NLP is in assisting with clinical decision support and evidence-based medicine. While this isn't yet the case, the integration of AI technologies with the entire ecosystem of data available will provide a means of collaborative support to clinicians as they evaluate patients.

One area where each of these five benefits of working with an HSP can have the greatest impact—by helping providers focus on their core competency rather than getting entangled in administrative friction—is coding. We talked at length about the complexity of the coding process in the chapter 3 subsection Breaking the Code. The answer to the challenges that we discussed in chapter 3 lies in the HSP's ability to combine deep expertise in process management, a broad understanding of claims across multiple providers and payers, and AI and NLP.

The fundamental challenge in the coding process is the lack of trust between providers and payers, which leads to both doing the best they can to protect themselves (Culprit #8, Defensive Medicine). Think back to the term we used in chapter 3, the battle of the coders. Think of this as a sort of tug-of-war (Illustration 5.4.1). Both sides are pulling as hard as they can to move the rope in their direction in order to gain even a slight advantage. There's no malice or fraud involved; both parties are playing by the rules they've been given. But without transparency into the other side's processes, documentation, or decision-making, all they can do is pull as hard as possible.

Now, what if one side of that tug-of-war yelled over to the other side, "Stop pulling for a minute so that we can share our strategy with you to see if there's a way to resolve this?" What would your first thought be if you were on the side being asked that question? If you're like most people, it would likely be along the lines of, "How can I trust them to not suddenly pull when I let go?" That's effectively what's happening within the current system.

However, let's change the relationship between provider and payer by introducing an HSP as a trusted intermediary that has the ability to access and understand all of the information available to both sides—the patient data, documentation, doctor's notes and lab results—then query the patient's health

The Battle of The Coders

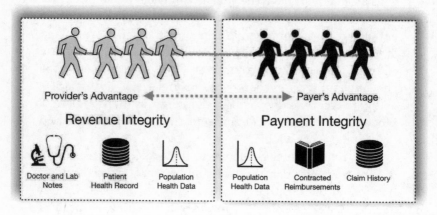

Illustration 5.4.1 Today's claims processing is often portrayed as a battle between provider and payer in which each side is attempting to shift the advantage to their side of the equation using their proprietary data and making assumptions about the other party's process. Providers want to increase revenue integrity to make sure they get paid fairly. Payers want to increase payment integrity to make sure they only pay for covered claims. This is not borne of malice or fraud, but rather a system that does not provide transparency into each side's processes or data and as a result generates distrust.

record, and determine how all of this maps to a payer's coverage (Illustration 5.4.2). What if the HSP could then make determinations about claims with coder involvement only in extreme outlier cases where human judgment or consultation was needed? By the way, over time, that algorithm would learn and require increasingly less human judgment.

I realize that this may sound a bit Orwellian at first glance. But the HSP's algorithms would have access to significantly more data about how claims are processed, what constitutes medical necessity, and the probabilities of the outcome associated with millions of other diagnosis and treatment combinations across vast collections of claims data.

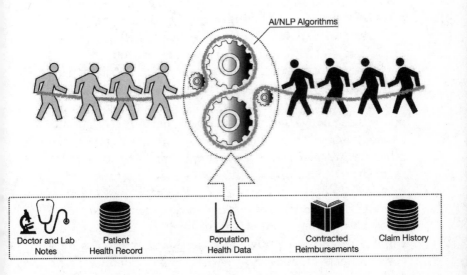

Illustration 5.4.2 An HSP could act as a trusted intermediary with access to all of the necessary data and documentation from either party to determine accurate and fair reimbursements, alleviating the tension and cost in the current model of coding and claims. Most importantly, it reduces the friction that otherwise typifies the claims process.

If you're asking, "But how can we trust an algorithm?" I'd suggest that the problem is that trust is exactly what's currently missing in the system. In many cases, providers and payers are effectively being asked to second-guess each other's responses. Transparency is virtually nonexistent. Each operates as a black box. And, as if all that wasn't enough to explain the current level of dysfunction, the amount of data needed to make sense of a claim is steadily increasing and exceeding the capacity of humans tasked with making the

209

right decisions. Is an algorithm perfect? Absolutely not. But it's much closer to it than the current state of affairs.

If you're still fearful, let me allay your concerns a bit. What I'm describing will not happen in one large fell-swoop redesign of healthcare and its many administrative processes. However, these changes are already happening and will continue to gain momentum as their benefits to providers, payers, and patients become more obvious and prevalent.

It's also worth noting that a similar argument about trust and risk is being used by those opposed to autonomous vehicle (AVs) or driverless cars. However, what is often left out of these conversations is that fact that AVs will not just be intelligent, but they will be able to communicate with each other. As human drivers, we are simply unable to do that with other drivers. The result is that we are constantly trying to guess what another driver will do, whether they will play by the rules of the road or try to jump a red light or stop sign. We are in a very similar tug-of-war in which we all try to gain a slight advantage. Not only does that disappear when cars are constantly communicating their status and intentions with each other, but traffic also goes away since cars can now coordinate their proximity to each other, traverse intersections and rotaries flawlessly, and increase the overall velocity of traffic flow.

What's especially interesting about the driverless car analogy is that when you look at traffic patterns on the roads today, friction is constantly present in the form of congestion, traffic delays, and accidents. With intelligent self-driven automobiles, all of this goes away.

In many ways, the role of the HSP is to be a trusted intermediary who makes sure everyone plays by the rules and constantly coordinates all available data to achieve the best outcomes for provider, payer, and patient.

The HSP model also has another benefit; it creates a more competent workforce by compressing the capability curve of an industry.

Collapsing the Capability Curve

Most vertically integrated organizations can be thought of as having a distribution of capabilities that range from those that are performed with distinction to those that are dangerously inept. We can categorize these capabilities broadly on what I call a capability curve (Illustration 5.5).

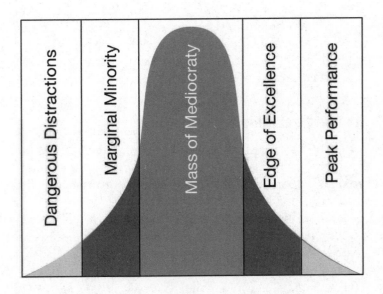

Illustration 5.5 Vertically integrated organizations, which try to take ownership of all activities from core to noncore, create a bell curve of capabilities that reflect a broad range of skills that also imply a much higher level of risk in their operations. The objective of the smartsourced organization is to eliminate or at least mitigate these risks by compressing its operation into the two right-most segments of the bell curve.

The Dangerous Diversions

These are the processes and tasks that a healthcare organization simply should not be involved in at all because they have negligible impact on any aspect of clinical operations or patient experience. Generally, these are tasks that end up being collocated with the organization for the sake of convenience. Good examples are valet parking or the cleaning service for linens and scrubs. While every aspect of a hospital's operation has the potential to impact the patient (after all, who wants poorly washed sheets?), the volumes involved and likelihood that a third party could do the job as well if not better are both high. Because these are typically also commodity services, there's little in the way of cost differential to keep them in-house. However, they can create big headaches in terms of peripheral risk or maintenance of expensive equipment. Because of this, Dangerous Diversions are easy to shed and should be the first thing to outsource.

The Marginal Minority

While the processes categorized as Dangerous Diversions are typically outside of the scope of where an organization should be operating, processes that fall into the Marginal Minority suffer from a different problem. The capabilities needed here are not necessarily out of the scope of the organization, but require training time and apprenticeship that creates risk. These processes require a set of skills that take time to develop.

For example, a hospital cafeteria. I've long been fascinated by how tightly hospitals hold onto this as an in-house process, some to extremes. Overlook Medical Center in Summit, New Jersey, actually has eight beehives that their in-house food service maintains. Overall, less than one quarter of all hospitals fully or partially outsource food service.[7] That surprising statistic points to something that I've seen in many organizations that push back on the notion of partnering on processes that they've long been responsible for. It's what I call the illusion of value. If you try to convince a provider that harvests their own honey for patients to partner with a third party such as Aramark, the most likely response will be that, "We take great pride in delivering the best and highest quality food service to our staff, our patients, and their friends and families." The implication there is, of course, that value can only be delivered at that level of quality by the organization itself.

That sentiment actually has merit. However, it also speaks to a fatal flaw in pursuing these processes over time. The flaw is one that's rarely obvious and which we will see in the case of John Muir Health, which we profile in the next chapter. Those who take the most pride in their contribution to the value being created in Marginal Minority activities soon find that they have hit a glass ceiling. Since the organization's core competency isn't food service, they have little opportunity for long-term career growth, learning from others or sharing their knowledge with similarly dedicated peers. That creates an especially acute risk for an organization since their loss is not easily replaceable. Imagine being in charge of operations at Overlook Medical Center when your beekeeper chef decides to move on.

Smartsourcing provides a career path for these individuals. As we'll see when we discuss John Muir Health, if done correctly, smartsourcing allows these individuals to stay with the organization while also giving them a much more promising career path.

The Mass of Mediocrity

This is the area where many organizations have the greatest difficulty in making a decision to partner. They may sense that they are not fully capable to do the job, but the cost of their inadequacy is typically veiled or even considered an acceptable cost of doing business. In many industries, this is perpetuated until one or more players in the industry decides to change the benchmark. Otherwise, there is simply no competitive mandate to invest in change. Moreover, the processes that underlie the inadequacy may be so convoluted and poorly understood that the effort to re-engineer the process is far more daunting than dealing with the consequences of the inadequacy.

In the case of healthcare, these processes represent several critical areas that have a direct impact on patient experiences and outcomes as well as the provider's financial performance. The four areas that we outlined earlier in this chapter—revenue cycle, information technology, data analytics, and care management—are among the best examples of these.

The challenge in smartsourcing these areas is that they are so inherently complex and end up becoming so intertwined with various parts of the organization (think of all the functions that IT supports) that there is a natural reluctance to let go of them. The fear is that no other organization will understand their nuanced complexities well enough and that the risk of failure in transferring them is too great.

The Edge of Excellence

Every hospital must excel at its core of patient care. While the nature of the excellence may come in a variety of forms, from healthcare specializations such as oncology or cardiac care, to better models of integrated medicine, there is little hope for hospitals that cannot deliver better outcomes in the current move toward VBC. The irony is that we expect the edge of excellence to remain an edge, that is, to be the thin edge of the blade rather than to define a substantial part of the organization. This attitude is at the heart of why smart-sourcing has been so slow to catch on in healthcare. I would challenge the notion that this must be a thin edge and instead offer (as we've already pointed out on many occasions in this book) that the majority of the investment an organization makes should, and eventually must, exist in this and the next segment of the bell curve.

Peak Performance

Every organization, no matter how efficient, motivated, or exemplary, will have a core group of peak performers that occupy this segment of the bell curve. This may take the form of an extraordinary surgeon who is focused on innovation within his or her specialty. For example, the Cleveland Clinic where Dr. Brian Gastman, plastic surgeon and otolaryngologist, leads a team that specializes in face transplants. The Cleveland Clinic was the first hospital globally to attempt a face transplant. You would expect that such a complex procedure would require an extraordinary plastic surgeon. But that's not the way Dr. Gastman describes it. One transplant can involve forty clinicians, fifteen specialist doctors, and seventeen separate surgeries. According to Dr. Gastman, "I think our team approach is somewhat different than at other institutions. It's much bigger, both surgically and nonsurgically, with multiple redundancies built into our process. We try not to be highly dependent on just one or two people."

Dr. Gastman's comments speak to the importance of differentiating the notion of peak performers (individuals) from the core capabilities of a team or an institution, which differentiate it in the absence of a few peak performers. Peak performers can create a temporary advantage, but core capabilities and processes, the lessons learned, captured, and taught within the organization, those that can be executed with excellence by all performers, are much more vital to long-term success. What makes all of this especially interesting is that the Cleveland Clinic was founded by doctors that had served in World War I and come back with a keen sense for the importance of teamwork in battlefield hospitals. That ethos was the foundation of the Cleveland Clinic. Again, this speaks to the critical importance of core competency, which is most often woven into an organization's cultural DNA.

The value of smartsourcing in this case is that it allows the provider to focus their efforts on building these critical core competencies that differentiate them and continue to build on the core.

Although it is arbitrary to expect a normal bell curve distribution among these five segments, it is the case that every hospital or hospital system that expects to survive will need to deliver outcomes based on its ability to move its core capabilities from the left- to the right-hand side of the capability curve.

...the smartsourcing partner becomes a watchdog for operational excellence and cost reductions, while offloading the organization of this burden allows it to refocus attention on its core.

Basic technology infrastructure may help to alleviate some of the drag created by the first three segments and compress these, allowing an enterprise to focus more on its core capabilities. However, the ultimate ambition and objective of smartsourcing is to move hospitals almost fully into the two rightmost segments.

At first, this may seem to be overreaching. It's clearly not where most healthcare providers are today. However, the premise is not that an entire enterprise can be moved into the two rightmost segments in whole, but that it can be moved in parts over time.

But to do this, providers have to begin looking beyond the cost-cutting benefits of outsourcing alone and consider the entire scope of the smartsourcing decision and the metrics they need to establish in order to measure competency and performance across the entire organization. While more time will be spent in the following chapters on the frameworks and mechanisms for achieving this, the fundamental questions that need to be answered by a provider organization in order to understand where smartsourcing can be of potential value to an organization are:

- How core is each process of your business to your unique strategic differentiation?

- How competitive and innovative is your organization in each of these business areas?

- How cost-effective are you at the activities in each business area, and how much patient-customer value do these processes add?

- Can you identify smartsourcing partners that have a proven core competency in your noncore areas?

- Will these smartsourcing partners help to innovate your noncore activities while also providing ways in which to innovate them so that you will be able to align your organization with future healthcare trends?

- Have you found a smartsourcing partner that shares your organization's values and which you can trust to co-invest with in the future?

The answers to these questions offer a great deal of insight into those areas that are best suited for sourcing and those that must be the focus of internal innovation.

There is, however, an important caveat to this exercise, which has often been ignored at the peril of organizations pursuing outsourcing or smartsourcing; namely, outsourcing and smartsourcing imply absolution. Conventional wisdom favors shedding messy and expensive processes to third-party experts, who will operate in a black box. After all, that's why you want to be rid of them, right? They are too messy and cumbersome, so just let someone else carry the risk. Nothing is further from the truth.

In fact, smartsourcing requires a much more intimate bond of trust, collaboration, and accountability between the organization and its partner. This should result in higher levels of innovation in core as well as noncore processes. In many ways, the smartsourcing partner becomes a watchdog for operational excellence and cost reductions, while off-loading the organization of this burden allows it to refocus attention on its core. In addition, this opens the door to new opportunities for partnering on processes in the first three segments of our bell curve that otherwise may not have been considered as candidates.

Savvy smartsourcing partners not only encourage this sort of relationship, but also work collaboratively on an ongoing basis to identify the areas that are best suited to external innovation. Open collaboration and a high level of transparency in this exercise are critical to establishing the sort of communication,

> Innovation requires intimacy, and it is inherently a trust-based process that demands exceptional integrity from participants.

trust, and long-term understanding of the benefits that smart-sourcing can bring to the table. In many cases this means complete disclosure on the part of the smartsourcing provider of the costs and business models used to determine the pricing and performance benefits for a partnership.

However, transparency of this sort requires a solid appreciation for the process being smartsourced and a method by which to adequately describe, monitor, and manage the processes that you are expecting external partners to help with. It also requires a new level of trust and intimacy between organizations and their sourcing partners. Innovation requires intimacy, and it is inherently a trust-based process that demands exceptional integrity from participants.

For many organizations, taking this approach blurs the line of demarcation between partner and provider. In the words of one healthcare CIO I spoke with, the service provider becomes a "true technology teammate."

But on closer inspection, you'll notice that while the amount of each dollar spent on each function drops, it creates a vacuum. Nature and capital abhor a vacuum. What happens to the increased margin? This capital does not lay idle; it must be reinvested, but in what?

These savings are passed directly to the bottom line of the smartsourcing organization and can be reinvested into the core patient care function. This break point from the relatively meager returns of cost savings to the much greater returns of increased investment in innovation marks a change in the way providers view sourcing partnerships and their benefits from simple outsourcing relationships to smartsourcing.

The bottom line is that providers are in a battle for survival to build organizations that will allow them to deliver on the promise of a patient-centered healthcare system.

Smartsourcing helps providers to refocus their operations on their core mission and competencies, objectives which may have been long obscured by the complexity of managing in-house operations for noncore activities, but which have always been the essence of what constitutes high-quality healthcare.

We are now at a turning point. It is time for healthcare providers to reinvest not just in those areas that make their organizations better, but in those core competencies that make them great.

The New Employment

There's one final aspect of smartsourcing that is often passed over when describing its benefits: the relationship of current provider employees to the HSP. What's critical to understand about a smartsourcing relationship is that it's not the typical partnership in which two separate organizations work at arm's length in a transactional arrangement. Drawing a hard line between the provider and the HSP isn't possible, nor is it desirable. The whole point of smartsourcing is to allow the HSP to work seamlessly with the provider so that the result is not another silo but an integrated competency. This is what creates the economy of scope that we talked about earlier. In keeping with that, there are two fundamentally different employment structures in a smartsourcing arrangement.

The first is to bring in an existing workforce that is employed

A smartsourcing relationship is built on a foundation of trust and shared values. Communicating and preserving these values to employees who are being rebadged is critical.

by the HSP and to place them in the provider's organization. While using an external workforce is typical in outsourcing relationships, it's less than ideal in establishing the best foundation for smartsourcing since these resources will almost always be seen as outsiders, especially in a community hospital setting.

The second model is what's referred to as "rebadging," in which existing provider employees become HSP employees. For organizations that haven't been through this process, the notion of rebadging stirs all sorts of fears about the reaction of current employees to the idea of being suddenly rehired by a new organization. Understanding how this will impact the motivation, loyalties, and responsibilities between employee and employer is one of smartsourcing's most important questions.

Although the specific employment model will always need to be built to meet the requirements and constraints of each situation, there are three reasons why rebadging is most often the preferred option.

First, there is an inherent benefit to having individuals who carry the culture of the provider in order to form the foundation of the partnership. These individuals carry the cultural DNA of the organization into the smartsourcing relationship and provide a vital thread to tie the smartsourced activities to the core activities of the organization. Having seen this play itself out in dozens of situations, I can't emphasize enough the important role it plays in establishing a foundation for long-term success.

Second, employment is not only about the company name on a paycheck. It involves the more complex emotional issues of camaraderie, being valued, recognition, a sense of principled and visionary leadership at the helm, and a foundation of employment certainty and stability. Ultimately, these factors will decide the primary allegiance of employees. A smartsourcing relationship is built on a foundation of trust and shared values. Communicating and preserving these values to employees who are being rebadged is critical. In cases such as John Muir's, where large parts of the organization are being rebadged, the communication plan to employees has to be clear, consistent, and compassionate.

Third, moving to the HSP provides developmental opportunities to employees that would not be available within the confines of the provider. This is one of the least well-understood and most overlooked aspects of rebadging under a smartsourcing arrangement. Yet, it's one of the most important to the employee. Since the HSP has deep competency in the areas being smartsourced, it will also have a career path and opportunities for advancement that almost always outweigh what would otherwise be available to an employee. Communicating that and emphasizing its value to the employee will help retain the best, brightest, and most motivated employees.

Fourth, the ability to invest in the tools and technologies which the provider's smartsourced employees are using increases substantially after smartsourcing. This may sound like a simple thing, but it can have significant consequences. In one case I'm aware of, the smartsourcing partner looked at the basic ergonomics of how rebadged employees were using their computer systems in one highly administrative function. The partner immediately realized that one of the impediments to the employees doing their job was the size of their computer screens, which still had not been upgraded to flatscreens due to the provider's IT equipment budget. By simply putting in place large flatscreen monitors, the partner caused employee satisfaction and efficiency to go up considerably.

Whatever the specifics of the employment model used, smartsourcing creates a new culture in an organization. The traditional bonds between employee and employer are blurred and altered in peculiar ways, raising questions about even some of the most basic aspects of corporate governance: whose policy do I really follow, the organization that pays me or the one I work for, or both? When asked who I work for, how do I respond? Will the HSP hold the same values as the ones I've bought into from my past employer? Understanding these issues is essential in order to reinforce behaviors that support quality and teamwork.

Will these sorts of advances allow HSPs to succeed where the healthcare industry in general has failed? I believe they will, but it will require reaching critical mass. Since the HSP model benefits from the dynamic of increasing returns (economies of scope), the more organizations within the healthcare industry that use it, the more valuable it becomes to participants.

As we close out this chapter, and before we delve into the future of healthcare, it's worthwhile to stop and look at how the combination of smartsourcing and HSPs is addressing the Ten Culprits we identified at the outset, and, as importantly, how it will shape the healthcare system of the future.

The table below summarizes the current and projected future benefits of the smartsourcing/HSP model. For each of the Ten Culprits, I've provided a short description of the impact that smartsourcing and HSPs are having and will have. Keep in mind that this is meant only as a high-level summary. In some cases, it's easy to foresee the changes to come; in others, it can be challenging.

For example, under Culprit #10, The Aging of America, it's clear that by reducing friction and administrative overhead, smartsourcing will enable the scaling of current clinical and nonclinical systems to keep pace with the increasing complexity and volume of care for the over-sixty-five demographic. What's not as clear is exactly how we will deal with all of the nuanced changes that will have to occur in everything from how we transport older patients who don't have access to their own transportation, to the need for AI-based case managers that can act as autonomous advocates for patients suffering from illnesses such as Alzheimer's and who cannot advocate for themselves.

#1 The Anonymous Patient	• Now: Smartsourcing not only provides a repository of all of the patient's data, but can use advanced technologies for predictive analytics, such as AI and NLP, to identify patterns and markers in patient data that need further evaluation.
	• Future: An HSP will be able to identify patient identity across multiple providers and payers, creating a single source of truth for patient history and advocacy.
#2 The Asymmetry between Costs and Outcomes	• Now: Smartsourcing the revenue cycle streamlines claims and billing, significantly reducing denials while providing immediate access to costs and likely outcomes.
	• Future: By working across many providers and payers, along with access to a vast collection of public health data, an HSP can build models that leverage the knowledge of best practices, identify risks and align them with payments, track outcomes, and better support value-based healthcare.
#3 The Episodic Care Conundrum	• Now: Smartsourcing creates an integrated view of the patient's many touchpoints within a health system in order to provide greater coordination of care. This is especially important as ambulatory care management increases in volume.

	▪ Future: Since an HSP can span multiple providers and has access to large populations of patients, a patient's EHR and associated documentation history can not only follow the patient, but also can be correlated against public health trends to identify risk factors for the patient's specific context.
#4 The Complexity Crisis	▪ Now: HSPs significantly reduce the friction created by the current highly fragmented model of healthcare by unifying patient data, integrating it with the various touchpoints within a healthcare system, and streamlining the patient experience.
	▪ Future: Through the use of predictive analytics, universal population health data, and comprehensive lifetime patient data, HSPs can identify health risks to individuals and populations well in advance. This enables a new era of preventative medicine to emerge.
#5 The Missing Link	▪ Now: An HSP coordinates all of the pieces of the healthcare system that need to be synchronized among patients, payers, and providers to minimize costs and optimize outcomes.
	▪ Future: HSPs span healthcare's more complex ecosystems that consist of multiple inpatient and outpatient providers to allow for frictionless movement of patients throughout the ecosystem while tracking outcomes across the patient's lifetime.

#6 Drifting from the Core	▪ Now: By significantly reducing administrative waste and friction, smartsourcing allows providers to focus on their cores while innovating across the entire value chain.
	▪ Future: The HSP becomes a partner in building new business models for the delivery of healthcare by leveraging data and technology in a way that aligns with the changing demands of the market.
#7 The Tragedy of the Commons	▪ Now: HSPs eliminate the need for gaming of the system, up- or down-coding, denials, and surprise billing, and they align interests across providers, patients, and payers.
	▪ Future: HSPs support the creation of a healthcare system that maintains the option of provider/payer choice for the patient-consumer while providing all of the perceived benefits of a single-payer model with interests aligned around a patient-centric ecosystem.
#8 Defensive Medicine	▪ Now: An HSP offloads the burden of excessive coding and documentation from the doctor or clinician so that they can focus on caring for the patient with greater certainty that patient data and records are consistent. The use of AI also identifies patterns or markers in documentation that need further attention and flags these for review by the clinician, corrects inconsistencies in documentation, and reduces the burden of EHR documentation on the clinician.

	• Future: AI used against large population data sets becomes a clinical collaborator with the physician in identifying predictive patterns of risk and suggested treatments with high levels of accuracy that precisely align risks and costs with outcomes.
#9 The Primary Care Crisis	• Now: Smartsourcing reduces administrative friction in documentation, coding, and claims processing, allowing the clinician to spend more time focusing on the patient and alleviating physician burnout. • Future: Smartsourcing provides a holistic view of the patient to deliver and coordinate the most effective healthcare services and the best outcomes. A single EHR also provides the ability to analyze patient data and to create predictive and preventative diagnostics and interventions based on personal and public health data.
#10 The Aging of America	• Now: By reducing friction and administrative overhead, smartsourcing enables the scaling of current clinical and nonclinical systems to keep pace with the increasing complexity and volume of care for the over-sixty-five demographic. This provides for greater ability to care for a population with higher incidence of comorbidity and multiple specialists and to analyze patient data to create predictive and preventative diagnostics and interventions based on personal and public health data.

- Future: HSPs provide autonomous advocates that are fully aware of a patient's history and medical records, and which integrate into the patient's lifetime journey through the health-care ecosystem.

SMARTSOURCING, CHAPTER 5: RECAP AND LESSONS LEARNED

Smartsourcing is founded on the premise that the cost and friction of maintaining a large vertically integrated infrastructure of noncore activities is greater, and less effective, than the cost of coordinating an external value chain with the same activities among partners whose cores are in these same areas.

For community hospitals and hospital systems that expect to survive into the next decade and beyond, there are only two viable options: to be acquired and become part of a behemoth healthcare provider system with access to shared services and higher reimbursement rates, or to smartsource everything that's not core and become a coordinator of an ecosystem of core competency providers.

- Smartsourcing is not about economies of scale; it is about economies of scope.

- Smartsourcing is not just about data and technology; it is about competency.

- Smartsourcing is not about ownership; it is about partnership.

- Smartsourcing is not just about cost cutting; it is about innovation.

- Smartsourcing is not about cheap labor; it is about smart, educated, and motivated workers.

- Most importantly, smartsourcing is not a theory.

We learned that the greatest risk in traditional outsourcing is focusing exclusively on costs and ignoring the importance of a concurrent innovation initiative.

Providers that smartsource shift from internal economies of scale to external economies of scope, which benefit from a free market of myriad coordinated resources, most of which are not owned by the organization but orchestrated by it.

Michael Porter's conceptual framework of the value chain has influenced the shift to economies of scope, facilitated by advances in communications, network bandwidth, technology, the internet, and the economics of frictionless partnering.

The cost of maintaining vertically integrated infrastructure is greater than the cost of coordinating external value chains.

The evolution of the zaibatsu and keiretsu, collections of companies who owned stock in each other, developed a very sophisticated manner of partnership that included both inter-reliance and interoperability. This can be used as a framework to think about a smartsourced healthcare system.

Providers have to begin looking beyond the cost-cutting benefits of outsourcing alone and consider the entire scope of the smartsourcing decision and the metrics they need to establish in order to measure competency and performance across their entire organization.

HSPs can bridge the gap of separate data silos by providing a common EHR platform or translation links between different EHR platforms, creating continuity of care for a patient across providers and over his or her lifetime.

HSPs create a trusted intermediary that can remove the friction inherent in tasks such as coding by accessing and understanding the full spectrum of data available to both provider and payer.

HSPs deliver value by investing in the administrative areas of a provider's business in a way no single provider ever could. They are transformational in that they can take investment risks that no single provider, insurer, or payer would ever undertake on their own.

Rebadging a provider's talent as part of a smartsourcing arrangement helps to provide continuity and ongoing alignment with the mission and vision of the provider organization. In this regard, a smartsourcing relationship is not the typical partnership in which two separate organizations work at arm's length in a transactional arrangement, but instead is a much more intimate and transparent arrangement were both parties are aligned in achieving the same goals.

PART THREE: THE FUTURE

*"Knowing is not enough; we must apply.
Willing is not enough; we must do."*

—GOETHE

CHAPTER 6
IN SICKNESS AND IN HEALTH

John Muir Health

Twenty-seven years ago, Dr. Stephen Shortell coined the term "holographic organization" in reference to health systems that are integrated so well that, as with a hologram, any part of the overall system would contain the information necessary to reflect the entire system.

In his book, *Remaking Health Care in America*, Dr. Shortell defined three integration categories: functional integration (concerning operations and administration); physician integration; and clinical integration, which is best described as the coordination of all the resources needed to care for a patient.

Dr. Shortell's message was simple; while the value of healthcare was historically determined primarily by how well it healed those who were sick, it is now even more importantly determined by how it keeps patients well to begin with and reduces the likelihood of their being readmitted after they have been treated. Both of those objectives require an integrated network of services that work in harmony across the entire spectrum of a patient's healthcare needs.

When I envision Dr. Shortell's description of the holographic organization in the context of a fully integrated healthcare system, what springs to mind is an image depicting thousands of patients at a hospital on an immense hologram, juxtaposed against a backdrop of all of the clinical and administrative complexity we've described throughout the book. If you break off any single patient image, you see not only that patient, but the entirety of the healthcare system supporting the patient.[i]

At the heart of this vision of integrated healthcare is an organization that is culturally aligned with the values of patient-centric treatment, operational excellence in administering patient care, and integration across clinical and nonclinical activities in a way that allows every part of the healthcare process to have an awareness of and an ability to communicate and coordinate care with every other part.

That may sound like a utopian ideal, but it is the only viable and sustainable vision for healthcare in the long run, and one that is already taking shape in many community-based healthcare providers. In this chapter, we'll look at the evolution of community hospitals by using an example of a Northern California-based healthcare system, John Muir Health.

Bringing It Home

In 1965, a group of California doctors came together to build a community hospital through the use of funding from the Hill-Burton Act, which, you may recall from chapter 4, was established to help support the creation of community and rural hospitals.

---

i   Holographic photography captures light patterns in a way that preserves the entirety of the image in every piece of the holographic image. For each piece of the hologram, you see a slightly different perspective of the same image.

Originally founded as John Muir Memorial Hospital, today that hospital system has grown into John Muir Health (JMH), a mid-tier coalition of three hospitals that serve the communities surrounding Contra Costa County, California. The hospital system is the result of a merger between the original John Muir Medical Center (started in 1965) and Mount Diablo Medical Center.

The origin story behind John Muir Health is one that speaks to the deep belief of so many healthcare professionals who pursue medicine: that healthcare is about being good servants to and stewards of their patients. The doctors who founded John Muir Memorial Hospital were the same ones who once made house calls with their little brown bags. They had started their practices long before many of the technologies that are today available. Ambulances did not exist—neither did para-medics. If you had an emergency, you would call the fire department, which could only administer oxygen. Without a doctor appearing on the scene to release the patient, or pronounce them deceased, patients could not be moved.

> ...John Muir Health stood out as a role model for the way in which community hospitals will need to approach healthcare in the coming decades.

Defibrillators had not yet been invented and even CPR had yet to be used in resuscitating patients whose heart had stopped beating.

One of those doctors who was part of the core group that launched John Muir Memorial was Dr. Marvin Epstein. In a book he wrote to recount those early years, *In Sickness and Health*, Dr. Epstein writes of what life was like for him as a physician in the 1950s.

...there were no cell phones and pagers then, but someone had organized a small FM radio network for mobile service. I suppose this began as a necessary service for contact with ambulances, but a number of physicians also were in the system....When I went into practice I was committed to one hundred percent availability, since I knew that this was critical for the growth of a practice—and thus I decided to join the radio network. It meant buying a transmitter-receiver, installing the boxes in the trunk, running a line from the unit of the microphone to the dashboard, putting an appropriate antenna on the car, and getting an FCC license! When I left the house in the morning I would get in the car, start the engine, turn on the transmitter, and then call the exchange, "This is car four, I'm on my way to Concord Hospital," or wherever I might be going. So, I was available all the time, and got the calls via that method from the emergency room patients without doctors.

From these humble beginnings, and a deep sense of commitment to patients, John Muir Health was born.

Today, John Muir Health's facilities include two acute care hospitals, including the county's only Level II trauma center along with specialty practices in orthopedics, cancer care, cardiovascular care, robotic surgery, neonatal intensive care and high-risk obstetrics, rehabilitation and critical care, neuroscience, behavioral health, and a seventy-three-bed psychiatric hospital.

Over a thousand physicians in seventy-four separate locations throughout the communities served make up the John Muir Physician Network. Due to California regulations, these physicians are not employed by John Muir Health, but rather by John Muir Medical Group, John Muir Cardiovascular Medical Group, John Muir Specialty Medical Group, or are independent physicians in small and large group practices. John Muir Health also runs seven urgent care centers.

> What's not to like about doing it better, faster, and at a lower cost so that you can invest your resources where it counts—in the clinic where the beds are?

In doing research for this book, John Muir Health stood out as a role model for the way in which community hospitals will need to approach healthcare in the coming decades.

As a community hospital system, there are several things that cause John Muir Health to stand out among its peers.

1. With a total of eight hundred beds, its size is clearly at the large end of the spectrum, based on our definition of a community hospital. This is important because I wanted to focus on how providers can build scalable healthcare solutions in order to allow for growth through mechanisms other than becoming part of large hospitals with thousands of beds which rely on economies of scale rather than economies of scope.

2. John Muir Health has been doing exceedingly well financially. Its foray into smartsourcing is not driven by a crisis mentality, but rather by a strategic decision to focus more of its valuable resources

on the core of patient care. This is critical since the vision behind smartsourcing is not to provide a temporary fix, but to create a systemic change in the architecture of the healthcare system.

3. John Muir Health is obsessed with being patient-centered in every aspect of its business. While putting the patient at the center is not a new concept, John Muir Health has built every aspect of its healthcare system with relentless focus on the patient. This is something you not only hear echoed by every doctor, clinician, and administrator at John Muir Health, but which is also manifested in every aspect of the physical layout of the facilities, admissions, the billing systems, and the care process.

In an interview, Cal Knight, current CEO of John Muir Health, summed up the driving passion behind smartsourcing: "What's not to like about doing it better, faster, and at a lower cost so that you can invest your resources where it counts—in the clinic where the beds are? That's what it's all about, how to maximize the investment of these hard-earned dollars in places where it really can help take care of patients."

Granted, it's easy for a CEO to say the words. Many do. What's impressive here is the degree to which an institution as large as John Muir Health can align nearly every aspect of its care and its business along that same compass setting.

One small example is the layout of the intensive care rooms. Anyone who has been in a hospital, especially an ER or ICU, is familiar with what's called a headwall, a unit mounted to the wall at the head of the bed that contains a series of ports where various medical devices and instruments can be attached. For example, oxygen or a vacuum tube. In several of

John Muir Health's ER and ICU rooms, there is no head-wall. Instead, units called Stryker booms, which have the same ports along with a variety of instruments for monitoring a patient, are hung from the ceiling on pivoting arms that allow them and the bed to be positioned in any manner necessary to accommodate the patient. This might seem like a small accommodation, but it allows everything in the room to revolve around the patient. It's an apt metaphor for the core philosophy behind nearly every person, process, and piece of equipment at John Muir Health.

Healthcare is local and it's very, very personal. Nationalizing it, if you will, either on a privatized basis or in a government-sponsored model, leads you directly away from the relationships.

Most people are likely also familiar with the way that nurses' stations are set up on each floor or unit of a hospital to monitor patients' vital signs. Typically, each nurses' station is responsible for monitoring several patients at the same time. Anyone who has spent even a few hours in a hospital, as a patient or visitor, is familiar with the sound of alarms going off due to a malfunctioning IV, an elevated heart rate, or a patient call button. Many times, these alarms will go on for some time before being attended to as nurses prioritize their activities. For a patient anxious about an incessant alarm or, worse yet, in a situation where they need immediate help and are unable to call a nurse, there is little to do but wait. John Muir Health has created a control room in which staff nurses monitor patients across multiple facilities and all of their vital signs on video monitors 24/7. They have the ability to escalate a call to an on-duty nurse and also to communicate with the patient by audio while seeing the patient's condition.

It's like a mini NORAD, always on the lookout for threats to the patient across the entire John Muir Health system.

Clearly, these are not innovations unique to John Muir Health. Each one is used in many other hospitals. But the integration of all of these approaches and their orchestration into a truly patient-centered model is impressive.

Cal attributes the strong ethos of putting the patient at the center with the culture that comes with a local community hospital, which puts a premium on the patient relationship, something that, according to Cal cannot be achieved at significantly large scale. "Healthcare is local and it's very, very personal. Nationalizing it, if you will, either on a privatized basis or in a government-sponsored model, leads you directly away from the relationships. It's really the relationships in the community that make a difference. Our people are who they are and do what they do because they love to help those patients in the community who trust them with their care."

Obviously, the culture of John Muir Health cannot simply be replicated in any other provider's context. Every organization has its own cultural legacy that informs and guides its decisions. However, in speaking with other community hospitals, I found that that the strong sense of purpose to build lifelong relationships with patients and to maintain an independence that allows the institution to create systems, processes, and a culture aligned with that purpose is a frequently recurring theme.

Unfortunately, we've already seen the many ways in which these well-meaning or-

...the US healthcare system tallies up $750 billion in wasteful spending each year on healthcare. To put that into perspective, it's the amount spent for the healthcare of all veterans for the past fifty-one years.

ganizations can be distracted from that mission by the attention required to manage the administrative overhead inherent in healthcare.

What makes the John Muir Health case study especially interesting is that its leadership acknowledges that, despite its exceptional operational excellence across both its clinical and nonclinical operations, without a smartsourcing strategy, its ability to stay independent and continue to provide care is at risk.

In Cal's words, "We have a profound responsibility to be here for future generations: your children, your grandchildren, their grandchildren. Our employees think about that. They want this place to be successful. It will be here for future generations."

If an institution such as John Muir Health is at risk, you have to wonder, how thin is the lifeline that every other community hospital is clinging to?

The Patient's Journey

Understanding how John Muir Health is using smartsourcing strategically requires first having an understanding of the tremendous inefficiency of the patient's journey through the current healthcare system.

According to a recent 2019 study published in the *Journal of the American Medical Association (JAMA)*,[1] the US healthcare system tallies up $750 billion in wasteful spending each year on healthcare. To put that into perspective, it's the amount spent for the healthcare of all veterans for the past fifty-one years.[2]

That waste breaks down to the following categories and the estimated potential savings:

Estimated Cost of Waste	Estimated Annual Savings
Failure of care delivery, $102.4 billion to $165.7 billion	$44.4 billion to $93.3 billion
Failure of care coordination, $27.2 billion to $78.2 billion	$29.6 billion to $38.2 billion
Overtreatment or low-value care, $75.7 billion to $101.2 billion	$12.8 billion to $28.6 billion
Pricing failure, $230.7 billion to $240.5 billion	$81.4 billion to $91.2 billion
Fraud and abuse, $58.5 billion to $83.9 billion	$22.8 billion to $30.8 billion
Administrative complexity, $265.6 billion[ii]	$132.8 billion (see footnote)

What's especially shocking about these numbers is where the US health system stands out most when compared with other countries: administrative costs.

A 2018 article published in *Modern Healthcare* looked at normalized costs across various national health systems. According to Yale University's Elizabeth Bradley and Lauren Taylor in their book, *The American Health Care Paradox: Why Spending More Is Getting Us Less,* if you compare the total of what the US spends on healthcare with what European countries spend on social services and healthcare combined, you'll find that the amounts are relatively equal.

However, according to the article, "the [areas] where the U.S. was wildly out of line was in administrative costs

---

ii   The authors did not identify specific savings for administrative complexity due to the fact that they could not find any generalized studies about estimated savings for this category. The savings are the author's estimate.

(8 percent[iii] of spending compared with 1-3 percent in other countries) and pharmacy costs ($1,443 per capita versus $466-$939 in other countries). Moreover, physician salaries in the U.S. were significantly higher ($218,173 for a generalist here compared with $86,607-$154,126 in other countries)."[3]

Assuming that physicians' salaries will remain relatively stable, and leaving pharmacy costs out of the equation for the time being,[iv] there is clearly an opportunity to lessen the administrative burden.

The Revenue Cycle

One of the first areas where John Muir Health is focusing its smartsourcing efforts is an obscure process that most people have never heard of. It's called the *revenue cycle* and it's also one of the most crucial areas where administrative friction frustrates and slows the patient's healthcare experience, as well as adding costs and administrative support burden. Simply put, the revenue cycle consists of the various tasks involved in managing the claims that a provider submits to a payer in order to determine what gets paid for and how.

This sounds simple; it's far from it. Making sure insurance claims are coded, submitted, managed, and paid quickly is critical and creates an enormous amount of administrative friction for providers. Smaller providers are especially susceptible to the drag this puts on resources, since it is likely

---

iii   The 8 percent noted is very conservative when compared with most of the literature estimates for administrative costs, which are most often projected at between 25–30 percent of total healthcare costs. In all other examples in the book, I've used the 30 percent figure for total administrative costs.

iv   I'm not discounting the impact of pharmaceutical costs and the fact that they need to be addressed as part of any comprehensive set of healthcare reforms. However, that conversation is far too detailed to do justice to within the scope of this book.

> ...successfully nego-
> tiating the revenue
> cycle is a monumental
> task that has repercus-
> sions throughout every
> aspect of the patient's
> experience...

that they do not have a significant number of dedicated staff focusing just on the revenue cycle. So, the same person who acts as receptionist, schedules appointments for patients, and calls in their prescriptions is also handling submission of claims to insurers. While that's not true for larger mid-tier providers, the revenue cycle still has the potential to become a burden. The sheer volume of claims, the dollar amounts involved, and the back-and-forth between provider and insurer can be the determining factors in whether a hospital is profitable or not.

The Revenue Cycle is the process by which a provider gets paid for services rendered to a patient. Although it sounds like a straight-forward process, it is one of the costliest and most resource- and time-consuming tasks for administrators. It's also one of the most frequently outsourced. However, outsourcing by simply lifting and shifting this process to another organization at a lower cost does little to help alleviate the friction it causes through the provider/patient experience. This makes the revenue cycle a prime target for smartsourcing.

In addition, successfully negotiating the revenue cycle is a monumental task that has repercussions throughout every aspect of the patient's experience and directly impacts the quality and cost of the care. If you think back to many of the cases we've covered in the book so far, each one is somehow tied to the revenue cycle and the payment or nonpayment of claims.

As we delve into the revenue cycle, I'll start with a simple analogy that illustrates the role that a relatively invisible component can have on the efficiency of a much larger process.

A Turn of the Screw

I grew up in the sixties and seventies. At that time, learning how to work on an automobile was a rite of passage—in large part due to the fact that few of us had the money to buy cars that didn't need ongoing maintenance, and even fewer of us could afford the services of a "real" mechanic. This was well before the internet and YouTube. So, we learned by doing. With a set of screwdrivers, a socket wrench set, and a pair of vice grips, we became shade tree mechanics.

But there was one part of those 1960s-era engines that challenged even the most experienced among us: the dreaded carburetor.

Carburetors are very simple in principle; they mix air and fuel. An internal combustion engine needs both gasoline (fuel) and air in just the right mixture. However, the

> Just as the relatively invisible aspects of a carburetor's adjustments dictate an automobile's overall engine performance...the revenue cycle's performance and efficiency have a profound effect on the entirety of healthcare, from the patient's experience to the quality of care provided to the cost of that care.

ratio changes depending on the operating conditions and the demands being put on the car. The carburetor controls and adjusts the fuel-air mixture to keep the engine running smoothly.

The trick to tuning a carburetor is adjusting a series of tiny screws on the carburetor's body, which, in turn, determine the proportions of the fuel-air mixture. If you don't adjust these tiny screws, the car simply will not operate. Or if it does, it will stall, sputter, backfire, and use much more gasoline than it needs to. In short, if the carburetor is not tuned correctly, the entire engine will run rough and be incredibly wasteful.

So, what does that have to do with healthcare? Just as the relatively invisible aspects of a carburetor's adjustments dictate an automobile's overall engine performance, its cost to operate, and the quality of the ride, the revenue cycle's performance and efficiency has a profound effect on the entirety of healthcare, from the patient's experience to the quality and cost of care provided.

With inefficiencies in the revenue cycle being the primary contributor to overall waste of $265.6 billion in overall administrative waste, this is one of the most obvious processes to smartsource.

The Revenue Cycle

Scheduling   Exam/Visit   Submit Claim   Claim Processing   Remittance

Illustration 6.1 The pieces of the revenue cycle seem straightforward individually, but together they can be one of the costliest and most important aspects of healthcare administration since the efficiency of the cycle determines how often and how quickly claims are paid and has direct repercussions on the patient experience.

The challenge with the vast majority of conventional revenue cycles is that they have been developed and are run in-house. The hospitals, clinics, or private practices that use them often operate under the illusion that they are the best ones to run their particular revenue cycle, given its complexity and the impact it can have on critical aspects of the business such as cash flow and profitability.

When you trace back many of the frustrations in poor patient experience, such as surprise medical bills, the often obscure and difficult nature of processing claims and how they are coded, and the inevitable denials of claims, it becomes clear that the revenue cycle plays a critical role in the perceived quality of healthcare.

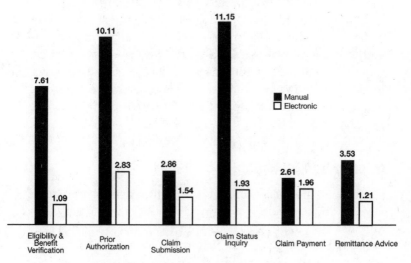

Illustration 6.2 Each of the activities in this illustration represents an opportunity for significant savings. Shown here are data about the cost of an individual transaction in either manual or electronic form. CAQH projects total potential industry savings of moving to a fully electronic process for the revenue cycle at $9.7 billion.[4]

By the way, I've left out the most interesting part of the carburetor analogy. It's the fact that the auto industry created an eminently more reliable and easy-to-adopt solution to carburetors: fuel injection, which completely replaced the archaic, fussy carburetor with computer-controlled electronic jets that did their job perfectly time and time again.

Because of fuel injection, the automobile industry has been able to achieve levels of fuel efficiency that would simply have been impossible otherwise. We've seen the evolution of more responsive engines that can operate for longer intervals between maintenance and which can be computer-controlled to incredibly fine levels of precision using sensors that constantly provide feedback and allow for real-time onboard adjustments.

We're seeing something that is uncannily similar in the evolution of healthcare processes such as the revenue cycle, information technology, and other nonclinical operations in healthcare as providers come to the realization that the methods used to run and maintain in-house operations are unable to scale at the same rate as the increasing complexities of delivering healthcare. In this regard, smartsourcing acts as a means to futureproof a healthcare provider's administrative system.

Information Technology

The second area where John Muir Health is smartsourcing is information technology systems (IT), an area where providers end up building large in-house practices that are perpetually behind the curve given how fast technology is advancing and the struggle to get and retain exceptional IT talent.

It's important here to draw a distinction between the three major categories of IT. The first is support for basic functions such as the help desk and infrastructure (all of the computers, devices, networks, and software). The second is outsourcing the actual processes that are used to support nonclinical functions such as admitting and billing. The third are the processes that are used to support clinical operations such as a patient's EHR and lab and diagnostic test orders. Each of these three is an essential part of running IT; however, the second two—supporting the clinical and nonclinical processes—are not candidates for traditional outsourcing. This is likely why healthcare experienced a steep decline in IT outsourcing after an initial flurry of activity prior to 2004. The lessons learned during that early foray into IT outsourcing are now fueling a second boom of activity.

A *Black Book* study[5] found that 73 percent of all surveyed hospitals and health systems with over three hundred beds and 81 percent of provider organizations under three hundred beds are pursuing IT outsourcing initiatives. According to an article in *Healthcare Finance News*, given that to break even, the average costs of hospitals will have to be reduced by 24 percent by 2022,[6] it's not surprising that interest in IT outsourcing is as high as it is.

However, IT outsourcing in healthcare is not a new phenomenon. Outside of peripheral outsourcing arrangements for basic services—food service, cleaning, laundry—it is the oldest and most-often-outsourced part of healthcare. IT outsourcing itself is over thirty years old. The first instance of a company outsourcing its IT was Kodak in 1989. At that time, one of the principle reasons to outsource was that the number of options for computer hardware and software was outrageously difficult to navigate. A similar, and in some ways even more complicated, situation has taken place in healthcare with the flurry of healthcare-specific technology solutions and devices that need to be managed for even a small provider.

There are well over three hundred thousand consumer apps available for healthcare alone. Over a thousand are for prescribing, diagnosis and treatment, practice management, coding and billing, point of care, drug reference guides, medical calculators, clinical guidelines, literature search portals, simulating medical procedures, and hearing or vision tests. Managing this level of variability is one thing; being able to provide guidance on the best practices is another altogether.

The two biggest risk factors in outsourcing any of these processes are, first, that the majority of providers (73 percent) outsource primarily to gain access to trained staff and technology, and that traditional outsourcing models are based on service level agreements (SLAs), which define in very rigid terms how the sourcing partner's performance will be measured.

Most providers who outsource primarily to obtain access to talent are doing so for one or more of the following reasons: quick wins that lower overall labor costs; help managing peak load demand of a call-support center; or the basic management of their devices, network, and cloud infrastructure. While each of those is a reasonable objective, none of them are innovative. Instead they each preserve the status quo of current processes. It's important to point out that this sort of outsourcing arrangement always has a relatively short contractual timeframe of about five years, which means that the process and overhead of selecting an outsourcing partner repeats regularly.

The second risk is a poorly defined service level agreement. Having an SLA in place is essential since performance metrics need to be in place for those tasks where there are explicit ways in which to measure success. These may include uptime of network and computer resources, backup and recovery of data, security, and response time.

While what I just described may work for something like a help desk, where first-call close rates and customer satisfaction can be measured, or a network that is measured based on uptime, it does not work in cases where ongoing innovation of the process is needed because innovation, by definition, changes the performance metrics.

Even in the case of something as well established as EHRs, providers need to be especially careful to identify a smartsourcing partner that's willing to understand the organizational and human factors that are critical to the successful use of technology in a clinical setting. They also need to work cooperatively with the provider and users to create systems that not only support existing systems, but work toward innovations that support a future model that is better aligned with the provider's longer-term objectives—for instance, being more patient-centered.

A seminal article by Drs. Patrick Ober and William Applegate, "The Electronic Health Record: Are We the Tools of Our Tools?," described the reaction of a medical resident to the EHR's role in a clinical setting.

> *What had always been considered to be the most immutable aspect of medicine was under assault. The patient was no longer the most important thing in the examining room. The machine, rather than the patient, had become the center of the doctor's focus. "I can remember my first encounter with one of my clinic patients using Epic," our house officer observed. "It was possibly one of the lowest times of my residency. Armed with this Rolls Royce of EHRs, I felt miles away from my patient." Our resident, in his wisdom, pointed out that our disgruntlement with the EHR was not simply a product of imperfect software or an error-laden*

code that was hurriedly being patched. The distress was seated much deeper. It was visceral. It arose from the medical profession witnessing an undermining of what has always been the soul of medicine, the doctor patient relationship.[7]

Outsourcing the implementation of technology may work in a purely transactional industry, such as retail, but not in the practice of medicine, which is ultimately about the use of technology to support the care of the patient. This may seem too subtle a point. It's not.

In my own experience leading the innovation lab at Perot Systems from 2004-2007, I saw firsthand the enormous impact that healthcare IT outsourcing could have, but also the significant challenge it presented. In 2009, Perot was ranked as the leading provider of IT outsourcing solutions to healthcare. Much of that was due to having a deep competency in technology and to its approach to smartsourcing, which focused on building intimate partnerships with providers that delivered innovative value.

What I learned in that time was that while IT may be an obvious area to outsource, it is also one of the most important areas for developing a deep partnership that recognizes the importance of long-term innovation on the part of the sourcing partner. One of the principle influences for the original *Smartsourcing* book was observing the critically important role of a trusted partner as a co-innovator.

The idea behind a smartsourcing partnership was to include innovation reviews as a mandatory part of the ongoing relationship. These reviews would involve monthly, in some cases weekly, reviews of both incremental and disruptive innovations that could be used to create greater value for the processes being smartsourced and recommendations to innovate ancillary processes that were not within the original scope of the relationship or which did not even exist when the relationship was first defined.

One last thing to point out is the critical importance of smartsourcing in defending against cyber threats. In 2019, cyberattacks will cost the healthcare sector $4 billion. The average cost to recover from one cyberattack is $1.4 million.[8]

In a cybersecurity leadership class I teach at Boston University, I've presented students with the hypothetical case of a hospital that has suffered a ransomware attack which results in patients' lives hanging in the balance. In the simulation, doctors are pleading with IT and the hospital's administration to do whatever it takes before patients suffer the real-life consequences of the attack. IT is scrambling to figure out a way to decrypt patient records and bring a hacked CT scanner back online while administrators are loath to pay up for fear of giving in to someone so blatantly unethical as to hold the well-being of patients in the balance. Many of my students would react to the exercise with the same sort of doubt: "Who could possibly do something so unethical?" Then, in 2017, the WannaCry ransomware attack hit global health systems with a particular focus on Britain's National Health Service. The simulation was no longer hypothetical. WannaCry would disable access to a hospital's IT systems until a ransom was paid in Bitcoin cryptocurrency. At least 180,000 British Pounds were paid[9] to attackers by hospitals that desperately needed to get back online in order to regain access to clinical and nonclinical systems.

The EHR has become one of the most valuable prizes for hackers. According to Experian, a complete electronic health record can sell on the dark web for as much as $1,000. Compare that with the value of an SSN at $1, or credit card at $30.[10] The ways in which this data can be used are as creative as they are terrifying. One situation reported in the

UK's *Independent* recounted how a senior security threat researcher at IBM, John Kuhn, had his EHR stolen, and was billed $20,000 for a stomach surgery that he hadn't had. As it turns out, his record had been sold to someone who did in fact have surgery while passing himself off as John. John had to show his stomach to the hospital staff to prove that he had not had the surgery.[11]

The challenge in dealing with cyber threats is that they require dedicated resources with the ability to use the most advanced threat detection technologies, identify risks across an entire industry, and constantly reinvest in innovation. Few, if any, hospitals or hospital systems have that level of competency, technology, industry-wide perspective, and dedication to keep up with the fast-changing landscape of cybercrime.

Some of the most important questions to ask in selecting a smartsourcing partner are:

- How do I attract and retain talent for IT positions that are in high demand across so many industries? For John Muir Health, this was an especially challenging proposition, since they are located near Silicon Valley, one of the most competitive parts of the world for IT talent. Imagine having to compete against Google, Facebook, Apple, and uncounted startups that are all vying to attract and retain the best and brightest IT professionals. A smartsourcing partner can provide these individuals with a career track, peer comradery, and upward mobility within their profession—something even the largest hospitals would be unable to do.

- How do I ensure continuous innovation of information systems beyond agreed-upon SLAs and other metrics meant to measure performance against current systems and processes?

- How do I leverage the best practices and experiences of other providers in building a world-class set of solutions that will keep pace with the constantly changing opportunities and demands of new technologies, applications, and user experiences?

- How will they provide world-class protection from the increasing menace and risk of cyber threats?

Ultimately, the objectives of every provider considering partnering to smartsource IT should be to first reduce the number of internally controllable costs by shifting them to externally coordinated costs, and second, to transfer the internal burden of noncore IT to the partner. Over time, this means that the role of the chief information officer (CIO) changes from the owner of all IT processes to a coordinator of internal and external IT processes.

Data Analytics

One of the fastest-growing areas for healthcare, and an area of focus for John Muir Health in better understanding trends among its local population, is that of data analytics. In healthcare, data analytics is the use of large collections of data about either individual patients or patient populations, which are used to better understand the current healthcare needs of patients, to evaluate the provider's performance in meeting those needs and to predict future healthcare trends and risks.

Analyzing data to perform these tasks is not a new concept. One of the reasons for using the ICD codes we talked about in chapter 3 is to provide classifications that can be used to better understand healthcare trends among large populations in regional and global contexts. For example, a hospital may want to identify all of its high-risk patients for certain diseases, such as diabetes, in order to determine if it is correctly aligned with its patients' needs.

What is new is the amount of data available about both the individual patient and the population at large. As much as 30 percent of all data that exists today is attributed to the healthcare industry. That's approximately seven zettabytes or seven million million terabytes! The healthcare industry has the greatest year-over-year growth rate of any other industry, at 36 percent compound annual growth rate.

The problem in fully leveraging that data, however, is threefold. First, the majority of it resides in the many separate silos of both providers and payers. Second, patient-specific data does not always follow the patient from provider to provider and payer to payer, so there is no "patient record." Rather, there are uncounted "patient records." Third, outside of government entities that look at broad trends for public health and policy, such as the Centers for Disease Control (CDC) and the World Health Organization (WHO), no single entity is responsible for identifying how all of this data is connected.

Even within a single provider's system or network, the way in which data is stored and accessed may vary widely. Although larger hospital systems (what we've called the behemoths) can exert substantial pressure on their health-care system members to use a single EHR, that still doesn't mean that the data in the EHR is being adequately protected and analyzed.

In addition to the data that providers and payers possess, there are now numerous startups gaining traction that produce wearable sensors and mobile devices used to track patient behaviors and integrate them with provider data.

For example, Madison, Wisconsin-based Propeller Health uses a sensor that attaches to an inhaler that can be linked to a smartphone to track a patient's use of their inhaler for asthma and chronic obstructive pulmonary disease (COPD).

The data is then shared with the provider or merged with data from the CDC to identify triggers, such as high pollen counts in a particular geography, and proactively manage these conditions. According to Propeller's CEO, David Van Sickle:

> We've always cared deeply about the individual burden of managing a chronic disease, and now we have an opportunity to help foster yet another community of people who are in this together, individuals and their families who are trying to manage a debilitating disease, and empower them to achieve a better quality of life, learning from what others like you have discovered.
>
> Plus, there's a ton of healthcare reform happening in the Medicare market and among ACOs (Accountable Care Organizations), and there's a real need among many providers and payers to focus on their Medicare population, many of whom have COPD. It's an important economic disease category for them. The cost to the nation to care for people with COPD is now $50 billion, with $30 billion in direct healthcare expenditures.
>
> About half of the patients who seek treatment in the ER for COPD report having had symptoms for at least four days. So, there's a lot of incentive among our customers to focus on COPD among their 65 and older members, to help them avoid the ER in the first place [hospitals aren't typically reimbursed for readmissions for the same illness that occur within thirty days].

Mobile and wearable solutions such as Propeller's may end up being among the greatest sources of data and trusted evidence about a patient's disease's progression, their behaviors, and adherence to a prescribed therapy or a pharmaceutical. But again, progress is stifled by the existence of myriad unconnected repositories of data. Simple standards for data interchange, such as the X12 standard for transmission of data between providers and payers, only define the way a subset of data needs to be formatted for interchange. The data still has to be mapped to the specifics of every provider's and payer's in-house data storage standards. In other words, the goal of creating a coordinated and comprehensive view of the patient continues to be elusive.

With a 36 percent yearly growth rate, the volumes of data involved in healthcare data analytics require a level of investment that is well beyond the resources of even the largest healthcare providers. However, what smartsourcing and the HSP can offer is the ability to manage this mushroom cloud of data and to integrate it with a provider's existing systems in order to create a 360-degree view of the patient. Providers can then augment the population data for their community with a much broader set of data that has been anonymized and represents data gathered across multiple providers. In the case of Optum, an independent division of UnitedHealth Group that provides smartsourcing solutions to healthcare providers, the HSP has over 250 million such records that can be used to identify historical, real-time, and predictive trends in population health.

The following are the primary areas where smartsourcing at John Muir Health will play a critical role in leveraging the use of data analytics.

Admissions Data and Staffing

One of the largest challenges hospital administrators face is determining and projecting staffing levels. Most providers still do this based on the recommendations of clinical personnel, such as a nurse manager or a shift supervisor. For example, one nurse I spoke with insisted that staffing always needs to take a full moon into account. These decisions can be more intuitive than they are evidence-based.

The irony is that all of the data needed to track admissions, the patient journey, diagnosis, treatments, and staffing needs to attend to a patient are already being captured, but not integrated in a way that allows evidence-based recommendations to be made from analysis. Longer-term trends can also be gleaned from the analysis of historical data using what's referred to as "time series analysis" and is basically identifying trends over time that are triggered or related to environmental or contextual factors. For instance, increases in ER admissions for seasonal high pollen counts.

Readmissions

Another way that this data is useful is in determining factors for readmissions. The ACA imposes strict penalties through CMS for readmissions within a thirty-day window. From 2013 until 2017, that cost to hospitals alone rose from $290 to $528 million. In 2019, Medicare cut reimbursements to 2,583 hospitals due to their having exceeded allowable readmission guidelines.[12] The value of data analytics in managing readmissions comes from the ability to identify patients who have a higher likelihood of readmission in order to provide adequate care and interventions to either reduce readmissions or to identify when they are warranted due to medical necessity.

For example, the University of Washington used data analytics (an algorithm they dubbed the "Risk-o-Meter") to identify which congestive heart failure patients were likely to be readmitted to the hospital inside of the thirty-day readmission period. The algorithm uses a form of AI to rank patients. The predictive models used both qualitative and quantitative metrics such as body-mass index (BMI), blood pressure, age, gender, and other illnesses or conditions the patient may have. The results are presented as a simple color-coded risk score of yellow, red, or green.

In the case of smaller community hospital systems, such as John Muir Health, it's not just the penalties for readmissions which are at issue, but just as important is that because these hospitals are local providers, patients are much more likely to use the emergency department as a source of primary care. Being able to identify these patients in advance and to then undertake the proper interventions to help them is critical for both the health of the patient and making the best use of the hospital's resources.

Real-Time Alerts and Clinical Decision Support

The use of data as a predictor of clinical events or high-risk situations is an area where healthcare is lagging behind many other industries. In transportation, for example, real-time telemetry has been significant in reducing the cost of commercial transport (trains, rail, airplanes) and increasing reliability. As is the case for Propeller Health's inhaler monitors, some personal devices can capture real-time data in the field and transmit it to a patient's PCP, who can then take action to support the patient's well-being. As we already saw in this example, this may be one of the most significant shifts in how data is used in medicine. Consider that up to 30 percent of all healthcare costs have been attributed to missed or incorrectly diagnosed conditions, creating a total yearly waste of $750 billion![13]

Enhanced Patient Engagement and Physician Relationship

As we saw in the earlier case of the medical resident who was beyond frustrated with the way in which an EHR distanced him from the patient, the unintended consequence of many technologies used in the administration of healthcare can be to create a more frustrating and less efficient experience for both the patient and the clinician. A smartsourced solution should consider the importance of preserving the patient-physician relationship while also increasing the quality of outcomes. One way this can be achieved is by using some of the already-mentioned approaches to enhance the patient's engagement in his or her healthcare. Most people using a smartphone or a wearable device today are accustomed to tracking their daily steps. It's a small step (unavoidable pun) to go from that to devices that encourage the patient to track other habits and behaviors that can aid the patient's physician in diagnosing illnesses, diseases, or risk factors. For instance, poor sleep habits and an elevated heart rate are often indicators of long-term cardiovascular problems.

Longitudinal Patient Analysis and Disease Cures

This last point is one that represents what could well be the holy grail of data analytics. I recall several years ago, when I was working with several individuals who ran the Partners HealthCare Research and Venture Licensing group (RVL). One of the topics they were discussing at the time was the critical importance of longitudinal patient data which could be used to identify issues within a population that no researcher would know to ask about. In a large longitudinal data set, AI and pattern-matching algorithms can be used to locate patterns that are invisible to human analysts and data scientists. These observations could lead to cures for some of today's deadliest diseases, such as cancer. A blue-ribbon panel under the Obama administration identified this as one of the top priorities of cancer research.[14]

Ambulatory Care

The final area where John Muir Health will be relying on smartsourcing to move into the future is also one of the most significant trends in medicine, especially as it applies to the changing role of the hospital: that of ambulatory care. We've referred to ambulatory care on several occasions so far. Simply put, it is the care of patients without the need for admission to a hospital. There are two ways to think of ambulatory care. One is the traditional type of care given in a clinical setting, such as a doctor's office, a walk-in clinic, an urgent care center, or an outpatient surgical setting. The other includes nontraditional settings such as a virtual setting, or via connected sensors and wearable or home-based diagnostic equipment, in digital kiosks, or home visits by doctors and clinicians. In either case, the aim is to minimize the need for overnight stays in a hospital.

Unfortunately, the mistaken notion of ambulatory care that many people have was reinforced when hospitals started to put up billboards with what were promised to be real-time ER wait times posted. For many larger hospitals, the ER is a feeder to hospital admissions. Even if that was not that case, and if we were to assume that the wait times are always accurate (something that's frequently contested),[15] driving patients to the ER is the last thing the healthcare system should be doing, since it is also the costliest, least convenient, and most resource-intensive use of healthcare.

During a single year, there are 130 million ER visits. That comes to about 43 visits per 100 persons (this doesn't mean 43 percent of people, since many people will visit an ER multiple times each year).[16] The number of these visits that is avoidable is hotly debated. One study found that between 13.8 and 27.1 percent of visits are avoidable and could be treated within other ambulatory settings.[17] Another widely quoted study puts that at 3.3 percent.[18]

Whatever the case, it is clear that at an average cost of just under $1,400 per visit, the ER contributes approximately $130 billion to the annual cost of healthcare. The objective of ambulatory care is to provide less costly and more effective ways to address the healthcare needs of a population, and an industry, that has become addicted to the ER.

Keep in mind that none of this means hospitals are going away, but rather that their role is changing from being centers of diagnosis and observation to centers of caring for the most critically ill. This is also not just an issue of costs. While hospital admission is among the most expensive forms of diagnosis and treatment, with an average three-day stay coming in at $30,000,[19] it is also one of the least effective ways to provide care for patients who often present the greatest risk and overall cost to a provider.

For example, John Muir Health has a contract with Humana, a large health insurer, for 7,500 Medicare patients. However, 250 of those patients account for 51 percent of all costs for the entire group. According to Mike Thomas, EVP and chief transformation officer at John Muir Health, the typical path for these patients has been to admit them, observe them, discharge them, and then readmit them. It's a vicious cycle that drives up costs and does little to put the patient on a long-term trajectory for wellness.

The challenge in shifting to an ambulatory model of care with these patients requires identifying who they are and then delivering services in a way that acknowledges the different nature of their care. At John Muir Health, that means creating collaborative, multi-disciplined case management teams that will meet with these patients for up to an hour (versus the typical fifteen-minute visit), evaluate the full complexity of the case, and counsel the patient on their best healthcare options. This will be done as often as needed, even weekly. The result is not only more personalized, but can also be delivered at a fraction of the cost of hospitalization and with far better outcomes.

Effective ambulatory care also ties back to the importance of having the ability to segment a patient population in ways that allow a provider to identify the high-risk categories of patients and also build treatment programs that are uniquely suited to each population segment. That means that John Muir Health is analyzing a broad range of data about its patients in order to identify the healthcare needs of specific groups. That may mean that patients happen to work for the same employer, reside in the same geography, or have the same socioeconomic context.

Another way in which ambulatory care is changing has to do with a topic we brought up earlier, the decline of the use of the PCP model. Recall that we talked about how many patients have shunned the PCP, due either to economic pressures, or, in the case of millennials, changing ethos and attitudes regarding the necessity for a PCP.

Much of this is driven by the fact that we are increasingly experiencing what's termed a multi-channel engagement model in virtually every other aspect of how we interact with product and service providers. It's a given that phone-based, web-based, mobile texting and in-app messaging, or email self-service should be part of any consumer experience. But multi-channel is about more than the option to alternate between whichever channel is most convenient at the time. The more important aspect of it is that the customer journey should follow you through all of those channels in one continuous thread.

So, for example, if you visit your doctor at her office and then call to speak with the on-call doctor later that evening, you would expect that both doctors would have access to your health record. The same should apply to a clinician, such as a nurse, involved in home care, who should have access to all of the patient's relevant information remotely in the patient's home. This ability to access patient data should apply to any combination of channels over any period of time. This goes back to the importance of creating continuity of care rather than remaining subject to the effects of Culprit #3, The Episodic Care Conundrum.

Having this sort of continuity of care requires more than sharing the same EHR; it means having an entire ecosystem whose technology infrastructure supports the patient throughout their clinical and administrative journey.

Trying to do any of what I just described without a smartsourcing partnership in place would be next to impossible for the vast majority of hospitals and hospital systems, which is why the case for smartsourcing is so important to make. Ambulatory care is not just an interesting adjunct to the healthcare system, it represents a fundamental shift in how patients experience healthcare, the quality and personalization of the care they receive, the way in which care is delivered to differing segments of the population, and the quality of outcomes. This is nothing less than a switch from the industrial era of one-size-fits-all healthcare to an era of hyperpersonalized medicine available anytime, anywhere.

IN SICKNESS AND IN HEALTH, CHAPTER 6: RECAP AND LESSONS LEARNED

In this chapter, we focused on ways in which smartsourcing and HSPs can be used to help providers remove the distraction of noncore operations in order to both better focus on their core and innovate their noncore. We used John Muir Health, a Northern California community hospital as a model for how and where providers can apply smartsourcing and HSP partnerships.

We introduced the term "holographic organization," to reflect a health system that is integrated so well that any part of the overall system reflects the values, mission, and process of the entire system.

We also looked at four areas where John Muir Health is smartsourcing: the revenue cycle, IT, data analytics, and ambulatory care, and discussed how each of these are prime candidates for smartsourcing in providers struggling with or distracted from their core by administrative processes.

CHAPTER 7
THE FUTURE OF HEALTHCARE

James Jackson has been a fisherman for his entire life. It's how he supports his family, and to listen to him talk about it, you get a clear sense that it's a source of immense pride for James that he can do what he loves while providing for his family. But all of that nearly ended one morning.

As James was getting ready to go to work, he found himself unsteady. After inexplicably stumbling twice, he realized something wasn't right and headed to the local ER, where James was told that he had chronic kidney disease which would require him immediately starting dialysis.

A typical dialysis regimen requires three days a week of four hours each hooked up to a dialysis machine, which does the critical work of filtering toxins from the blood that is otherwise performed by healthy kidneys. Like many

> As she reviewed his record, it became apparent to Cherie that something about his medication list didn't make sense.

people who are facing the prospect of dialysis, James considered how drastically his life would change being tethered to a machine as his lifeline for three days out of the week. His career and his livelihood were in jeopardy. He was devastated.

Today, chronic kidney disease affects one out of seven adults[1] and it takes more than fifty thousand lives each year,[2] more than breast or prostate cancer. It's called the silent killer since it often shows no symptoms until it's too late to do anything other than dialysis or a kidney transplant. Both are expensive; however, the lifetime costs, outcomes, and quality of life are all far better if transplantation is an option taken early—ideally before dialysis starts.

The costs for either option are steep. An uninsured kidney transplantation averages $260,000. Yearly costs for dialysis range from $40,000–$72,000. However, dialysis has risks. The longer a patient stays on dialysis, the greater the risks of kidney failure, cardiovascular problems, and infections.[3] According to Ty Dunn, MD, surgical director of kidney and pancreas transplantation at Penn Medicine's Transplant Institute, "Not many people live more than ten years on dialysis. On the other hand, I tell patients that they can expect, on average, fourteen to sixteen years of function from a kidney that comes from a living donor. In low-risk patients who do well that first year following the transplant and who really take care of themselves, that number can reach twenty years or more."

James was fortunate. His case manager, Cherie Jones, an RN and certified diabetes educator, was using a case management system that relied on an AI-enabled predictive capability from Optum. When James's record flashed on her screen's inbox of patient work for the day, a predictive algorithm indicated that he had markers for end-stage renal disease (ESRD). As she reviewed his record, it became apparent to Cherie that something about his medication list didn't make sense. She ordered additional lab tests for James, which showed that his kidney function was clearly diminished but holding strong enough that dialysis wasn't needed. Knowing that transplants after dialysis were rare, she immediately reached out to James, who had already had the equipment for home dialysis delivered to his house and was waiting to begin his treatments. Cherie explained to James that not only did he not yet need dialysis, but that if they managed his condition carefully, he stood a much better chance for a successful transplant. Shortly thereafter, James received his transplant from a living donor and is now once again living a normal life.

James's example is the way healthcare should work; by using data in the context of a patient's history, applying advanced analytics to flag cases that need to be further evaluated, and then taking informed action in order to achieve the best outcomes for the patient while simultaneously reducing costs, everyone benefits.

The challenge is to extend the sort of care that James received to everyone who is in a situation where complex coordination of data about the patient, the options available, and the risks involved can be balanced to achieve the best possible outcomes.

While James's experience is not yet the standard of care that we may expect, it is going in the right direction—the direction we set out on when I said in chapter 1 that healthcare is on the precipice of enormous transformation, which will bring unprecedented opportunity to positively impact our quality of life in dramatic ways.

James's case is just a glimpse of what that future will look like. In this chapter, we'll take a look at some of the other ways that smartsourcing, HSPs, and hospital transformation will create new opportunities to deliver higher-quality healthcare that's both affordable and accessible.

As we do that, it's important to keep in mind that fixing US healthcare is not so much a destination as it is an ongoing journey. There is no single static solution, policy, or business model that will "fix" healthcare since both the technologies of healthcare and the needs of the populations it serves are constantly changing. The objective of healthcare should be to adapt to these changing needs by improving the rate at which we can innovate healthcare and then make these innovations available to the broadest possible population. That has been and always will be a process of evolution.

> ...what needs to be factored into that conversation is that today's healthcare system is simply not built to deal with a future in which today's demographic minority becomes tomorrow's majority.

As we find cures for some diseases, we will undoubtedly be faced with new challenges. As medicine extends our lifespan, we will need to also extend the quality of those extra years. That will cost more; it's the price we will need to pay for the benefit of living longer, more productive, and more enjoyable lives. But that doesn't mean that the price we will pay has to include all of the inefficiencies and constraints of the industrial-era model of healthcare that we are saddled with today. The assumptions that we have built the healthcare system around over the past one hundred years have changed dramatically, as have the tools and technologies available for the practice of medicine.

Stop and consider that only 54 percent of men in 1935 could expect to live to the age of sixty-five. Today that number is 80 percent.[4] If you lived till sixty-five in 1940 (the first year Social Security benefits were paid out), you could expect to collect for thirteen years. Today you would collect for twenty years.[5]

As life expectancy increases, so will the numerous coexisting conditions that an older population has to deal with. As our ability to diagnose and treat diseases increases, so will the cost associated with these illnesses. For example, a gene therapy for cystic fibrosis, announced as this book is being written, promises to benefit 90 percent of patients with the disease. The cost of the treatment is $300,000 a year.[6]

The challenge is that as the demographic changes, the new technologies we've talked about will continue to drive up the cost of healthcare. On the one hand, we could rightfully say that such is the responsibility of a civilized society. However, what needs to be factored into that conversation is that today's healthcare system is simply not built to deal with a future in which today's minority becomes tomorrow's majority.

According to a 2017 report by the National Academy of Medicine, over 50 percent of US healthcare spending is for only 5 percent of all patients, and 20 percent is for the sickest 1 percent of patients.[7] (See Illustration 7.1.) These patients, defined as "high-needs" patients, are increasing rapidly as the over-sixty-five cohort also increases. Today, 55 percent of those over sixty-five are considered high-needs patients (with three or more chronic diseases and functional limitations). If that trend continues (as we first said in chapter 2) and the sixty-five-and-older cohort doubles to make up half of the US population by 2060, we will have as many patients in the high-needs category as we have total patients today.

Based on that trend, the US healthcare system will grow

> ...over 50 percent of US healthcare spending is for only 5 percent of all patients, and 20 percent is for the sickest 1 percent of patients.

to the point where it constitutes nearly 40 percent of the US government's yearly spending by 2040 (Illustration 7.2). Keep in mind that this does not take into account all of the money spent on US healthcare, just the portion spent by the government.

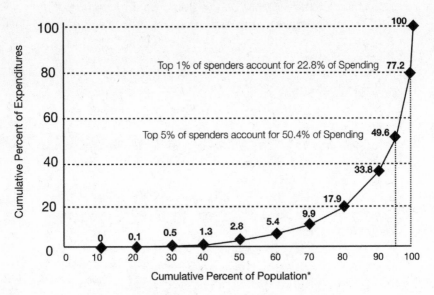

Cumulative Healthcare Expenditures by Percent of Population

Source: https://meps.ahrq.gov/data_files/publications/st506/stat506.shtml
*Cumulative percent of non-institutionalized civilian population

Illustration 7.1 Healthcare costs are dramatically skewed toward the sickest of the patient population, with 1 percent of patients accounting for 22.8 percent of all healthcare spending and the top 5 percent accounting for 50.4 percent of spending on healthcare.[8]

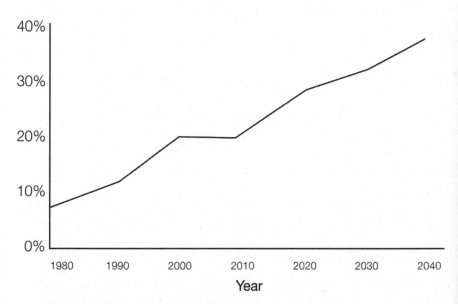

Federal Healthcare Spending as a Percent of the Federal Budget

Source: Committee for a Responsible Federal Budget

Illustration 7.2 Under the federal government's current policies the Congressional Budget Office projects that the share of the federal budget spent on mandatory healthcare programs will increase from less than 10 percent in 1980 to just under 40 percent in 2040.

It all points to the unyielding fact that we've repeated often in the book: the industrial-era model of healthcare is simply no longer sustainable. Tomorrow's healthcare, hospitals, and doctors will have the same mission that they have always had, to keep us healthy and to heal us when we're not. But tomorrow's healthcare, hospitals, and doctors will not look like what we have today; to survive, they can't.

That may sound like a tough future to predict, but there are some aspects of it that are already coming into focus. Four

> ...we still want to feel the very human presence and emotional connection of a physician or nurse face-to-face with us as we have difficult and complex discussions about our health.

of those will most define the landscape for change over the coming decades. These are what I call the Disruptors: The Existentialists, Ambulatory Care, Personal Digital Advocates, and The Hospital in the Cloud.

Although these four areas do not represent a comprehensive review of the technologies or innovations that will shape the future of healthcare, they are key to aligning it with the changing needs of patients, the evolution of HSPs, smartsourcing, and the transformation of hospitals.

One thing to keep in mind as we delve into some of these disruptors is that while technology increasingly gives us ways to be nonlocal in how we engage with healthcare providers, the notion of a hospital, a doctor's office, or a clinic as the place we go to get healthy does not go away. There are many things that technology cannot yet circumvent, and foremost among them is the plain and simple fact that we are humans made of flesh and blood who still need the locality of medicine, diagnostics, and surgical centers. And, perhaps most importantly, we still want to feel the very human presence and emotional connection of a physician or nurse face-to-face with us as we have difficult and complex discussions about our health.

I could easily go far afield in this last chapter and describe how technology will make this physicality moot with the advent of therapies that cure diseases at the level of our genome and obviate surgery, how holographic images will replace the physical presence of a physician, or how autonomous clinical robots, driven in autonomous vehicles, will perform home visits for the elderly.

I'm as tantalized by these futures as anyone else, and I have little doubt that many of us will someday live in that future, and that it will be far stranger than anything I could predict here. But I'll leave that to the science fiction writers for now. The focus of this book, and the promise I made at the outset, is to look at the practical application of technologies and methods that would put US healthcare on the right track within the next five to ten years. And that's where I'd like to keep our focus as we close out this last chapter.

The Existentialists

The greatest threat of disruption for any industry typically comes from outsiders—those who are unencumbered by the legacy of the past and have no sacred turf on which to tread lightly. And few industries are as ripe for disruption as healthcare. It's a $3.5 trillion-dollar industry, one of the largest line items on most people's personal budgets, a source of continuous frustration for patient-customers, an industry that's constantly criticized in the media for its inefficiency, an increasing burden on the bottom line of nearly every business, and, as we've seen throughout this book, desperately in need of innovation. So, it's hardly a surprise that many of the largest tech companies in the US have strategies in place to play in the healthcare space. Discounting the impact these hyperscale tech players will have on healthcare is a proven folly.

The book-selling and publishing business was not disrupted from within its ranks. The music industry wasn't upended by a large record label. The movie and cable entertainment industry wasn't disrupted by a major Hollywood studio. Amazon, Apple, and Netflix were all outsiders that

> Just consider that each person will generate enough healthcare data during their lifetime to fill three hundred million books.

were barely taken seriously by incumbents in each of these industries, and yet they were able to not only change the business models in each case, but also create customer experiences that were unimaginable before they came along.

In the case of healthcare, a very similar scenario is starting to play itself out. Over the next five years, tech giants such as Google, Apple, Amazon, and even Facebook will step in and attempt to use their scale, technologies, and most importantly, their access to behavioral data to create new approaches to how the patient-customer engages with the healthcare system.

The scale of the opportunity eclipses anything we can today imagine. Just consider that each person will generate enough healthcare data during their lifetime to fill three hundred million books.[9]

The three areas where these companies, and many others that are lesser known—for now—will have the greatest impact are likely to be wearables and monitoring, behavioral and lifestyle data and risk, and data storage and analytics.

Wearables and Monitoring

By 2022, over 25 percent of the US adult population will have a wearable health-tracking device.[10] Unlike their early counterparts, which simply stored data having to do with distance walked, stairs climbed, hours of sleep, or calories burned, today's devices are (or soon will be) able to monitor vital signs, blood sugar, potassium, and oxygen levels, take ECGs, and even detect certain cancers.

That's all very impressive, but what's missing is a clear connection from the device to the patient's record, and ultimately to provider systems. If I tell my doctor during my annual physical that my Apple Watch shows an arrhythmia, his response is not going to be "let me take a look at your Apple Watch," but "let's do an EKG in the office." However, that's going to change over the next few years as the value of that real-time data becomes apparent. Apple is already working with providers such as Stanford University School of Medicine to study the accuracy and impact of an Apple Watch wearable ECG monitor on 419,000 participants.[11]

What we are creating with these devices, in an ad hoc manner, is a shadow medical record, or what *Wired* magazine writers Kevin Kelly and Gary Wolf first called the Quantified Self in 2007.[12] Over time, the volume and value of this data will increase dramatically. According to Statista, global wearable monthly data traffic has increased from 15 petabytes per month in 2015 to 335 petabytes per month in 2020. The question will soon be, how is the value of that data realized and who benefits from it? Providers certainly aren't oblivious to its value. At Atrium Health, formerly Carolinas HealthCare System, data from up to seventy different health tracking devices can be stored by patients as part of their medical record.[13]

> If providers are reluctant to embrace it and collaborate with technology vendors who develop [wearables], it will only accelerate the move to patient-owned electronic healthcare records.

> ...anyone who's ever owned a wearable that tracks even their most basic activity in the form of steps taken, miles walked, or calories burned has experienced the slight effects of behavioral modification resulting from the regular reminders from their wearable on their progress toward goals.

As wearables become more sophisticated in their diagnostic applications and the data they produce more comprehensive and reliable, consumers (and technology vendors) will have more data about their health-care than their healthcare providers. One study by the AMA on digital health found that although 85 percent of doctors saw the potential benefit of wear-able technology, less than 30 percent were using it with their patients.[14] It's inevitable, however, that over time, this data will prove much too valuable to ignore, at least for the patient if not the provider. If providers are reluctant to embrace wearables and collaborate with technology vendors who develop these devices, it will only accelerate the move to patient-owned electronic healthcare records (something we talk about later in this chapter). Given the propensity of millennials to shun PCPs, expect that the power to use this data in a self-service approach to medicine will end up being a point of serious contention if it's not addressed through progressive approaches on the part of providers to integrate wearable technology and data with the model of a far more ambulatory healthcare system.

Behavioral Data, Lifestyle, and Noncompliance

With the prevalence of patient-owned data from wearables, we will also have more available data from which to identify patterns that provide valuable data about lifestyles and habits. This has always been one of the hardest areas of patient engagement for doctors to manage. Many clinicians see even offering advice on lifestyle to be outside of their scope of responsibility or believe that it simply will not be followed. Only a slight majority of physicians (61 percent) and nurses (53 percent) said they always offer such advice.[15]

According to the CDC, only one out of four patients who are prescribed drugs for high blood pressure actually take them, and 20–30 percent never even have their prescription filled. A 2012 report by U.S. Surgeon General, Regina M. Benjamin, estimated the total healthcare costs of medication non-adherence to be between $100 and $300 billion a year.[16] This also results in direct costs of $500 billion for hospitals that are penalized by Medicare for readmissions.

There's more to this problem than wearables can fully address. Much of it comes down to a basic distrust of pharmaceutical companies and an inherent unwillingness to change lifestyle. However, anyone who's ever owned a wearable that tracks even their most basic activity in the form of steps taken, miles walked, or calories burned has experienced the slight effects of behavioral modification resulting from the regular reminders from their wearable on their progress toward goals. The other, and perhaps more powerful, behavioral modification technique is that of peer groups. Many users of wearables join informal groups that compete for the most activity in a day, week, or month. In my own case I was recently (proudly) comparing my Apple Watch activity statistics with a friend's when he suggested we compete for steps and promptly sent me a request to do so. In the spirit of full transparency, and with a bit of irony, I'm ignoring the request until this book is done.

This, too, is part of how the notion of healthcare is changing from a relationship purely between provider and patient to one that is diffused into many aspects of our lives that help to improve outcomes but have little to do with the traditional notion of healthcare. Again, the transformation of healthcare is in part something that will need to change from the inside out, but at least as much of that change will come from the existential disruptors that are completely outside of the healthcare industry.

Another novel way in which wearables could be used is as a means of aligning patient-doctor incentives by increasing what's termed healthcare literacy. Simply put, healthcare literacy is the ability of patients to better understand their medical conditions and available options. One way to do that is through the use of wearables and predictive models that help put the doctor and patient on the same page.

For example, one model that's been proposed and researched notifies the patient and the doctor of a health condition after an event recognized by a wearable, after an office visit involving a diagnosis or treatment plan, or whenever a claim is submitted. An algorithm that has access to the patient's EHR uses information about the patient, their history, current condition, and the doctor's findings or diagnosis to identify current evidence-based medicine or health articles related to the patient's condition. The doctor then forwards this information to the patient who, in turn, needs to review the information and then demonstrate adequate knowledge of it. Think of this as a sort of online training program that has a short quiz at the end. Part of the incentive for both doctor and patient to do this is a financial incentive of some nominal but reasonable amount. For example, the patient may have their office visit deductible waived and the doctor may receive some equal amount of compensation.

Although this approach may sound trite, research has shown that forms of it do work in populations that have been studied in controlled tests. In one peer reviewed study published in the Journal of Medical Internet Research, over 1500 patients and 100 physicians were tracked over a five-year period from 2013 through 2017. During that time, hospitalizations and emergency room visit rates per 1000 decreased 32 percent and 14 percent respectively.[17]

...during a 2014 West African outbreak of Ebola in Senegal, mobile data from the French wireless carrier Orange used anonymized and aggregated data from 150,000 customers to identify patterns that emerged and which could be used to identify the pandemic's progress and spread.

Public Health Data Storage and Analytics

In the short term, much of the value and benefit of wearables will come from the two areas we've already talked about. However, there is a longer-term benefit that will eclipse much of what we've already described and which will upturn many of the ways in which the healthcare system provides value in what's termed public health.

According to the American Public Health Association, public health "promotes and protects the health of people and the communities where they live, learn, work and play."[18] This includes a variety of activities from promoting vaccinations, to tracking disease outbreaks, educating people on health risks, safety, and nutrition, to raising awareness about the use of tobacco products and vaping.

...MIT used autonomous robotic devices that crawled through the Boston and Cambridge sewer systems to sample sewage and... provide real-time data about health issues down to the street level of a neighborhood.

Until recently, the tools used to identify public health issues were primarily manual means of data collection through surveys, pools, point-of-care data capture in a clinical setting, pharmaceutical-use data, and self-reported data from patients. All of this made public health an analytical discipline that relied on data from past experiences rather than real-time data. This is broadly called data analytics in healthcare and most other industries that rely on historical data analysis. With the advent of not only wearables and mobile devices but also the proliferation of behavioral tracking through internet-based interactions with social media, GPS, and web search, a new discipline, which I call *prelytics*, or predictive analytics, is emerging.

For example, during a 2014 West African outbreak of Ebola in Senegal, mobile data from the French wireless carrier Orange used anonymized and aggregated data from 150,000 customers to identify patterns that emerged and which could be used to identify the pandemic's progress and spread.[19] (An interactive version of this data shows an up-to-date animation of how the pandemic has spread around the globe and can be found at the URL in the footnote below.)[v] While this data was still retrospective and not real-time, the same approach is being used in real time to track the spread of flu epidemics.[20]

---

v   "Ebola Outbreaks," 2014, https://healthmap.org/ebola/#timeline.

Prelytics is one of the most powerful tools available to the public and the healthcare industry as they overcome one of the greatest sources of friction for most providers: predicting staffing levels, pharmaceuticals, and resources needed to handle what can be significant fluctuations in the capacity needed to address public health issues. The implications of having this sort of real-time data are far-reaching. One project I've seen at MIT used autonomous robotic devices that crawled through the Boston and Cambridge sewer systems to sample sewage and determine the health habits, pathogens, and other fluctuations in these samples that could provide real-time data about health issues down to the street level of a neighborhood.

When I first saw MIT's invention, I was immediately reminded of the 1854 outbreak of cholera in London, which took the lives of more than ten thousand people. A local London physician, Dr. John Snow, is ultimately credited with stopping the epidemic by using data to identify that the predominant cases centered on a water pump located just outside of a home on London's Broad Street, where it was likely that the first case of cholera (the index case) was that of an infected infant girl whose mother had used the cistern outside of her front door on Broad Street to rinse the baby's diarrhea-soaked diapers. The cistern, it appears, was seeping into an adjacent pump used by the community for fresh water. Dr. Snow's recommendation was to simply remove the handle from the pump, something that was at first met with less than enthusiasm by the local board of guardians of St. James's parish, in which Broad Street was based.[21]

Just as interesting is that the only way to determine if shutting down the pump was effective was to wait and see, something which promoted talk about how the outbreak had probably run its course anyway and was not slowed and ultimately stopped due to the pump's handle being removed.

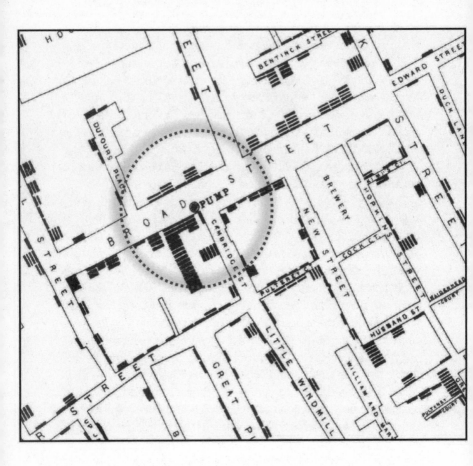

Illustration 7.2.1 Dr. Snow's hand-illustrated map of London's Broad Street and the surrounding area with notations (the short stacked black bars) representing deaths in the area due to symptoms of what was then an unknown epidemic. Note the large bar at the intersection of Broad Street and Cambridge Street and the proximity of the pump used by the community's residents for fresh water. As the story is often told, the pump was operated by cranking a handle up and down. Dr. Snow's solution was to simply to remove the handle. In fact, Dr. Snow's map was not the means through which the cause was determined, but rather meant to simply illustrate and effectively communicate the already assumed causes of the epidemic.

Data analytics hasn't changed much in principle since that time. Sure, we are analyzing amounts of data with computers that dwarf, almost comically, the data available to a nineteenth-century physician, but the process has always been retrospective. And the delta in time between identifying a possible cause of a health issue and taking action to correct it has always made the relationship between cause and effect more difficult to determine. The ability we now have to observe an act in real time is a line of demarcation that, once crossed, opens up entirely new ways to think about the challenges of public health. We can better correlate causes to their effects and treatments to their outcomes.

However, I'll once again bring you back to the question: who will own this data and how will they extract value from it?

Large companies such as Apple, Google, Amazon, JPMorgan, and Berkshire Hathaway are beginning that process by evaluating the option of building their own healthcare networks for their employees in which they are the payers and, in some cases, owners of the providers. The impetus here is that the cost of healthcare has become so steep for large corporations that it is in their best economic interests to build their own solutions. Will these become role models for the rest of the healthcare industry? Will they become competitive weapons for talent in the same way that post-WWII employers used health insurance as a benefit to attract employees?

One thing is certain: the current state of how we use technology to identify health risks and predict health outcomes is falling behind fast. And when that happens, free markets have a way of rectifying the laggards and building new solutions that take the incumbents completely by surprise. Call it the Uber-ization of industry. Uber didn't just refine the taxi experience, it decimated it by reimagining what a frictionless experience would look like.

While all of this existential change is occurring, there is also a great deal of internal change that will be reshaping healthcare.

The Shift to Ambulatory Care

One of the most important and widespread shifts in health-care, which will be enabled by new advances in the technology of remote monitoring, diagnostics, and treatments, is ambulatory care—the move away from inpatient hospital care to outpatient care. Few things will define the line of demarcation from the past into the future of healthcare as profoundly as this fundamental shift in the way healthcare is delivered. Consider that from 1995 to 2016, the average length of stay at a community hospital dropped by 15 percent, from 6.5 days to 5.5 days.[22] Across all community hospitals, the number of inpatient days per 1000 people dropped by 18.75 percent from nearly 800 to approximately 550 (Illustration 7.3).

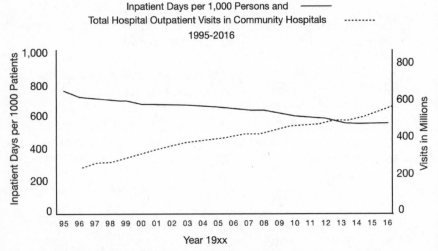

Inpatient Days per 1,000 Persons and ──────
Total Hospital Outpatient Visits in Community Hospitals ·········
1995-2016

Source: Analysis of American Hospital Association Annual Survey for 2016 for community hospitals
US Census Bureau National and State Population Estimates, July 1 2016

Illustration 7.3 As inpatient days per thousand persons have decreased, outpatient visits have increased in almost direct proportion.[23]

At the same time, hospital revenues have been steadily shifting from inpatient to outpatient services (Illustration 7.4). Much of this is enabled by new technologies that allow remote patient monitoring through wearables, sensors, and mobile devices, what are collectively often called the Internet of Things (IoT). Information from IoT-enabled devices and sensors provides not only real-time monitoring capability, but also data which can be used to predict health issues and risks

Comparison of Outpatient vs. Inpatient Revenues 1995-2016

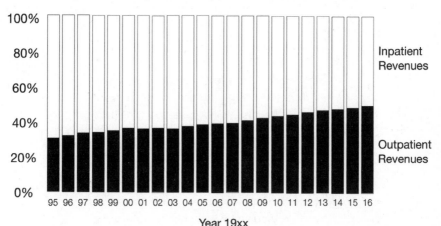

Illustration 7.4 Hospital revenues have been steadily shifting from inpatient to outpatient services.

For example, David Park, the founder and CEO at VirtuSense, which developed sensor-based systems to help prevent falls, described how sensors can have an enormous impact on healthcare for an aging population.

> *In the US alone, one in three seniors reported falling each year. Our mission, simply put, is to reduce falls so seniors can age well. We're*

doing that by deploying predictive and pre- ventive solutions for homes and senior living facilities. We're also planning to deploy these fall prediction and prevention solutions for hospitals. We do it using machine vision, artificial intelligence, and data analytics. The big goal is trying to provide successful aging through innovative technologies and data analytics. This has tremendous impli- cations for the health industry because the mega trend that we're all riding is the aging of our population globally; it's going to impact our society, healthcare, and govern- ment for decades to come.

Albert Einstein College of Medicine studied three hundred to four hundred seniors over more than the three-year time period, and they've determined that if a senior has a gait speed of .7 meters per second or slower, then they are 54 percent more likely to fall over the next twelve months. So, we build gait analysis that observes you during the course of your day. If you're moving slower than that, then a warning is triggered.

The advent of these sorts of remote sensor-based appli- cations enable new pathways for the delivery of healthcare outside of a traditional clinical setting.

But these are not just futuristic scenarios. Home health- care is already an area of intense growth as the population ages. According to the CMS Office of the Actuary, the US Medicare system will spend approximately $108.8 billion on home healthcare in 2019. By 2027, that's expected to reach nearly $190 billion, making home healthcare the fastest-growing segment of Medicare spending.[24] However, what that masks, and the greater problem, is the enormous economic burden that it already creates for informal caregivers.

According to a comprehensive 2015 study by the National Alliance for Caregiving and AARP,[25] there were 43.5 million adults that had been caregivers to an adult or child in the twelve months prior to the study. What's even more startling is that a 2015 AARP report, "Valuing the Invaluable,"[26] estimated the economic value of home caregivers' unpaid contributions at approximately $470 billion in 2017, up from an estimated $375 billion in 2007. To put that into perspective, it's approximately the same as Wal-Mart's total yearly revenues, or about 10 percent of all federal spending.

The strain put on the lives, work routines, and health of these caregivers creates a ripple effect that is much larger than even the direct economic value of their time. Caregivers over the age of fifty experience on average lost wages and benefits of $303,880 during their lifetime, as well as the additional reduction in their Social Security benefits as a result of lower wages.[27] They suffer from increased risk of cardiovascular events due to higher cortisol levels and report higher levels of depressions and psychological illness, and one often-quoted study[28] went so far as to conclude that caregivers had a 63 percent higher chance of mortality than non-caregivers. The label used to describe this is "Caregiver Syndrome," a term first coined by Dr. C. Jean Posner, a neuropsychiatrist in Baltimore, Maryland, who defined caregiver syndrome as "a debilitating condition brought on by unrelieved, constant caring for a person with a chronic illness or dementia."[29]

The graying of the population will only amplify the home healthcare burden on the entire healthcare system as well as the added socioeconomic toll it takes at large.

However, ambulatory care is not without its challenges. According to Ann Scott Blouin, RN, PhD, executive vice president of customer relations at The Joint Commission (an independent, not-for-profit organization that accredits and certifies twenty-two thousand health care organizations and programs in the US) there are at least three areas where ambulatory care presents challenges to the current health-care system.[30]

- Diagnostic errors are more common.

- Test results from earlier inpatient stays often go "astray."

- Inpatient and ambulatory EHRs often don't talk to each other.

As the network of ambulatory care services continues to grow and diffuses healthcare into the community and the home, creating a hospital without walls, we will experience much more opportunity for the creation of friction among all of the touchpoints of these expanded healthcare networks.

Smartsourcing is critical in enabling expanded ambulatory care because it provides greater control over the many administrative aspects of each of these challenges. Ambulatory care, by its very nature, is highly distributed, both geographically and also in terms of the many processes involved, which necessitates a much larger and richer ecosystem of facilities, resources, personnel, touch points, and devices. According to Definitive Healthcare, there are currently 9,280 ambulatory surgical centers (ASCs); that's 1.5 times as many ASCs as there are hospitals. And those ASCs already perform 56 percent[31] of all surgeries. But even this is barely a glimpse of the magnitude of the change to come in ambulatory care as both hospitals and physicians are charged with moving their services closer to the patient. We'll talk more about this virtualization of healthcare later when we look at the hospital in the cloud. But for now, consider what healthcare might look like when consultations, diagnostics, and even many procedures, which now require a clinical setting, take place in the patient's home or an assisted living facility. While it may seem we are far from that sort of reality, that is the direction healthcare is moving in, and the next two innovations will bring us closer to that future.

Digital Healthcare Advocates

One of the most serious flaws in the current healthcare system, which leads to higher costs, redundancy, errors, and episodic care, is the lack of continuity of care and coordinated care for someone who does not have an advocate that can provide critical information when they are physically, emotionally, or cognitively impaired. Consider that patients over sixty-five years of age have seen an average of 28.4 individual doctors during their lifetime, including primary care, specialists, hospital physicians, and urgent care providers.[32] At the same time, the CDC reports that less than 6.3 percent of all doctors use a fully functional EHR in their practice.[33] The combination of those two factors alone would imply that the adequate transfer of patient data among these providers is woefully inadequate.

As the population ages, the prevalence of dementia and related neurological and cognitive diseases among the population will also increase. This creates a mandate to look at advocacy

> The irony is that the worse the illness, the greater the costs and complexity that need to be managed, and the less able the patient is to manage them.

in an entirely different way, as an essential component of the healthcare system.

While EHRs were meant to address this, they only do so within very narrow cases where the patient is already part of a healthcare system and all of his or her diagnostic records, treatments, and medications are available within that same healthcare system. That presents several challenges.

First, people change PCPs regularly, which means that the transfer of records may or may not happen during each of those handoffs. Even in the case of referrals from a PCP to a specialist, over 70 percent of specialists rank the quality of the health records they receive during a transfer as fair or poor.[34]

Second, despite the fact that most providers who have an EHR use one of the two leading systems, Epic or Cerner, even within a single hospital system, there are often differing and incompatible implementations of the same EHR.

Third, payers who may have access to procedures and treatments while they have covered that patient are not necessarily sharing that data with other payers or providers. (CMS has recently proposed changes to MyHealthEData[vi] that are intended to improve patient access and sharing of patient data.)[35]

Dr. Ilana Yurkiewicz, a physician at Stanford University, tells the story of one of her patients, Michael Champion, who was brought in by ambulance when his wife had noticed that Michael had a 102.4-degree fever after a weekend of being increasingly more lethargic.[36]

Michael was a veteran with a history of diabetes and a stroke that had left him with a feeding tube and the need for

---

vi   MyHealthEData is an initiative announced under the Trump administration that aims to empower patients by ensuring that they control their healthcare data and can decide how their data is going to be used.

daily catheters. With his limited ability to communicate, his wife Leah was his advocate—as Dr. Yurkiewicz called her, "a living, breathing medical record."

Dr. Yurkiewicz recounts how after treating Michael, she was meticulous in performing Michael's discharge to rehabilitation care:

> *I typed out a discharge summary outlining each of his medical problems. I spelled out his antibiotics plan. I wrote his new insulin regimen—an additional injection every six hours and extra doses with his tube feeds, on top of his usual morning dose. I summarized what we were thinking, what we had done, and what needed to be done next. Whenever possible, I had learned to bolster that sheet. I used simple and straightforward language. I bolded. I double-checked my medication list. I knew this sheet was often the only guidance a nursing facility would receive. If I didn't write something here, it very often didn't exist.*
>
> *But I also knew that even if I did write it down, it might not be read by the caregivers and health care professionals who would treat him next. And I knew that only fragments of their notes and charts were likely to get passed down the line of Michael's care, too."*

Days later, Michael ended up back in her ER, despite Leah's protestations at the nursing care facility regarding Michael's deteriorating condition. When Dr. Yurkiewicz examined Michael, she found that his blood sugar was four times higher than normal. The insulin Dr. Yurkiewicz had pre-scribed in the transfer was simply not being provided while Michael was at the nursing facility. Reading that, you'd like to think that Michael's situation is a rarity. Dr. Yurkiewicz's comments aren't that comforting. "Sometimes, it's remark-able that things turn out well so much of the time, given all the places they could go wrong."

The complexity of managing patient records and relying on them in many clinical settings is compromised by all of the issues we've outlined: the lack of transferability due to many differing formats and standards that even electronic records are stored in; the inherent mobility of patients through many providers; and the complexity and volume of data and docu-ments in the records themselves.

According to Dr. Yurkiewicz, "When a patient with a complex medical history like Michael arrives under my care, it's like opening a book to page 200 and being asked to write page 201. That can be challenging enough. But on top of that, maybe the middle is mysteriously ripped out, pages 75 to 95 are shuffled, and several chapters don't even seem to be part of the same story."

This lack of continuity of care that this creates is at the heart of the Episodic Care Conundrum that we have been describing throughout the book.

The role of a digital healthcare advocate in this capac-ity would be threefold: to provide continuity of care through access to all of the patient's historical and current healthcare information and to coordinate care with clinical staff, spe-cialists, and the patient's primary care provider (PCP); to provide early warnings of potential health problems based on changes in behavior and habits that could be indicative of an underlying undiagnosed condition; and to monitor the patient and ensure their compliance with prescribed pharma-ceuticals, therapies, and other treatments.

The other aspect of advocacy often needed by the patient is help in navigating insurance companies and claims. This can be hard enough to do when you are healthy and have the mental, emotional, and physical capacity to do the work involved, but it's typically the last thing someone battling an illness can afford. The irony is that the worse the illness, the greater the costs and complexity that need to be managed, and the less able the patient is to manage them.

While there are already many companies and individuals providing advocacy as a service, an alliance of professional health advocates with over six hundred members, and even advocacy certification, what's much more interesting is envisioning the role of advocate being filled, at least in part, by AI.

In the next section of this chapter, we'll introduce the idea of a hospital in the cloud as being a portfolio of services that can be disaggregated and then reconstituted as needed. It's not much of a stretch to go from that to an app that plugs into the hospital in the cloud which has access to a patient's healthcare and insurance records, the ability to monitor the patient's health, is integrated with data analytics that are able to benefit from public health data, and communicates with the patient, designated family and friends of the patient (FOPs), and doctors or clinicians.

To take that even one step further (albeit a large step), the digital healthcare advocate could be the ultimate form of hyperpersonalization by also using the unique genome of each individual to identify the specific healthcare needs of each patient.

Driven by the astounding drop in the cost of gene sequencing, the ability to explore how various therapies and treatments affect an individual based on their personal genome promises to create a sea change in the future of medicine from the "standard of care" approach, which used a one-size-fits-all model of medicine, to a hyperpersonalized model where each patient is unique in how their genetic profile defines the treatment with the best outcomes for that patient.

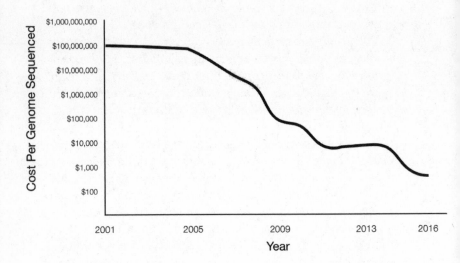

Decrease in Cost Per Genome Sequenced 2001-2016

Illustration 7.5 The amazing drop in the cost of sequencing the human genome, which has plummeted from three hundred million dollars in 2000 (the cost of the original genome sequencing) to under ten million dollars in 2007, to one million dollars in 2008, to under one thousand dollars today. The expectation is that the cost will have dropped to under one hundred dollars within the next five to ten years. The rate of decrease in the cost exceeds even that which is predicted by Moore's law when projecting the exponential advances of semiconductor technology.[37]

Cancer treatments have been among some of the most promising that are following this approach, using genetic markers to indicate the type of pharmaceuticals and therapies that particular cancers in specific patients respond to. To date, there are over 1,800 genes that have been identified as markers of specific diseases, 2,000 genetic tests, and more than 350 clinical trials for genome-specific biotechnology therapies.[38]

Given the rate of population change we've described, the continuously increasing complexity of care, the lack of adequate PCP coverage, and the personalization of healthcare, having a digital advocate isn't just something that will be a nice-to-have; it's imperative in creating a sustainable healthcare system.

The Hospital in the Cloud

The last disruptor is what I call the hospital in the cloud, and it comes from a much larger trend in technology and business over the past decade—the advent of cloud-based models for the use of software, computing, and data storage. Most often, the idea of cloud computing is presented as a way to purchase and use technology services, such as software applications, computer power, or data storage, as needed, in the volume needed, and where needed. This creates a much more cost-effective way to consume the resources required for an organization's information technology systems, but it also does something we've been talking about from the start of this book: allows organizations to get out of noncore activities, such as IT, and to focus on their core.

> Imagine you are asking financial advice. You call the 1-800 number, and Warren Buffett answers the phone. This is the vision we're trying to create with telehealth.

Many hospitals are already well under way in moving their technology to the cloud. According to David Vawdrey, VP of analytics and clinical systems at NewYork-Presbyterian hospital, "By 2022, we're expecting to move the majority of our applications and infrastructure to the cloud, leaving just 20 percent on-premises. Imagine you are asking for financial advice. You call the 1-800 number, and Warren Buffett answers the phone," Vawdrey said. "This is the vision we're trying to create with telehealth."[vii,39]

In our use, *a hospital in the cloud* refers to a much more important and significant aspect of the cloud. By disaggregating the various services that a traditional hospital delivers, along with new ambulatory offerings such as virtual medicine, these services can be re-aggregated as needed and delivered to the patient in a variety of settings. Think of this as a personalized set of healthcare services that are built to suit each patient wherever and whenever—a portable hospital for one.

In its simplest form, a hospital in the cloud provides:

- A set of managed virtualized administrative and clinical services.

- Integration of EHRs, documentation, and analytics across disparate EHRs.

- Data analytics for care management and public health.

- Protection against cyberthreats.

- The ability to use advanced technologies such as AI and NLP to eliminate the friction and high-overhead tasks such as medical coding and claims submissions.

- Collaborative AI to help clinicians identify health markers and provide predictive diagnostics.

---

vii   In this case, the term telehealth is being used in a generic manner as a reference to any service the hospital may be delivering or an interaction between a patient and the hospital via voice or data telecommunications.

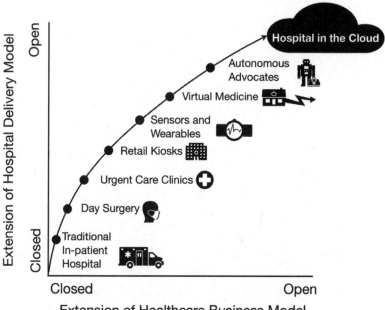

The Evolution Towards a Hospital in the Cloud

Illustration 7.6 The evolution toward a hospital in the cloud includes new business models for healthcare as well as new methods of delivering patient healthcare services. Over time, the various services that make up a traditional hospital are disaggregated into individual services. These can be delivered to the patient as a customized and hyperpersonalized healthcare system that understands the patient's needs and the context of their lifestyle and that can integrate many of these services in a localized way that maximize convenience and optimal outcomes. Note that smartsourcing is not shown on the illustration since it is an underlying enabler rather than a care delivery model.

The obstacle to deploying a hospital in the cloud isn't nearly as much that of the technology as it is the reluctance of providers to give up control of vertically integrated functions. That's especially true of large provider systems which are trying to create very large self-contained healthcare eco-

> The obstacle to deploying a hospital in the cloud isn't nearly as much that of the technology as it is the reluctance of those organizations that currently own and control patient data.

systems. But, as we've already pointed out, evidence doesn't support these larger systems lowering costs or improving outcomes.

However, the trend toward consolidation into increasingly larger and fewer mega-providers seems to continue unabated. During the past five years (2014–2019), there have been, on average, one hundred mergers per year.[40,41] At the same time, hospitals have been closing at the rate of thirty per year.[42] And two-thirds of all community hospitals are already part of a hospital system.[viii,43] With only those three dynamics at play, it's hard to see how the notion of a freestanding hospital will survive beyond the next decade.

So, if consolidation doesn't reduce costs or improve outcomes, why is it being done? The reason is purely the perverse way that healthcare economics work. As we described earlier, scale enables providers to exact higher reimbursements. These higher reimbursements provide greater capital to large providers for further consolidation, and the cycle continues. This is like the depiction of the mythical Ouroboros, a snake or serpent that loops back to devour itself.

Smaller mergers and consolidations that bring together a handful of smaller providers are not the issue. These smaller mergers help in creating better patient access to specialists, managing complex care, and operational efficiencies from shared systems. The concern is at the high end, where

---

viii   According to the AHA "A System is defined by AHA as either a multihospital or a diversified single hospital system. A multihospital system is two or more hospitals owned, leased, sponsored, or contract managed by a central organization."

mega-hospital systems drive up healthcare costs (without evidence of better outcomes), shift the focus from the patient to efficiency, and focus on operational excellence over innovation. While there may be limited cases, such as Mayo, where a single integrated provider requires scale in order to be able to handle highly complicated cases that involve many specialists and the immediacy of extensive in-house labs, imaging, and diagnostic capabilities, this is only a fraction of healthcare.

And it's not just consolidation through acquisitions that's concerning. Other options for consolidation have been discussed, such as a single provider national healthcare system.

While there is currently precedent for this model in the way the VA (Department of Veterans Affairs) provides healthcare, any attempt to nationalize that same approach has so far been met with enormous pushback from Americans, who place a high premium on choice. This model is also the least likely to provide the sort of healthcare innovations that result from a competitive free market.

Another popular option is the single-payer model fashioned after Medicare, or a variation of it, as a private-public model in which there is both the option of national healthcare for anyone who wants it and private healthcare for those who do not and can afford to pay for private insurance. Again, these both limit choice for the overwhelming majority of people, while the latter also creates social bifurcation and elitism—two more things that do not play well to the American psyche.

What all of these models have in common is that they shift the focus toward a more consolidated industry at a time when just the opposite is true of nearly every other industry. Think back to the illustration we used in chapter 5 (Illustration 5.3) that showed how industries were increasingly moving into the upper right-hand quadrant where partnerships were held together by strategy to deliver a service personalized to the customer. Each of the options that we just described are pushing healthcare back into the lower left-hand quadrant where ownership and undifferentiated product was the norm. Recall that the lower left-hand quadrant of this model represents the industrial-era model of economies of scale, while the upper right-hand quadrant represents economies of scope.

The greatest risk to healthcare is that we stifle its evolution into a post-industrial-era model that takes advantage of the economies of scope offered through new technologies and methods such as smartsourcing and HSPs.

Instead of consolidation, imagine a healthcare system in which the basic building blocks of a hospital are virtualized and available in the cloud. These building blocks are, at the very least: revenue cycle, IT, analytics, public health, remote diagnostics and sensor-based technologies, and even the patient-owned EHR. In this future, everything that today causes friction and distraction from the core competency of the provider is available as a service. Hospitals can now focus on their cores while being assured of the best possible efficiency for their operations and their business.

In the absence of this sort of hospital in the cloud, the industry will continue to create larger walled gardens that wield greater power over payers, while limiting patient choice and innovation. You may have noticed that I'm being careful in my word choices by saying "limit" rather than "eliminate." That's because the insidious nature of walled gardens is that they provide just enough innovation to keep customers (or in this case patients) within their walls as long as possible.

This is precisely the case with many users of technology who are locked into a particular platform such as Apple, Google, or even Facebook; they end up being held hostage by the fear of losing their content and the highly integrated nature of the many apps that link to their platform.

It's not coincidental that this approach has also resulted in devices whose value commands much higher price tags.

Apple, with the most restrictive walled garden, commands a steep premium from its users who are accustomed to happily paying prices that are two to three times higher for mobile phones, laptops, and tablets than for non-Apple alternatives. That may be a point of some irritation when it comes to our mobile devices, but it's an extraordinarily dangerous path to go down for healthcare.

Ultimately, moving the administration and operations of a hospital into the cloud as a series of best-of-class services, hosted and managed by an HSP, will allow healthcare to become fully integrated with all of the advances that we've been discussing, from wearables and behavioral tracking to public health and prelytics. And all of this while alleviating the burden of administration.

It's naive to expect that the sort of transformation I'm describing will be anything but enormously disruptive to the many providers already pursuing a strategy predicated on massive consolidation as well as those organizations who feed off the inefficiency of the current system.

Decorating the Box

As I was writing this last chapter and considering how to close the book, I was reminded of three things.

The first is what I said at the very beginning of this chapter, that healthcare is not a solvable problem. It's not formulaic and there is no single "fix." It's a constantly moving target; what the philosopher Sir Karl Popper called a cloud problem versus a clock problem. The latter is mechanical and linear, the former is constantly moving and evolving. Technology changes, populations change, lifestyles change, generational expectations and attitudes change, social and economic context changes.

The second is what I said at the very outset of the book, that we are on the precipice of great positive change in how

> Like a patient who stubbornly refuses to accept her illness despite the many obvious symptoms, many healthcare providers and payers will continue to ignore the signs for change which line the road into the future.

healthcare can improve the quality of our lives. As I was writing the book, the many stories of how the healthcare system had failed people like Nataline, Isabella, Wanda, and so many others who I talked with that never made it into the book, brought me to realize just how much work there is to be done. I'll admit it was at times depressing to hear and to retell their stories. Toward the middle of the book, I felt the way many first-year medical residents do: overwhelmed, dog-tired, and thinking I had come down with every malady I'd read or heard about.

There is no immediately obvious way to stop the dysfunction of the current healthcare system and the collateral pain it causes so many of our fellow citizens. But what encouraged me more than anything else was hearing the stories of many patients, like James at the beginning of this chapter, for whom the system had worked, and speaking with the incredibly dedicated clinicians I met at institutions like John Muir Health. It's cliché to say, but the problem with healthcare is overwhelmingly not the people but a system in which well-meaning and dedicated healers are detracted from their core purpose and mission.

The last thing that struck me, and the last thought I'll leave you with, is a pearl of wisdom imparted to me by my son, Adam, when he was twelve years old.

I was working in my home study on a speech I was about to give on the topic of creative thinking. As Adam walked into my office, I was pencil-sketching a drawing of the classical depiction of a man trying desperately to get out of a box.

Adam looked over my shoulder, studied the drawing, and went on to tell me how they had just talked about "getting out of the box" in one of his classes. I smiled to think that we were somehow on the same wavelength. Like father, like son, or something like that. Then, very innocently but astutely, he asked, "Hey, Dad, what do you do if you can't get out of the box?" I thought about the many ways I could answer, the opportunity to pass on wisdom from a lifetime of work in helping very smart people do the same. Instead, I decided to explore his viewpoint on the matter. So, I turned it back on him and said, "I don't know, Adam, what would you do?"

Without missing a beat, he beamed. "I'd just make sure it's decorated nicely!"[ix]

That's exactly what we've done with the US healthcare system. We've accepted the walls of this box as immovable, and we've tried to work within the parameters of a system that has grown organically to the point where its complexity is simply no longer sustainable within the same confines that it and we have evolved within; an industrial age whose precepts were put in place to create scale and volume, at the price of huge inefficiency. To follow on with my analogy, a more apt description of the well-decorated box, in the case of healthcare, would be a hoarder's attic filled with artifacts from the last one hundred years that we can't seem to get rid of. It's time for an intervention, or at least a yard sale.

The complexity of healthcare and the changing demands of the population are a mandate for us to step outside of the constraints of the last one hundred years to reimagine and rebuild a future for healthcare that allows the entire system—patients, providers, and payers—to focus on what's most important, what has always been the noble aspiration of every caregiver: the health and well-being of, you, the patient.

---

ix   I should point out, in fairness to Adam, that I'm sure he'd eventually find his way out of the box!

THE FUTURE OF HEALTHCARE,
CHAPTER 7: RECAP AND LESSONS LEARNED

The assumptions that we have built the healthcare system around over the past one-hundred years have changed dramatically, as have the tools and technologies available for practice of medicine.

Only 54 percent of men in 1935 could expect to live to the age of sixty-five. Today that number is 80 percent. If you lived till sixty-five in 1940 (the first year Social Security benefits were paid out) you could expect to collect for thirteen years. Today you would collect for twenty years.

Healthcare costs are dramatically skewed toward the sickest of the patient population with one percent of patients accounting for 22.8 percent of all healthcare spending and the top five percent accounting for 50.4 percent of spending on healthcare.

Over the next five years, tech giants such as Google, Apple, Amazon, and even Facebook will step in and attempt to use their scale, technologies, and most importantly their access to behavioral data to create new approaches to how the patient-customer engages with the healthcare system.

Medical data is expected to double every seventy-three days by 2020, and each person will generate enough healthcare data during their lifetime to fill 300 million books.

By 2022 over 25 percent of the US adult population will have a wearable health tracking device.

With the advent of not only wearables and mobile devices but also the proliferation of behavioral tracking through Internet-based interactions with social media, GPS, and web search, a new discipline is emerging, which I call prelytics, or predictive analytics.

Large companies, such as Apple, Google, Amazon, JP Morgan, and Berkshire Hathaway are beginning that process by evaluating the option of building their own healthcare networks for their employees in which they are the payers and in some cases owners of the providers.

One of the most important and widespread shifts in healthcare, which will be enabled by new advances in the technology of remote monitoring, diagnostics, and treatments, is ambulatory care—the move away from inpatient hospital care to outpatient.

As the population ages, the prevalence of dementia and related neurological and cognitive diseases among the population will also increase. This creates a mandate to look at advocacy in an entirely different way: as an essential component of the healthcare system.

Digital healthcare advocates will evolve to provide continuity of care, provide early warnings of potential health problems based on changes in behavior and habits, and to monitor the patient and ensure their compliance with prescribed pharmaceuticals, therapies, and other treatments.

The evolution toward a hospital in the cloud includes new business models for healthcare as well as new methods of delivering patient healthcare services. Over time, the various services that make up a traditional hospital are disaggregated into individual services. These can be delivered to the patient as a customized and hyperpersonalized healthcare system that understands the patient's needs and the context of their lifestyle, and which can integrate many of these services in a localized way that maximize convenience and optimal outcomes.

ENDNOTES

1   E. Mazareanu, "Global Outsourcing Market Size 2000–2018," Statista, July 22, 2019, https://www.statista.com/statistics/189788/global-outsourcing-market-size/.

Chapter 1

1   Christine Sinsky et al., "Allocation of Physician Time in Ambulatory Practice: A Time and Motion Study in 4 Specialties," *Annals of Internal Medicine* 165, no. 11 (2016): 753–60.

2   Maria Obiols, "The World's Richest Companies 2018: Global Finance Cash 25," *Global Finance*, September 1, 2018, https://www.gfmag.com/magazine/september-2018/global-finance-cash-25-2018.

3   Anil Kaul, K. R. Prabha, and Suman Katragadda, "Size Should Matter: Five Ways to Help Healthcare Systems Realize the Benefits of Scale," PricewaterhouseCoopers, 2016, accessed November 11, 2019, https://www.strategyand.pwc.com/us/en/reports/size-should-matter.pdf.

4   MedicalBag, "Standard Panel Size of 2500 Patients Per Doctor Is Not Optimal in Primary Care Setting," Haymarket Media, September 9, 2019, https://www.medicalbag.com/home/business/standard-panel-size-of-2500-patients-per-doctor-is-not-optimal-in-primary-care-setting/.

5   "Minority Health," Kaiser Family Foundation, accessed November 11, 2019, http://kff.org/state-category/minority-health/.

6   "Physicians Spend Two Hours on EHRs and Desk Work for

Every Hour of Direct Patient Care," Physicians for a National Health Program, accessed November 11, 2019, https://pnhp.org/news/physicians-spend-two-hours-on-ehrs-and-desk-work-for-every-hour-of-direct-patient-care/

7   Jackson Healthcare, "Gallup Poll Quantifies U.S. Physician Opinions on the Scope of Defensive Medicine," HealthLeaders, February 25, 2010, https://www.healthleadersmedia.com/welcome-ad?toURL=/strategy/gallup-poll-quantifies-us-physician-opinions-scope-defensive-medicine.

8   Leslie Hill, "Practice of Defensive Orthopaedic Medicine Costs U.S. $2 Billion Annually," Research News@Vanderbilt, February 9, 2012, https://news.vanderbilt.edu/2012/02/09/defensive-orthopaedic-medicine/.

9   Joanne Finnegan, "Worse Than Ever: Physician Shortage Could Hit 120K by 2030," FierceHealthcare, April 12, 2018, https://www.fiercehealthcare.com/practices/physician-shortage-could-hit-120k-by-2030-aamc-darrell-g-kirch.

10   "Economic Report: Inbound Medical Tourism in the United States," *Medical Tourism Magazine*, accessed November 11, 2019, https://www.medicaltourismmag.com/article/economic-report-inbound-medical-tourism-in-the-united-states.

11   Arthur Chambers, "Trends in U.S. Health Travel Services Trade" (USITC Executive Briefing on Trade, August 2015).

12   Annalisa Merelli, "A History of Why the US Is the Only Rich Country without Universal Health Care," *Quartz*, July 18, 2017, https://qz.com/1022831/why-doesnt-the-united-states-have-universal-health-care/.

13   Bradley Sawyer and Daniel McDermott, "How Does the Quality of the U.S. Healthcare System Compare to Other Countries?" Peterson-Kaiser Health System Tracker, March 28, 2019, https://www.healthsystemtracker.org/chart-collection/quality-u-s-healthcare-system-compare-countries/.

14   University of Maryland School of Medicine, "Nearly Half of US Medical Care Comes from Emergency Rooms," *Science-*

Daily, October 17, 2017, https://www.sciencedaily.com/releases/2017/10/171017091849.htm.

15   J. M. Legramante et al., "Frequent Use of Emergency Departments by the Elderly Population When Continuing Care Is Not Well Established," *PLoS One* 11, no. 12 (2016), https://journals.plos.org/plosone/article?id=10.1371/journal.pone.0165939.

16   "New Findings Confirm Predictions on Physician Shortage," Association of American Medical Colleges, April 23, 2019, https://www.aamc.org/news-insights/press-releases/new-findings-confirm-predictions-physician-shortage.

17   "Trendwatch Chartbook 2018: Trends Affecting Hospitals and Health Systems" (American Hospital Association), 21, https://www.aha.org/system/files/2018-07/2018-aha-chartbook.pdf.

Chapter 2

1   Pauline W. Chen, "When Insurers Put Profits Between Doctor and Patient," *New York Times*, January 6, 2011, https://www.nytimes.com/2011/01/06/health/views/06chen.html.

2   A. Jain et al., "Long-Term Survival after Liver Transplantation in 4,000 Consecutive Patients at a Single Center," *Annals of Surgery* 232, no. 4 (2000): 490–500.

3   Louise B. Andrew, "Physician Suicide," Medscape, August 1, 2018, https://emedicine.medscape.com/article/806779-overview.

4   Daniel S. Tawfik et al., "Physician Burnout, Well-Being, and Work Unit Safety Grades in Relationship to Reported Medical Errors," *Mayo Clinic Proceedings* 93, no. 11 (2018): 1571–80, https://www.ncbi.nlm.nih.gov/pmc/articles/PMC6258067/.

5   Steffie Woolhandler and David U. Himmelstein, "Single-Payer Reform: The Only Way to Fulfill the President's Pledge of More Coverage, Better Benefits, and Lower Costs," *Annals of Internal Medicine* 166 (8) (2017): 587–588, https://annals.org/

aim/fullarticle/2605414/single-payer-reform-only-way-fulfill-president-s-pledge-more.

6   Ibid.

7   Melanie Evans, "What Does Knee Surgery Cost? Few Know, and That's a Problem," *Wall Street Journal*, August 21, 2018, https://www.wsj.com/articles/what-does-knee-surgery-cost-few-know-and-thats-a-problem-1534865358.

8   "Who Bears the Cost of the Uninsured? Nonprofit Hospitals," KelloggInsight, June 22, 2015, https://insight.kellogg.north-western.edu/article/who-bears-the-cost-of-the-uninsured-nonprofit-hospitals.

9   Elisabeth Rosenthal, "Those Indecipherable Medical Bills? They're One Reason Health Care Costs So Much," *New York Times*, March 29, 2017, https://www.nytimes.com/2017/03/29/magazine/those-indecipherable-medical-bills-theyre-one-reason-health-care-costs-so-much.html.

10 Justin Mccarthy, "U.S. Women More Likely Than Men to Put off Medical Treatment," Gallup, December 6, 2017, https://news.gallup.com/poll/223277/women-likely-men-put-off-medical-treatment.aspx.

11 John Tozzi and Zachary Tracer, "How Sky-High Deductibles Broke the U.S. Health Insurance System," *Los Angeles Times*, https://www.latimes.com/business/la-fi-health-insurance-deductible-20180626-story.html.

12 Susan Morse, "Health Systems Need to Collect Patient Balances," *Healthcare Finance News*, accessed November 11, 2019, https://www.healthcarefinancenews.com/news/health-systems-need-collect-patient-balances.

13 Lorie Konish, "This Is the Real Reason Most Americans File for Bankruptcy," CNBC, February 11, 2019, https://www.cnbc.com/2019/02/11/this-is-the-real-reason-most-americans-file-for-bankruptcy.html.

14 "Consumer Credit Reports: A Study of Medical and Non-Medical Collections," Consumer Financial Protection

Bureau, December 2014, https://files.consumerfinance.gov/f/201412_cfpb_reports_consumer-credit-medical-and-non-medical-collections.pdf.

15   Robert Pearl, "Why Major Hospitals Are Losing Money by the Millions," *Forbes*, November 7, 2017, https://www.forbes.com/sites/robertpearl/2017/11/07/hospitals-losing-millions/#323a24dd7b50.

16   David Cutler, "Why Does Health Care Cost So Much in America? Ask Harvard's David Cutler," *PBS NewsHour*, November 19, 2013, https://www.pbs.org/newshour/nation/why-does-health-care-cost-so-much-in-america-ask-harvards-david-cutler.

17   Lawrence P. Casalino et al., "What Does It Cost Physician Practices to Interact with Health Insurance Plans?" *Health Affairs* 28, no. 4 (2009): w533, https://www.healthaffairs.org/doi/10.1377/hlthaff.28.4.w533.

18   Elisabeth Rosenthal, *An American Sickness: How Healthcare Became Big Business and How You Can Take It Back* (New York: Penguin, 2017): 245–48. Kindle.

19   Austin Frakt, "Hospital Mergers Improve Health? Evidence Shows the Opposite," *New York Times*, February 11, 2019, https://www.nytimes.com/2019/02/11/upshot/hospital-mergers-hurt-health-care-quality.html.

20   Zack Cooper et al., "Does Hospital Competition Save Lives? Evidence from the English NHS Patient Choice Reforms," *Economic Journal* 121, no. 554 (2011): 228–60, https://onlinelibrary.wiley.com/doi/full/10.1111/j.1468-0297.2011.02449.x; and Daniel P. Kessler and Mark B. MacClellan, *Is Hospital Competition Socially Wasteful?* (Cambridge, MA: National Bureau of Economic Research, 1999).

21   "2018 Employer Health Benefits Survey," Kaiser Family Foundation, October 3, 2018, https://www.kff.org/report-section/2018-employer-health-benefits-survey-summary-of-findings/.

22   Jared Bilski, "This Alarming Healthcare Trend Has Increased 87% in the Past Four Years," HRMorning, August 8, 2018,

https://www.hrmorning.com/news/this-alarming-healthcare-trend-has-increased-87-in-the-past-four-years/.

23   Bradley Sawyer and Gary Claxton, "How Do Health Expenditures Vary across the Population," Peterson-Kaiser Health System Tracker, January 16, 2019, https://www.healthsystemtracker.org/chart-collection/health-expenditures-vary-across-population/#item-people-age-55-and-over-account-for-over-half-of-total-health-spending_2016.

24   "An Aging Nation," U.S. Census Bureau, April 10, 2017, https://census.gov/library/visualizations/2017/comm/cb17-ff08_older_americans.html.

25   "Facts and Figures," Alzheimer's Association, accessed November 11, 2019, https://www.alz.org/alzheimers-dementia/facts-figures.

26   Mary Rechtoris, "86% of Physicians Are Still Paid under Fee-for-Service Payment Model: 5 Takeaways," *ASC Review*, October 27, 2016, https://www.beckersasc.com/asc-coding-billing-and-collections/86-of-physicians-are-still-paid-under-fee-for-service-payment-model-5-takeaways.html.

27   Trisha Torrey, "How Health Care Capitation Payment Systems Work," Verywell Health, October 29, 2019, https://www.verywellhealth.com/capitation-the-definition-of-capitation-2615119.

28   Sandra G. Boodman, "For Millennials, a Regular Visit to the Doctor's Office Is Not a Primary Concern," *Washington Post*, October 6, 2018, https://www.washingtonpost.com/national/health-science/for-millennials-a-regular-visit-to-the-doctors-office-is-not-a-primary-concern/2018/10/05/6b17c71a-aef3-11e8-9a6a-565d92a3585d_story.html.

29   "Did You Know? CFM56 Engine's Performance, Extended Time-on-Wing Advantage," AviationWeek.com, November 29, 2016.

30   Andrew Guthrie Ferguson, "The Truth about Predictive Policing and Race," The Appeal, December 7, 2017, https://

theappeal.org/the-truth-about-predictive-policing-and-race-b87cf7c070b1/.

31   David Lazarus, "Insurer Pats Itself on the Back for Approving a Medical Claim It Twice Denied," *Los Angeles Times*, February 15, 2019, https://www.latimes.com/business/lazarus/la-fi-lazarus-healthcare-gunshot-insurance-claim-denial-20190215-story.html.

32   Jordan Weissmann, "We're Getting Ripped Off," *Slate*, September 27, 2019, https://slate.com/business/2019/09/health-insurance-us-kaiser-study.html.

33   David Belk, "Outpatient Charges," The True Cost of Healthcare, 2020, accessed January 15, 2020, http://truecostof-healthcare.org/outpatient_charges/.

34   These are actual ICD codes Y92.253 and V97.33, respectively

35   American Hospital Association and PricewaterhouseCoopers, *Patients or Paperwork? The Regulatory Burden Facing America's Hospitals* (Chicago: American Hospital Association, 2001).

36   "Stratified, Personalised or P4 Medicine: A New Direction for Placing the Patient at the Centre of Healthcare and Health Education (May 12, 2015)," Summary of a joint FORUM meeting, Academy of Medical Sciences, the University of Southampton, Science Europe, and the Medical Research Council, https://acmedsci.ac.uk/download?f=file&i=32644.

37   Melissa Rohman, "JAMA: U.S. Spends the Most on Healthcare—and Imaging Is a Reason Why," *HealthImaging*, March 14, 2018.

38   JoNel Aleccia, "State Laws Ban Surprise Medical Bills: She Got One for $227K And Fought Back," Kaiser Health News, March 22, 2019, https://khn.org/news/even-with-insurance-she-faced-227k-in-medical-bills-what-it-took-to-get-answers/.

39   Ibid.

40   Ibid.

41   Ryan Jaslow, "Gallup Poll: 3 in 10 Americans Skip Medical

Care Due to Cost," CBS News, December 14, 2012, https://www.cbsnews.com/news/gallup-poll-3-in-10-americans-skip-medical-care-due-to-cost/.

42   David Muhlestein, Robert S. Saunders, and Mark B. McClellan, "Growth of ACOs and Alternative Payment Models in 2017," *Health Affairs*, June 28, 2017, https://www.healthaffairs.org/do/10.1377/hblog20170628.060719/full/.

43   J. H. Thrall, "Unintended Consequences of Health Care Legislation," *Journal of the American College of Radiology* 8, no. 10 (2011): 687–91, https://www.sciencedirect.com/science/article/pii/S1546144011003322.

44   Lewis A. Lipsitz, "Understanding Health Care as a Complex System: The Foundation for Unintended Consequences," *Journal of the American Medical Association* 308, no. 3 (2012): 243–44, https://www.ncbi.nlm.nih.gov/pmc/articles/PMC3511782/.

Chapter 3

1   Tolentino v. Health Care Service Corp., 3:14-cv-00017 (5th Cir., Texas Southern District, 2016), https://www.courtlistener.com/recap/gov.uscourts.txsd.1147247.22.0.pdf.

2   "History of Hospitals," PennNursing, accessed November 11, 2019, https://www.nursing.upenn.edu/nhhc/nurses-institutions-caring/history-of-hospitals/.

3   Ibid.

4   "History of Tufts Medical Center," Tufts Medical Center, accessed November 11, 2019, https://www.tuftsmedicalcenter.org/about-us/history.

5   "Fast Facts on U.S. Hospitals, 2019," American Hospital Association, accessed November 11, 2019, https://www.aha.org/statistics/fast-facts-us-hospitals#community

6   "Hospital Service in the United States: Twelfth Annual Presentation of Hospital Data by the Council on Medical

Education and Hospitals of the American Medical Association," *Journal of the American Medical Association* 100, no. 12 (1933): 887–972.

7   "5 Statistics about Hospital Capacity Over Time," *Becker's Hospital Review*, March 17, 2015, https://www.beckershospitalreview.com/patient-flow/5-statistics-about-hospital-capacity-over-time.html.

8   "Fast Facts on U.S. Hospitals, 2019," American Hospital Association, accessed November 11, 2019, https://www.aha.org/statistics/fast-facts-us-hospitals.

9   Richard E. Schumann, "Compensation from World War II through the Great Society," U.S. Bureau of Labor Statistics, https://www.bls.gov/opub/mlr/cwc/compensation-from-world-war-ii-through-the-great-society.pdf.

10   Nancy J. Niles, *Basics of the U. S. Health Care System* (Burlington, MA: Jones & Bartlett Learning, 2019).

11   Dave Barkholz, "Insurance Claim Denials Cost Hospitals $262 Billion Annually," *Modern Healthcare*, June 27, 2017, https://www.modernhealthcare.com/article/20170627/NEWS/170629905/insurance-claim-denials-cost-hospitals-262-billion-annually.

12   Ibid.

13   Philip Betbeze, "Claims Appeals Cost Hospitals up to $8.6B Annually," HealthLeaders, June 26, 2017, https://www.healthleadersmedia.com/finance/claims-appeals-cost-hospitals-86b-annually.

14   Jacqueline LaPointe, "Top 4 Claims Denial Management Challenges Impacting Revenue," Rev Cycle Intelligence, March 10, 2017, https://revcycleintelligence.com/news/top-4-claims-denial-management-challenges-impacting-revenue.

15   Barkholz, "Insurance Claim Denials Cost Hospitals $262 Billion Annually."

16   "AHA Data Show Hospitals' Outpatient Revenue Nearing Inpatient," *Modern Healthcare*, January 3, 2019, https://www.

modernhealthcare.com/article/20190103/TRANSFORMA-TION02/190109960/aha-data-show-hospitals-outpatient-revenue-nearing-inpatient.

17   Martha C. White, "Hospitals Made $21B on Wall Street Last Year, but Are Patients Seeing Those Profits?" NBC News, February 7, 2018, https://www.nbcnews.com/business/business-news/hospitals-made-21b-wall-street-last-year-are-patients-seeing-n845176.

18   Jeff Goldsmith, "How U.S. Hospitals and Health Systems Can Reverse Their Sliding Financial Performance," *Harvard Business Review*, October 5, 2017, https://hbr.org/2017/10/how-u-s-hospitals-and-health-systems-can-reverse-their-sliding-financial-performance.

19   Karen Pollitz, Cynthia Cox, and Rachel Fehr, "Claims Denials and Appeals in ACA Marketplace Plans," Kaiser Family Foundation, February 25, 2019, https://www.kff.org/private-insurance/issue-brief/claims-denials-and-appeals-in-aca-marketplace-plans/view/footnotes/.

20   Phillip Tseng et al., "Administrative Costs Associated with Physician Billing and Insurance-Related Activities at an Academic Health Care System," *Journal of the American Medical Association* 319, no. 7 (2018): 691.

21   LaPointe, "68% of Consumers Did Not Pay Patient Financial Responsibility," Rev Cycle Intelligence, June 27, 2017, https://revcycleintelligence.com/news/68-of-consumers-did-not-pay-patient-financial-responsibility.

22   "Devenir Research: 2017 Year-End HSA Market Statistics & TrendsExecutive Summary," (Devenir pamphlet, February 22, 2018), http://www.devenir.com/wp-content/uploads/2017-Year-End-Devenir-HSA-Market-Research-Report-Executive-Summary.pdf.

23   "2018 Employer Health Benefits Survey," Kaiser Family Foundation, October 3, 2018, https://www.kff.org/health-costs/report/2018-employer-health-benefits-survey/.

24 Emily Gee and Topher Spiro, "Excess Administrative Costs Burden the U.S. Health Care System," Center for American Progress, April 8, 2019, https://www.americanprogress.org/issues/healthcare/reports/2019/04/08/468302/excess-administrative-costs-burden-u-s-health-care-system/.

25 Kelly Gooch, "US Healthcare Prices Reflect Huge Administrative Costs: 6 Statistics," Becker's Hospital CFO Report, July 16, 2018, https://www.beckershospitalreview.com/finance/us-healthcare-prices-reflect-huge-administrative-costs-6-statistics.html.

26 "Occupational Outlook Handbook," US Bureau of Labor and Statistics, 2020, accessed January 16, 2020, https://www.bls.gov/ooh/healthcare/medical-records-and-health-information-technicians.htm.

27 KrisEmily McCrory, "The Danger in Treating Patients as Customers," Physicians Practice, August 9, 2018, https://www.physicianspractice.com/article/danger-treating-patients-customers.

28 Barbara Starfield, Leiyu Shi, and James Macinko, "Contribution of Primary Care to Health Systems and Health," *Milbank Quarterly*, October 3, 2005, https://www.ncbi.nlm.nih.gov/pmc/articles/PMC2690145/.

29 P. Franks and K. Fiscella, "Primary Care Physicians and Specialists as Personal Physicians: Health Care Expenditures and Mortality Experience," *Journal of Family Practice* 47, no. 2 (1998): 105–09.

30 Stephen J. Spann, "Report on Financing the New Model of Family Medicine," *Annals of Family Medicine* 2, Suppl. 3 (2004): S1–S21, https://www.ncbi.nlm.nih.gov/pmc/articles/PMC1466777/.

31 Joanne Finnegan, "Many Americans Don't Have a Primary Care Doctor," FierceHealthcare, January 12, 2017, https://www.fiercehealthcare.com/practices/many-americans-don-t-have-a-primary-care-doctor.

32   Sandra G. Boodman, "Spurred by Convenience, Millennials Often Spurn the 'Family Doctor' Model," Kaiser Health News, October 9, 2018, https://khn.org/news/spurred-by-convenience-millennials-often-spurn-the-family-doctor-model/.

33   Matthew Lee Smith et al., "Factors Associated with Healthcare-Related Frustrations among Adults with Chronic Conditions," *Patient Education and Counseling* 100, no. 6 (2017): 1185–93.

34   Thomas Koulopoulos and Dan Keldsen, *The Gen Z Effect: The Six Forces Shaping the Future of Business* (New York: Hachette, 2015).

35   James R. Knickman and Emily K. Snell, "The 2030 Problem: Caring for Aging Baby Boomers," *Health Services Research* 37, no. 4 (2002): 849–84, https://www.ncbi.nlm.nih.gov/pmc/articles/PMC1464018/.

36   Susan Morse, "Medicare Part A Will Run Out of Funds in 8 Years, Medicare Trustee Report Says," *Healthcare Finance News*, June 6, 2018.

37   "2018 Annual Report of the Boards of Trustees of the Federal Hospital Insurance and Federal Supplementary Medical Insurance Trust Funds" (Washington, DC,, June 5, 2018).

38   Judi L. McClellan and Richard Holden, "The New Workforce: Age and Ethnic Changes" (Washington, DC: US Department of Labor, Employment, and Training Administration, Biennial National Research Conference, 2003).

39   "Table V.A3. Social Security Area Population as of July 1 and Dependency Ratios, Calendar Years 1941–2095," US Social Security Administration, Office of the Chief Actuary, July 13, 2017.

40   "The 2017 Long-Term Budget Outlook" (Washington, DC: Congressional Budget Office, March 30, 2017).

Chapter 4

1   "Best Hospitals by Specialty," *U.S. News & World Report*, accessed November 11, 2019, https://health.usnews.com/best-hospitals/rankings.

2   Tom Sullivan, "Why EHR Data Interoperability Is Such a Mess in 3 Charts," Healthcare IT News, May 16, 2018, https://www.healthcareitnews.com/news/why-ehr-data-interoperability-such-mess-3-charts.

3   "Diversified Genius," Mayo Clinic History & Heritage, 2020, http://history.mayoclinic.org/historic-highlights/diversified-genius.php.

4   Jim Chappelow, "Diseconomies of Scale," *Investopedia*, September 9, 2019, https://www.investopedia.com/terms/d/diseconomiesofscale.asp.

5   Gee and Ethan Gurwitz, "Provider Consolidation Drives Up Health Care Costs," Center for American Progress, December 5, 2018, https://www.americanprogress.org/issues/healthcare/reports/2018/12/05/461780/provider-consolidation-drives-health-care-costs/.

6   Beth Jones Sanborn, "Nonprofit, Public Hospital Margins Hit 10-Year Record Low, Moody's Report Says," *Healthcare Finance News*, April 24, 2018, https://www.healthcarefinancenews.com/news/nonprofit-public-hospital-margins-hit-10-year-record-low-moodys-report-says.

7   "Hill-Burton Free and Reduced-Cost Health Care," Health Resources & Services Information, 2020, accessed January 16, 2020, https://www.hrsa.gov/get-health-care/affordable/hill-burton/index.html.

8   "Rural Hospital Closures Since 2010," Stroudwater, October 2019, http://www.stroudwater.com/?resources=infographic-rural-hospital-closures-since-2010-updated-jan-2018

9   Cristin Flanagan, "U.S. Hospitals Shut at 20-a-Year Pace, With No End in Sight," *Bloomberg*, August 21, 2018, https://www.

bloomberg.com/news/articles/2018-08-21/hospitals-are-get-ting-eaten-away-by-market-trends-analysts-say.

10   "History of Community Health Centers," Massachusetts League of Community Health Centers, 2020, accessed January 16, 2020, http://www.massleague.org/CHC/History.php.

11   "About the Health Center Program," HRSA Health Center Program, accessed November 11, 2019, https://bphc.hrsa.gov/about/index.html.

12   "History of Community Health Centers."

13   "Fast Facts on U.S. Hospitals, 2020," American Hospital Association, 2020, accessed January 16, 2020, https://www.aha.org/statistics/fast-facts-us-hospitals#other.

14   Alanna Moriarty, "How Many Hospitals Are in the US?" The Definitive Blog, February 27, 2019, https://blog.definitivehc.com/how-many-hospitals-are-in-the-us.

15   "100 Largest Hospitals in America," *Becker's Hospital Review*, August 15, 2011, https://www.beckershospitalreview.com/lists/100-largest-hospitals-in-america.html.

16   "The Modern Definition of a Community Hospital," *Becker's Hospital Review*, June 8, 2015, https://www.beckershospital-review.com/hospital-management-administration/the-mod-ern-definition-of-a-community-hospital.html.

17   "2018 Annual Health Care Cost Trends Report," Massachusetts Health Policy Commission, February 2019, https://www.mass.gov/files/documents/2019/02/20/2018 percent20Cost percent20Trends percent20Report.pdf.

18   Kaul, Prabha, and Katragadda, "Size Should Matter.".

19   Martin Gaynor, "Statement of Martin Gaynor, Professor, Carnegie Mellon University: Hearing on 'Health Care Industry Consolidation,'" in Physician Practices: Changes, Trends, and Implications (Hauppauge, NY: 2011): 139–69.

20   Stuart V. Craig, Matthew Grennan, and Ashley Swanson, "Mergers and Marginal Costs: New Evidence on Hospital

Buyer Power" Cambridge, MA: National Bureau of Economic Research, 2018).

21   Laurence Baker et al., "Physician Practice Competition and Prices Paid by Private Insurers for Office Visits," *Journal of the American Medical Association* 312, no. 16 (2014): 1653–62.

Chapter 5

1   Fred Schulte and Erika Fry, "Death By 1,000 Clicks: Where Electronic Health Records Went Wrong," Kaiser Health News, March 18, 2019, https://khn.org/news/death-by-a-thousand-clicks/.

2   Alok Prasad, "EMR & The American Recovery and Reinvestment Act of 2009," MedCityNews, March 8, 2014, https://medcitynews.com/2014/03/emr-ehr_arra-2009/.

3   "Physician Outcry on EHR Functionality, Cost Will Shake the Health Information Technology Sector," *Medical Economics*, February 10, 2014, https://www.medicaleconomics.com/health-care-information-technology/physician-outcry-ehr-functionality-cost-will-shake-health-information-technology-sector.

4   Edward R. Melnick et al., "The Association between Perceived Electronic health Record Usability and Professional Burnout among US Physicians," *Mayo Clinic Proceedings* (2019): https://www.mayoclinicproceedings.org/article/S0025-6196(19)30836-5/pdf.

5   Schulte and Fry, "Death By 1,000 Clicks."

6   Sullivan, "Why EHR Data Interoperability Is Such a Mess."

7   FSD Staff, "2016 Healthcare Census: Hospitals Raise Their Game," *FoodService Director*, May 16, 2016, https://www.foodservicedirector.com/operations/2016-healthcare-census-hospitals-raise-their-game.

Chapter 6

1   W. H. Shrank, T. L. Rogstad, and N. Parekh, "Waste in the US Health Care System: Estimated Costs and Potential for Savings," *Journal of the American Medical Association* 322, no. 15 (2019): 1501–09.

2   Colin Hung, "Wasted Healthcare Spending: A $750 Billion Opportunity," HCLDR (Healthcare Leadership Blog), July 15, 2018, https://hcldr.wordpress.com/2018/07/15/wasted-health-care-spending-a-750-billion-opportunity/.

3   Merrill Goozner, "Editorial: Waste Isn't the Cause of High Healthcare Costs," *Modern Healthcare*, March 24, 2018, https://www.modernhealthcare.com/article/20180324/NEWS/180329959/editorial-waste-isn-t-the-cause-of-high-healthcare-costs.

4   "2018 CAQH Index: A Report of Healthcare Industry Adoption of Electronic Business Transactions and Cost Savings" CAQH Explorations, 2018, accessed November 11, 2019, https://www.caqh.org/sites/default/files/explorations/index/report/2018-index-report.pdf.

5   "Providers to Adopt IT Outsourcing Solutions in 2016 as More Hospitals and Physician Practices Slide Deeper into Financial Uncertainty, Black Book Survey," *Black Book*, November 24, 2015, https://www.prnewswire.com/news-releases/providers-to-adopt-it-outsourcing-solutions-in-2016-as-more-hospitals-and-physician-practices-slide-deeper-into-financial-uncertainty-black-book-survey-300183692.html.

6   Jeff Lagasse, "Hospital Costs Should Be Cut 24 Percent by 2022 to Break Even, Outsourcing May Help, Survey Says," *Healthcare Finance News*, May 8, 2018, https://ramaon-healthcare.com/hospital-costs-should-be-cut-24-percent-by-2022-to-break-even-outsourcing-may-help-survey-says/.

7   K. Patrick Ober and William B. Applegate, "The Electronic Health Record: Are We the Tools of Our Tools?" *The Pharos* (Winter 2015).

8   Jessica Davis, "Data Breaches Will Cost Healthcare $4B in 2019, Threats Outpace Tech," HealthITSecurity, November 5, 2019, https://healthitsecurity.com/news/data-breaches-will-cost-healthcare-4b-in-2019-threats-outpace-tech.

9   Samuel Gibbs, "WannaCry: Hackers Withdraw £108,000 of Bitcoin Ransom," *The Guardian*, August 3, 2017, https://www.theguardian.com/technology/2017/aug/03/wannacry-hackers-withdraw-108000-pounds-bitcoin-ransom.

10 Brian Stack, "Here's How Much Your Personal Information Is Selling for on the Dark Web," Experian (blog), December 6, 2017, https://www.experian.com/blogs/ask-experian/heres-how-much-your-personal-information-is-selling-for-on-the-dark-web/?pc=soe_exp_twitter&cc=soe_exp_twitter___20180711_1663697558_expn&ref=soe_.

11 Zlata Rodionova, "Healthcare Is Now Top Industry for Cyberattacks, Says IBM," *The Independent*, April 21, 2016, https://www.independent.co.uk/news/business/news/healthcare-is-now-top-industry-for-cyberattacks-says-ibm-a6994526.html.

12 Jordan Rau, "New Round of Medicare Readmission Penalties Hits 2,583 Hospitals," Kaiser Health News, October 1, 2019, https://khn.org/news/hospital-readmission-penalties-medicare-2583-hospitals/.

13 "The Human Cost and Financial Impact of Misdiagnosis," PinnacleCare, 2016, accessed November 11, 2019, https://www.pinnaclecare.com/forms/download/Human-Cost-Financial-Impact-Whitepaper.pdf.

14 "Cancer Moonshot Blue Ribbon Panel," National Cancer Center, accessed November 11, 2019, https://www.cancer.gov/research/key-initiatives/moonshot-cancer-initiative/blue-ribbon-panel.

15 Marianne Aiello, "Why Hospitals Should Stop Advertising ER Wait Times," HealthLeaders, September 16, 2015, https://www.healthleadersmedia.com/strategy/why-hospitals-should-stop-advertising-er-wait-times.

16   J. G. Behr and R. Diaz, "Emergency Department Frequent
      Utilization for Non-Emergent Presentments: Results from
      a Regional Urban Trauma Center Study," *PloS One* 11, no. 1
      (2016).

17   Robin M. Weinick, Rachel M. Burns, and Ateev Mehrotra,
      "Many Emergency Department Visits Could Be Managed at
      Urgent Care Centers and Retail Clinics," *Health Affairs* 29,
      no. 9 (2010): 1630–36.

18   "How Many ED Visits Are Avoidable? About 3.3%, Study
      Finds," Advisory Board, September 12, 2017, https://www.
      advisory.com/daily-briefing/2017/09/12/ed-visits-avoidable.

19   "Why Health Insurance Is Important: Protection From High
      Medical Costs," HealthCare.gov, accessed November 11, 2019,
      https://www.healthcare.gov/why-coverage-is-important/pro-
      tection-from-high-medical-costs/.

Chapter 7

1   "Kidney Disease Statistics for the United States," National
      Institute of Diabetes and Digestive and Kidney Diseases,
      accessed November 11, 2019, https://www.niddk.nih.gov/
      health-information/health-statistics/kidney-disease.

2   "Kidney Disease," Centers for Disease Control and Preven-
      tion, accessed November 11, 2019, https://www.cdc.gov/nchs/
      fastats/kidney-disease.htm.

3   "Get the Facts on Kidney Transplantation Before You Start
      Dialysis," Penn Medicine, July 24, 2019, https://www.pen-
      nmedicine.org/updates/blogs/transplant-update/2019/july/
      kidney-transplant-facts-before-dialysis.

4   "Social Security History," Social Security Administration,
      accessed November 11, 2019, https://www.ssa.gov/history/
      lifeexpect.html; and "Survival to Age 65, Male (% of Cohort)—
      United States," World Bank, 2019, accessed November 11,

2019, https://data.worldbank.org/indicator/SP.DYN.TO65.
MA.ZS?locations=US.

5   Ibid.

6   "New Hope for Patients Living with Cystic Fibrosis after
      Scientists Unveil Therapy," NPR, November 1, 2019, https://
      www.npr.org/2019/11/01/775509387/new-hope-for-patients-
      living-with-cystic-fibrosis-after-scientists-unveil-therap.

7   Peter Long et al., eds., *Effective Care for High-Need Patients:
      Opportunities for Improving Outcomes, Value, and Health*
      (Washington, DC: National Academy of Medicine, 2017), 31.

8   Ibid.

9   "Watson Health: Get The Facts," IBM, accessed November 11,
      2019, https://www.ibm.com/watson-health/about/get-the-facts.

10   "Wearables 2019: Advanced Wearables Pick up Pace as Fit-
      ness Trackers Slow," eMarketer, accessed November 11, 2019,
      https://www.emarketer.com/content/wearables-2019.

11   Chris Welch, "Apple and Stanford's Apple Watch Study
      Identified Irregular Heartbeats in over 2,000 Patients:
      Only 0.5 Percent of Participants Received the Notifica-
      tions," *The Verge*, March 16, 2019, https://www.theverge.
      com/2019/3/16/18268559/stanford-apple-heart-study-results-
      apple-watch.

12   Wired Staff, "Know Thyself: Tracking Every Facet of Life
      from Sleep to Mood to Pain," *Wired*, March 22, 2009.

13   Brian Dolan, "Carolinas HealthCare Monitors Fitbit Data
      to Intervene with CHF Patients," MobiHealthNews, March
      1, 2016, https://www.mobihealthnews.com/content/caroli-
      nas-healthcare-monitors-fitbit-data-intervene-chf-patients.

14   Chris Notte and Neil Skolnik, "Where to Go with Wearables,"
      MDedge, October 31, 2018, https://www.mdedge.com/endocri-
      nology/article/178625/business-medicine/where-go-wearables.

15   Marcia Frellick, "Doctors, Nurses Give Lifestyle Advice
      but Are Skeptical It's Heeded," *Medscape*, March 29, 2018,
      https://www.medscape.com/viewarticle/894572.

16   Regina M. Benjamin, "Medication Adherence: Helping
      Patients Take Their Medicines as Directed," *Public Health
      Reports* (2012), 127(1): 2–3. doi:10.1177/003335491212700102.

17   Jeffrey C. Greene et al., "Reduced Hospitalizations, Emer-
      gency Room Visits, and Costs Associated with a Web-Based
      Health Literacy, Aligned-Incentive Intervention: Mixed
      Methods Study," *Journal of Medical Internet Research* (Octo-
      ber 2019): https://www.jmir.org/2019/10/e14772.

18   "What is Public Health?" American Public Health Associ-
      ation, accessed November 11, 2019, https://www.apha.org/
      what-is-public-health.

19   David Talbot, "Cell-Phone Data Might Help Predict Ebola's
      Spread," *MIT Technology Review*, August 22, 2014, https://
      www.technologyreview.com/s/530296/cell-phone-data-
      might-help-predict-ebolas-spread/.

20   Susan Hall, "Digital Data Makes Real-Time Flu Tracking a
      Reality: Smart Technology and Tracking Tools Make Deliver-
      ing Flu Resources and Information a More Current Endeavor
      for Public Health Officials," *HealthTech*, March 19, 2018,
      https://healthtechmagazine.net/article/2018/03/digital-da-
      ta-makes-real-time-flu-tracking-reality.

21   Howard Brody et al., "Map-Making and Myth-Making in Broad
      Street: The London Cholera Epidemic, 1854," *The Lancet* 356
      (July 2000): https://www.globalhealthlearning.org/sites/de-
      fault/files/page-files/Brody_SnowCholera%20article.pdf.

22   "Trendwatch Chartbook 2018: Trends Affecting Hospitals and
      Health Systems" (American Hospital Association), 31, https://
      www.aha.org/system/files/2018-07/2018-aha-chartbook.pdf.

23   Ibid., 30.

24   Robert Holly, "Home Health Spending Rate Projected to
      Surpass All Other Care Categories," Home Health Care
      News, February 20, 2019, https://homehealthcarenews.
      com/2019/02/home-health-spending-rate-projected-to-sur-
      pass-all-other-care-categories/.

25   "2015 Report: Caregiving In the U.S." (National Alliance for Caregiving and the AARP Public Policy Institute, June 2015), https://www.aarp.org/content/dam/aarp/ppi/2015/caregiving-in-the-united-states-2015-report-revised.pdf.

26   Lynn Feinberg, Susan C. Reinhard, Ari Houser, and Rita Choula, "Valuing the Invaluable: 2011 Update; The Growing Contributions and Costs of Family Caregiving" (AARP Public Policy Institute), accessed November 11, 2019, https://assets.aarp.org/rgcenter/ppi/ltc/i51-caregiving.pdf.

27   Eds. Richard Schulz and Jill Eden, "Economic Impact of Family Caregiving," chapter 4 in *Families Caring for an Aging America* (Washington, DC: National Academies Press, 2016).

28   Schulz and S. R. Beach, "Caregiving as a Risk Factor for Mortality: The Caregiver Health Effects Study," *Journal of the American Medical Association* 282, no. 23 (1999): 2215–19.

29   Andree LeRoy, "Exhaustion, Anger of Caregiving Get a Name," CNN Health, accessed November 11, 2019, http://edition.cnn.com/2007/HEALTH/conditions/08/13/caregiver.syndrome/index.html.

39   "The 5 Key Challenges for Providers Expanding Ambulatory Care: The Five Key Challenges You Should Know," Advisory Board, October 19, 2016, https://www.advisory.com/daily-briefing/2016/10/19/the-5-key-challenges-for-providers-expanding-ambulatory-care.

31   Judy Mathias, "AHRQ Releases Stats on Outpatient, Inpatient Surgeries," *OR Manager*, June 2, 2017, https://www.ormanager.com/briefs/ahrq-releases-stats-on-outpatient-inpatient-surgeries/.

32   "Survey: Patients See 18.7 Different Doctors on Average; Practice Fusion Surveys Patients, Highlights the Inefficiency of Paper Records and the Need for Electronic Medical Records in the US," Cision PR Newswire, April 27, 2010, https://www.prnewswire.com/news-releases/survey-patients-see-187-different-doctors-on-average-92171874.html.

33   Ibid.

33   Ateev Mehrotra, Christopher B. Forrest, and Caroline Y. Lin, "Dropping the Baton: Specialty Referrals in the United States," *Milbank Quarterly* 89, no. 1 (2011): 39–68.

34   "CMS Advances Interoperability & Patient Access to Health Data through New Proposals," CMS, February 8, 2019, https://www.cms.gov/newsroom/fact-sheets/cms-advances-interoperability-patient-access-health-data-through-new-proposals.

35   Ilana Yurkiewicz, "Paper Trails: Living and Dying with Fragmented Medical Records," *Undark*, September 24, 2018, https://undark.org/2018/09/24/medical-records-fragmentation-health-care/.

36   "The Cost of Sequencing a Human Genome," National Human Genome Research Institute (NHGRI), accessed October 7, 2017, https://www.genome.gov/27565109/the-cost-of-sequencing-a-human-genome/.

37   Dawn McMullan, "What Is Personalized Medicine?" *Genome*, August 3, 2014, http://genomemag.com/what-is-personalized-medicine/.

38   Sullivan, "Why Hospitals and Health Insurers Are Really Turning to the Cloud," Healthcare IT News, February 11, 2019, https://www.healthcareitnews.com/news/why-hospitals-and-health-insurers-are-really-turning-cloud.

40   "Hospital Consolidation: Trends, Impacts & Outlook," NIHCM, January 2020, https://www.nihcm.org/categories/hospital-consolidation-trends-impacts-outlook.

41   "2018 M&A in Review: The Year in Numbers," Kaufman Hall, 2018, https://mnareview.kaufmanhall.com/the-year-in-numbers?_ga=2.195083116.1177820953.1550596993-1216528080.1546983849.

42   Flanagan, "U.S. Hospitals Shut at 30-a-Year."

43   "Fast Facts on U.S. Hospitals, 2020," American Hospital Association, 2020, https://www.aha.org/statistics/fast-facts-us-hospitals#network.